Text and Genre
in Reconstruction

Willard McCarty is Professor of Humanities Computing and academic staff member of the Centre for Language, Discourse and Communication, King's College London, Editor of *Humanist* and of *Interdisciplinary Science Reviews*. He is recipient of the 2006 Richard W. Lyman Award, National Humanities Center and the Rockefeller Foundation, U.S., and of the 2005 Award for Outstanding Achievement, Computing in the Arts and Humanities, The Society for Digital Humanities / Société pour l'étude des médias interactifs, Canada.

Willard McCarty

Text and Genre in Reconstruction

*Effects of Digitalization on Ideas,
Behaviours, Products and Institutions*

Cambridge

2010

OpenBook Publishers

Open Book Publishers CIC Ltd.,
40 Devonshire Road, Cambridge, CB1 2BL, United Kingdom
http://www.openbookpublishers.com

© 2010 Willard McCarty. Contributors are free to re-publish their contributions in whatever other ways they choose.

Some rights are reserved. This book is made available under the Creative Commons Attribution-Non-Commercial-No Derivative Works 2.0 UK: England & Wales License. This license allows for copying any part of the work for personal and non-commercial use, providing author attribution is clearly stated. Details of allowances and restrictions are available at:

http://www.openbookpublishers.com

As with all Open Book Publishers titles, digital material and resources associated with this volume are available from our website:

http://www.openbookpublishers.com

ISBN Hardback: 978-1-906924-25-6
ISBN Paperback: 978-1-906924-24-9
ISBN Digital (pdf): 978-1-906924-26-3

Cover Image: Scribbly Gum, Brisbane Water National Park, New South Wales, Australia. Photograph taken by the Editor, August 2008. See page 187, this volume.

All paper used by Open Book Publishers is SFI (Sustainable Forestry Initiative), and PEFC (Programme for the Endorsement of Forest Certification Schemes) Certified.

Printed in the United Kingdom and United States by
Lightning Source for Open Book Publishers

*To Warwick Gould FRSL, FRSA, FEA,
Professor, Director and friend –
'But every now and then, just weighing in
Is what it must come down to...'*

Acknowledgements

All of us who have contributed to this volume, long in the making, would like to acknowledge with gratitude the help of many kinds given by the publisher and especially to its Managing Director, Dr Alessandra Tosi. The Editor in turn pays tribute to the authors, who have been magnificently cooperative and patient. Thanks are due to the Institute of English Studies (to its Director, for whom the dedication) and to the Centre for Computing in the Humanities, King's College London, and its Director, Professor Harold Short, for unstinting support of the Seminar from which most of the essays in this volume originated.

Contents

Contributors	viii
Introduction	
Willard McCarty	1
1. Never Say Always Again: Reflections on the Numbers Game	
John Burrows	13
2. Cybertextuality by the Numbers	
Ian Lancashire	37
3. Textual Pathology	
Peter Garrard	71
4. The Human Presence in Digital Artefacts	
Alan Galey	93
5. Defining Electronic Editions: A Historical and Functional Perspective	
Edward Vanhoutte	119
6. Electronic Editions for Everyone	
Peter Robinson	145
7. How Literary Works Exist: Implied, Represented, and Interpreted	
Peter Shillingsburg	165
8. Text as Algorithm and as Process	
Paul Eggert	183
9. 'I Read the News Today, Oh Boy!': Newspaper Publishing in the Online World	
Marilyn Deegan and Kathryn Sutherland	203
References	219

Contributors

John Burrows is Emeritus Professor of English at the University of Newcastle, NSW Australia, Director of the Centre for Literary and Linguistic Computing there from 1989-2001 and winner of the 2001 Roberto Busa Award for his work in literary computing. He is the pre-eminent scholar in computational stylistics, with numerous publications on questions of authorship in 17th through 19th-century English literature.

Marilyn Deegan, trained as an Anglo-Saxonist, is Emerius Professor of Humanities Computing, Centre for Computing in the Humanities, King's College London, and Director of Research Development. She is Editor, *Literary and Linguistic Computing*, co-author of *Digital Futures* (2002) and co-editor of *Digital Preservation* (2006). Formerly she was Professor of Electronic Library Research, De Montfort, and Director, Forced Migration Online, Refugee Studies Centre, Oxford.

Paul Eggert is an Australian Research Council professorial fellow, based at the University of New South Wales at ADFA in Canberra. He chairs the Board of the AustLit database, and has been involved in experimental electronic edition projects since the mid-1990s. He was founding general editor of the Academy Editions of Australian Literature (10 vols, 1996-2007). His edition, with Elizabeth Webby, of Rolf Boldrewood's *Robbery Under Arms* appeared in 2006. He wrote *Securing the Past: Conservation in Art, Architecture and Literature* (2009).

Alan Galey, is Assistant Professor in the Faculty of Information at the University of Toronto, where he also teaches in the Book History and Print Culture Program. His research focuses on the history and future of the book, specifically with regard to digital scholarly editing and theories of the archive. He is a co-leader of the Textual Studies team on the Implementing New Knowledge Environments (INKE) project, supported by the Social Sciences and Humanities Research Council of Canada (SSHRC), and holds a SSHRC research grant for a project titled *Archive and Interface in Digital Textual Studies: From Cultural History to Critical Design*.

Contributors

Peter Garrard, has held faculty positions at the Institute of Cognitive Neuroscience, London, and the University of Southampton. He is currently Reader in Neurology at St. George's, University of London. His numerous papers on cognitive neuroscience, language and neurodegenerative disorders are widely cited. His 2005 article in *Brain* on 'The effects of very early Alzheimer's disease on the characteristics of writing by a renowned author' (128.2) received worldwide media attention.

Ian Lancashire is Professor of English at the University of Toronto and a member of the Royal Society of Canada. In 2006 he won a prestigious Killam Research Fellowship in English Literature. He is a specialist in Renaissance drama, General Editor of *Representative Poetry Online* and *Lexicons of Early Modern English*, founding Director of the Centre for Computing in the Humanities there from 1984 to 1996, Canadian pioneer in the digital humanities, software developer and author of numerous books and articles. His *Forgetful Muses: Reading the Author in the Text* is forthcoming from the University of Toronto Press.

Peter Robinson is co-director of the Institute for Textual Scholarship and Electronic Editing, University of Birmingham, textual editor specializing in Chaucer, software developer and founder of Scholarly Digital Editions. Since the 1980s he has pioneered digital techniques for editing, most notably the use of philogenetic software applied to the study of large textual traditions. Currently he is working with the Institute for New Testament Textual Research, Birmingham, on both the Nestle-Aland 28 and the Digital Nestle-Aland editions. His *Canterbury Tales Project* is a normative starting point for scholars interested in digital editing.

Peter Shillingsburg, formerly Director of the Centre for Textual Scholarship, De Montfort, is Svaglic Professor of Textual Studies, Loyola University, Chicago. He is author of five books (most recently *From Gutenberg to Google: Electronic Representations of Literary Texts*) and numerous articles on editing, general editor of *The Works of W. M. Thackery* and editor of four other editions. He is a pre-eminent theoretician of digital editing practice.

Kathryn Sutherland is Professor and Reader in Bibliography and Textual Criticism, St Anne's College, Oxford. Her interests are in bibliography, textual criticism and literature 1750-1850. She is author of *Jane Austen's Textual Lives* (2005) and numerous essays on textual criticism and its digital aspects. Her book with Marilyn Deegan, *Transferred Illusions: Digital Technology and the Forms of Print*, was published in 2009.

Edward Vanhoutte is director of research at the Royal Academy of Dutch Language and Literature, Ghent Belgium, and head of the Centre for Scholarly Editing and Document Studies (CTB). He pioneered electronic textual editing in Belgium and the Netherlands, is Associate Editor, *Literary and Linguistic Computing,* and author and editor of books and articles on (electronic) textual editing and humanities computing.

Introduction
Willard McCarty

---

1. The Question in Principle

In his Alfred Korzybski Memorial Lecture, the great neurophysiologist Warren McCulloch relates a story from his youth. When in 1917 he entered Haverford College, a Quaker institution in the United States, Rufus Jones called him in and asked him about his intentions:

> 'Warren,' said he, 'what is Thee going to be?' And I said, 'I don't know.' 'And what is Thee going to do?' And again I said, 'I have no idea; but there is one question I would like to answer. What is a number, that a man may know it, and a man, that he may know a number?' He smiled and said, 'Friend, Thee will be busy as long as Thee lives.' I have been, and that is what we are about. (McCulloch 1988/1960: 2)

Changing what needs to be changed in the above quotation, the central complex of questions that work in digital textual studies has been orbiting all these years emerges: his 'we' is us, the writers and readers of this book, and conjoined to (rather than substituted for) 'number', is 'text' (and so 'book'). It is this complex of questions that is asked here again by some of the leading scholars in the field. What is text that we may read it in all its forms and genres, and find meaning in the statistical behaviour of its words? What are we that we may find the marks on the pages of books intelligible and put them there so that others of our kind may read?

Asking such big questions and claiming, as is so often done, that the digital medium has fundamentally altered the conditions for asking them are both apt to give pause. Haven't such questions always been asked or at least been implicit in scholarly work? Isn't the role of the editor much the same as it was in ancient Alexandria (and perhaps in even earlier times) and then added to in the centuries which followed? Waters muddied by decades of hype and kept that way by constant demands for innovation make responding to such reasonable objections quite difficult. Claims of revolutionary effects are clearly not good enough; arguments, such as are offered here, are badly needed. But neither can the fact of such claiming be simply dismissed with some form of the Preacher's sentence, that 'there is no new thing under the sun'. Change and continuity require each other to be meaningful; for both the meaning is in the detail.

Reduction of text to data is a trade-off: manipulability, including quantification and other transformations, is gained; meaning, and with it 'context' as a meaningful term, is lost. Effectively all would indeed be lost as far as the humanities are concerned if the change were one-way, the machine substituted for human intelligence. Nothing like that is the case for scholarship. Like other tools, computing augments it, gives it greater reach. Furthermore, because the computer is, as we will see, dynamically reconfigurable by design, it can in turn be augmented with new intelligence. Computing machines and scholarly intelligence change each other, recursively. A perfect illustration may be seen in John Burrows' essay, first in this volume.

What can this recursive machine do with text that is worthy of your notice? Let me propose the following features which make a genuine difference. Chief among these is (1) the automation which brings the timescale of forbiddingly laborious tasks within normal human bounds. From this fact of temporal advantage the rest can be derived. In particular, (2) the capacity to store and retrieve amounts of text large enough to permit access to and processing of unread but relevant material gives us the automated digital library, which remains an objective of research. On the theoretical side is (3) the conceptual language and ultimately software which gives us a standard, communicable way of describing processes of interest to us and of testing the descriptions, then implementing and distributing them. In consequence of the rigours of using this language, which requires complete and explicit specification, there arises (4) the struggle to articulate what normally goes without saying in our editions and editing practices. The mutability if not instability of the digital medium results in (5) the strong tendency for scholarship produced with it toward the conversational, improvisational and experimental. Hence, (6) the world-wide communication network implied by the above has developed, and is a necessity for exchange of scholarship at a pace commensurate with experimental, often collaborative work.

My principal claim is not about the reality of these features. That, I would suppose, is beyond dispute. Rather I claim that they make a genuine difference for two reasons: first, that nothing gets done if it is too laborious or time-consuming, and second, that beyond a certain level of complexity things begin to happen which could not be predicted logically, though we may foresee them. The essays in this volume exemplify and explore these differences actually made.

2. The Question Historically Considered

In the early days, when computing was rare within the humanities, it was deployed almost exclusively to take the place of long-established manual operations. The focus of the majority was on alleviating the burden of drudgery, reducing error and increasing the efficiency of scholars' time. A widespread fear of automation in the wider world and the deep worry of commentators that new means were obscuring humane ends were reflected among textual scholars by the curiously repeated and seemingly nervous reassurance that the purpose of the computer was not to replace but to support the humanist 'in the work which only he can accomplish', as Franklin J. Pegues said in a review of the 1964 IBM Conference on Literary Data Processing (1965: 107). In a prescient article in the inaugural issue of *Computers and the Humanities* two years later, the literary critic Louis Milic, amongst other things, complained that, 'satisfaction with such limited objectives denotes a real shortage of imagination among us. We are still not thinking of the computer as anything but a myriad of clerks or assistants in one convenient console' (1966: 4).

As in artificial intelligence and machine translation, early humanists began the 1960s with stirring visions and early successes only to plough into a morass of difficulties by mid decade. Then began the characteristic cycle of sifting for that which we now call 'evidence of value'. In 1976 – to choose one example out of many – the Aquinas scholar Roberto Busa noted the 'rather poor performance' of literary computing that had resulted from pursuing such limited objectives as Milic identified. To him the failure to do better pointed back to a profound ignorance of language, of 'what is in our mouths at every moment', and so to the need for fundamental research. Similarly, in an oft-cited article published two years later, Susan Wittig (1978) examined Margaret Masterman's stirring vision of a 'telescope of the mind' (Masterman 1962), observing how far short of it scholars had come. Like Jerome McGann more recently (2004b), she concluded that the fault lay with an utterly inadequate conception of text and recommended, like Busa, fundamental research into the question of what it is.

In the digital humanities ideas and machines interact asynchronously to deepen the fundamental problems, rather than solve them. While the revolution proclaimed for computing has turned out to be more a going around in circles than a liberation from the hard slog of scholarship, what matters for research is the nuclear bundle of questions that governs the orbital path. To be fair, the revolutionary path isn't a closed circle either. Our accumulating body of work demonstrates that it's more of a spiral. But paying attention to the forward-pointing axis means minding the questions at the centre.

3. The Contents

Seven of the nine essays collected here originated as papers delivered at the London Seminar in Digital Text and Scholarship from Autumn 2006 to Spring 2008. The remaining two essays were commissioned to complete the volume. Altogether the collection is arranged in two parts, the parts united by the question of text though divided by the perspectives they take on it.

The first part is analytic and microscopic, with a focus on text as a fundamentally probabilistic medium whose hidden devices the patient use of statistical tools is allowing us gradually to unravel, and so giving us new understanding of our relation to language. The second part is synthetic and macroscopic, concerned with how the digital medium affects, reflects and bodies forth ideas of textuality, and especially concerned with its transforming potential in both scholarly and popular genres. In both parts, contributors probe how what we thought we safely knew or had in hand, disintegrates when seen from the digital perspective, and places us, scholars, not merely in the position of witnesses and guessers but in the role of makers, for whom the emergent potentialities of the medium constitute essential information. As one of the authors, Alan Galey, points out, 'The digital humanities' most productive response [...] has been to ask 'why speculate when we can prototype?' – that is, to regard the future of the book as something we create, not just observe and comment upon.' (p. 108). Scholars are becoming end-*makers* rather than mere end-users of digital tools.

In the first part of this volume we hear from both sides of the same question – from two literary scholars engaged with the empirical aspects of writing (Burrows and Lancashire) and a cognitive neurologist, trained in the Classics, who studies literature in English (Garrard). The humanities, we know, do not progress by turning the uncertain into the certain, rather the opposite. But quantitative, even scientific approaches to the study of text, as here, while they provide an ever firmer basis for investigation of literature's relationship to the creatures we are, also pry open cans of wonderfully wriggly worms.

The essays of the second part place us imaginatively in the messy workshops, editorial workspaces and seminar rooms where experiments in the design of digital genres are taking place. We are made privy to the arguments, far from settled, indeed digitally unsettled, about what exactly it is that we think we are doing with texts. We are disabused of the silly but persistent notion that a solid, well-understood but obsolete physical object, the codex book, is being replaced 'real soon now' by another not so solid, not so well-understood but fabulously better object, the e-book, electronic newspaper or, in the case of textual scholarship, the digital edition. We are brought up against not only undoubted change but also uncertain and highly contingent outcomes. We are, by the uncertainty of it all and by its dependence on human choice as well as historical accident, invited to participate in the shaping of the future. The last 60 years of work with digital text inform the arguments of the contributors to this volume and remind us how much goes into the cultural assimilation of technical inventions.

3.1. Analysis of Text

In 'Never Say Always Again' John Burrows, the pre-eminent scholar of computational stylistics in the Anglophone world, reflects on 'the numbers game' by presenting three case studies to illustrate his most recent methods for discriminating authorship. His title-word 'game' is worth noting as a clue to his working method, which is experiment-like and seriously playful in its recursive alternation of statistical trials and literary-critical judgement. He says, without fanfare, 'that work by different authors, work in different genres, work of different eras, work in different national forms of English can all comprise statistically distinguishable groups' (p. 28). It is difficult to overestimate the significance of this statement, which announces the probabilistic quality of literature. We know from research in natural language processing that probabilistic methods have proven highly successful in automatic treatment of ordinary human discourse (cf.

Manning and Schütze 1999). However, we also know anecdotally and by studying linguistic corpora that such discourse is highly repetitive, and so we might be inclined to dismiss the success of probabilistic methods as trivial. But Burrows shows that the most artfully crafted prose, however much the *variatio sermonis* may have been the author's intention, yields to statistical methods at the deepest levels we know how to reach. Ian Hacking's *The Taming of Chance*, which Burrows cites, begins by declaring with equally quiet authority that '[t]he most decisive event of twentieth century physics has been the discovery that the world is not deterministic', that its principles of order are stochastic (1990: 1). In *Mind and Nature* Gregory Bateson argues that culture is transmitted by 'a sort of hybrid or mix-up' of replication and learning, and that learning 'gathers its solutions' out of the random play of the world (2002: 45). In other words, in terms of our subject, literary texts emerge from this mix-up of mimesis and random opportunity, hence are accessible stochastically, and hence are real as the physical world itself is. Burrows raises the troubling question of confidence – how much can we place in statistical analysis? Here is the beginning of an answer.

In 'Cybertextuality by the Numbers' Ian Lancashire constructs a theory of authoring from a synthesis of cybernetics, writers' self-testimony, cognitive psychology and computational text-analysis. The core of his argument, and a most valuable contribution to this volume, comes with his conclusion that authors, and so our species, have been able to overcome basic limitations of the human mind by means of writing. 'We have', he says, 'unrelentingly developed both cognitive and mechanical technologies consciously so as to gain control of our *making*' (p. 69). He uses computational models and tools to frame the problem of how writing happens and to provide a means of detecting evidence for the role it plays in human development. The cybernetic idea of the feedback loop, he argues, allows us to explain in detail how text is so much more than marks on the page. It is, among other things, an Engelbartian technology of augmentation, a creative extension beyond nature by means of art, and so creative of a new nature (Engelbart 1962). Nevertheless the phenomenology of tool-use as a whole for example in the writings of Michael Polanyi (1969) and, more recently, Walter Vincenti (1990), is highly relevant and helps to connect cybertextuality with a broad range of work elsewhere.

Following the classical approach of physiological research – to investigate a function of the body by studying a relevant pathology – Peter Garrard describes how the loss of structure and organization in consequence of

Alzheimer's, reflected in degeneration of linguistic abilities, may be used to infer the nature of healthy cognition. As a case study he describes research into the possible effects of Alzheimer's on the final novel of Iris Murdoch, *Jackson's Dilemma*, which presents a rare opportunity to study textual pathology before the author herself could have been aware of its effects and to compare the text against a large corpus of work very close to the author's original manuscripts. This is, Lancashire notes, 'a uniquely important case study' highlighting the modularity of mental language processing and, in this case, the working memory central to his study (p. 44). Garrard considers the criticisms and arguments surrounding *Jackson's Dilemma* carefully, but he finds both by a systematic top-down analysis from his hypotheses to the data, and by a bottom-up, data-driven approach, striking confirmations. In a nutshell, Garrard provides a fine instance, refreshingly clinical, of the fact that text embodies embodied thought.

3.2. Synthesis of Textual Genres

The particular focus of this volume's second half is the macroscopic or telescopic view from textual data to the forms we give them.

Alan Galey, in 'The Human Presence in Digital Artefacts', argues that this view begins with the tensions 'between the surface orderliness of scholarly resources and the stubborn irregularity of textual materials' (p. 93). These tensions are the daily concern of textual editors but not usually of their scholarly clientele, let alone the reading public. They reveal not only that any interface is cognitively thick and complex in proportion to the text it re-presents, but also that textual irregularities can never be completely modelled for or by computer processing. Models in the sense intended here, as elsewhere in the digital humanities, *always* simplify by omission of that which others may regard as important, and so are never all-encompassing. Galey shows that the technical concerns of design are inseparable from the irresolvable aesthetic, symbolic and hermeneutical dimensions of editorial work. Thus, he argues, there can be no *definitive* digital resource, no digital monument against time, not even in the sense of a single modelling device. Galey's argument from these stubborn irregularities, from what text *is*, concludes in an invitation to us to become (as I am fond of saying) end-*makers* in the designing of digital genres. As the great Australian ethnographic historian Greg Dening used to insist (1998), the point is to think present-participally rather than nominally – of the future of textual edit*ing* as a communal process.

Edward Vanhoutte's declared purpose in 'Defining Electronic Editions: A Historical and Functional Perspective' is to propose a definition of what an electronic edition is, and to frame it in terms of work done to date. Against the background of the history of electronic textual editing, he discusses Peter Robinson's model of cooperative, distributed editions and Peter Shillingsburg's knowledge sites (both discussed in following chapters), Espen Ore's self-sufficient archive and both Robinson's and Jerome McGann's models of the reproductive edition. Vanhoutte's defining method for the electronic edition follows from an application of Espen Aarseth's taxonomy of how texts are *traversed*. (Again, note the significant emphasis on readerly process rather than structural product.) The typologies inherited from editions in print do not suit the digital environment but offer a way forward. He speaks in combinatorial terms, of a set of interoperable tools the end-user would deploy to construct 'new genres of editions'. The question of what these genres might be reflects back on the question of what text *is* that allows it to be edited. The design of tools raises the question of operational primitives – or, less problematically, of commonplace operations discovered in practice, as (one suspects) most tools have been.

Peter Robinson's practical work over many years itself constitutes the raw material for an historical study of how ideas for editing in the digital medium have developed. His chapter for this volume, 'A specification towards distributed editions', thus represents as much experience with the conceivable alternatives as anyone could muster. Here he specifies what might be required to create the 'fluid, cooperative and distributed' scholarly editions that many scholars, such as Peter Shillingsburg in the following essay, have advocated. He proposes specific mechanisms to label components of such an edition, outlines how these components should be held on distributed-edition servers and how software tools on the reader's computer and on the server might interact. He sketches out the functionality readers and scholars require. In appendices he gives instances of how attributes of distributed editions may be used by various projects, describes the relations of components and discusses stand-off encoding, which Paul Eggert takes up in a following chapter. The manifest failure of the standalone 'e-book' to replace the printed codex, as Robinson illustrates in an opening anecdote, and the manifest success of distributed online resources lend strong support to his argument.

In 'How Literary Works Exist: Implied, Represented and Interpreted' Peter Shillingsburg writes as a digitally informed scholarly bibliographer and book historian with four decades of practical experience and theoretical reflection. His is a critical activist's project to tease out the nature of textual existence and representation in order to address not so much a digital future for the book but the future of the book in a digital world. He begins, then, where one must – with the codex, recipient of nearly two millennia of creative attention. He sees that, on the one hand, speculations about and experiments with the tools are weak and rootless without detailed knowledge of the book as it has been; and that, on the other hand, textual editors face an unavoidable challenge to migrate their skills and concerns to the digital medium. He takes the incursion of digital representation into textual editing as an urgent opportunity for understanding the book as a physical object, medium of communication and locus of understanding. The ontological question of what text *is*, he reminds us, may in its abstract formulation turn us away from the prior question of how we in fact actually encounter text and what the form of the codex has shown itself capable of doing. (Here practice corrects theory and forces us to revise it for another go at the stubborn truth of things.) He concludes that we should acknowledge editing as an attempt to deal with complex materials in a wide variety of ways; that editing in the digital world should serve as a foundation to be maintained and extended; and that a large and future community of scholars can contribute to basic, ongoing editorial work communally.

In 'Text as Algorithm and as Process: A Critique', Paul Eggert orbits the basic problem that complete explicitness and absolute consistency pose for representation and manipulation of cultural artefacts. The twin computational demand stirs up fundamental questions for the prospect of a digital edition, the central one being, he notes, what are texts and how do they function? Since text-encoding is central to edition-making, at least now and for the foreseeable future, the imperative to ask this question is undeniable, since every tag, however factual, signifies an interpretative intervention. 'We *have* to think about text, its material condition and its reception if we are to understand what it is that we are encoding when we say that we are encoding texts.' He takes strong issue with Jerome McGann's notion of the 'bibliographic code', arguing that there is no such renderable system of signifiers. However useful as a metaphor for thinking about and discussing textual features, there is nothing computationally tractable beyond it. (Here computational experience corrects theory and, as before, forces us to revise it for another go.) The full reality of text will always be elusive. He asks, how can we stabilise this fluid, ever-changing reality so that we can discuss texts and not just ourselves? Since totalising schemes of encoding can never be implemented, stand-off markup (which Eggert and colleagues at the University of New South Wales have pioneered) seems the best answer. The strategy he recommends then, is, like Shillingsburg's and Robinson's, communal, though the means of achieving it may be different as there is a need to provide an effective means for coordinating the many possible versions of the common source of interest: the work. The resulting artefact, one might say, would resemble the ancient variorum commentary, with superior organizational capabilities and collaborative distribution of work but the same objective of progressive accumulation.

The volume ends with a bridging study which takes us from the struggles of scholarly editing in academia to the struggles of newspaper publishing in daily life. Marilyn Deegan and Kathryn Sutherland, in '"I Read the News Today, Oh Boy!" Newspaper publishing in the online world', highlight the problem common throughout this volume: how the shift in media disintegrates everything concerned – understandings, behaviours, objects, institutions. Deegan and Sutherland chart 'a gradual decoupling of news from paper and print, with [...] hybrid signs of both experiment and formal nostalgia' along the way. Some reformations of old forms make obvious sense and find acceptance; others seem emotional curiosities. Deegan and Sutherland chart the shift from mass collective identification via a product constructed by expert editorial teams to mass individuation of dynamically constructed units of what is individually taken to be news. They consider what is gained and what is lost, and how reading habits are reforming – the habits, one might note, of those who also read literary works and use textual editions. 'What has changed', they conclude, 'is the scale and the fine-tuning of the newspaper's functions as its economies and its implied reading culture shift from paper to screen and as its conceptual model sets a standard for the electronic delivery of other textual forms than those associated with the news.'

4. The Future

Scholarly writings in which the computer figures tend to remind us indirectly if not directly that, as mathematicians have also discovered, to compute is to intervene in the world and so to bring ideas and arguments up against stubborn actualities. We soon learn that our obviously meaningful texts are to a significant extent beyond the processing abilities of the best machines we can devise or seem likely to devise. From the rigorous perspective of programming languages all of what one wants to do must be completely and consistently spelled out. But when it comes to text, we learn, it cannot be and will not be. The puzzle from the readerly perspective of the scholar is more that these fundamentally mathematical machines are as effective as they are turning out to be: 'unreasonably effective', as Eugene Wigner (1960), then Richard Hamming (1980) noted about mathematics itself in relation to the world we call real.

In the days when most of the authors and the editor of this volume were *imprinted* by computing (as the *OED* says of social animals, brought to 'a state of habitual recognition of or trust in another') user and computer were separated in space by a glass wall, input/output desk or other insuperable barrier, and in time, by hours or days of waiting for one's printout to be delivered. This is essentially the situation depicted in 1950 by Alan Turing for his famous test of machine intelligence (1950: 433-4) and by John Searle thirty years later for his equally famous Chinese Room argument (1980). Thus when computing, with the practical realities of its use, was compared with the codex as a new 'machine to think with' (Richards 1924: 1), it did rather poorly. It proved to be at best something on the side of the main action, a useful auxiliary device for certain highly limited kinds of investigation (often called drudgery), and simply unable to match the referential subtlety of a well-crafted edition in print. This is not, however, what computing is now, and not the computing that the authors in this volume address. Progress, intruding into the humanities, has brought us to a new place from which to consider and redefine old problems.

1. Never Say Always Again: Reflections on the Numbers Game[1]

John Burrows

For Harold Love: Vale.

In order to 'place' my argument, I declare myself, first and last, a student of English literature. I took up computing because it seemed likely to answer some of my questions. Perhaps it has, but only by opening up a thousand more. My object in this paper is to look back at the quarter-century I have spent in computational stylistics and to consider what such work entails. I must speak, accordingly, with some generality: yet I am neither a theorist nor a philosopher. Our heuristic procedures have much in common with those of experimental science: yet I am no scientist and have never claimed that work like mine lay in that domain. What I have to say is not offered as an apologia: yet I would like, if I can, to allay the doubts that such work arouses in many of our colleagues and to face some of the questions that they raise.

---

1 This paper was originally given at King's College, London, 25 October 2006, as the third biennial Wisbey Lecture and the Inaugural Lecture for the London Seminar in Digital Text and Scholarship, Institute of English Studies, University of London. The biennial Wisbey Lecture was initiated by Harold Short to honour the pioneering work of Roy Wisbey in the field of humanities computing. It is a pleasure to bring their names together and to acknowledge their successive achievements in and far beyond King's College.

1. Three Case Studies

I shall begin with an account of three cases where my tests seem to indicate that a particular text had two identifiable authors. Here, as also with parody and pastiche, the problem of attribution can be more delicate than usual. But if problems like these can be successfully resolved, we are better placed to handle the suggestion that a text is 'contaminated' whether that suggestion arises in reality or is introduced as a skeptical gambit.

In the first two cases, my results concur with well-founded documentary evidence. The third case is more contentious because the work in question has always been regarded as having a single known author. While these cases will occupy us for a little while, they are offered as preamble for a broader question. It was put to my friend and colleague, Hugh Craig, in a letter from an eminent Shakespeare scholar: How much confidence should I place in a result like this?

The question quite transcends its immediate occasion and goes to the heart of our whole endeavour. It should, I suggest, evoke a sense of scholarly obligation on both sides. It is always incumbent upon those who introduce new methods to proceed cautiously, to work with rigour, and to present their findings as plainly as they can. As we advance, it is increasingly incumbent upon other scholars in the humanities to put aside any instinctive aversion for unfamiliar forms of inquiry. Both parties can unite in an awareness that new methods are not always appropriate and that, like old ones, they can be misused.

The first of my three case-studies concerns *St. Ives*. When Robert Louis Stevenson died in 1894, his unfinished manuscripts included thirty chapters — over a hundred thousand words — of a romance about a French prisoner of war in Napoleon's day. After escaping from Edinburgh Castle, the eponymous hero goes into England to claim his inheritance from a dying uncle, a wealthy grandee of the *ancien regime*. Our hero then quixotically returns to Scotland to clear his name and claim the hand of his beloved. Back in Edinburgh after many an astonishing escapade, he is stranded by the author's untimely death. He is rescued by Arthur Quiller Couch (1863-1944), who added thirty thousand words and saw the whole work published in 1897. While it is a lively specimen of an adventure story, both authors give it an extravagantly mock-heroic air. Whenever St Ives blunders, his enemies are at the ready. Whenever he is most in need, the very man he needs is waiting round the corner. Not so much a subversion of the genre as a mildly 'camped-up' version of it.

As a framework of comparison for determining whether it is possible to show who wrote which part of *St. Ives*, I began with a 72,000-word sample from the novels and stories of each target-author. All of this material was downloaded from the Project Gutenberg.[2] It was supported by 12,000-word samples from the work of thirty other authors born within forty years before and forty after Stevenson's own date of birth. In each case, the selection drew on at least three pieces by a given author. These thirty selections came from our own archive, entered by keyboard over the years. Apart from all this were two samples of narrative by Stevenson and Quiller Couch selected from works not used above. They, too, came from the Gutenberg Project and incorporated about thirty thousand words by each author. Like *St. Ives*, all the samples chosen were of retrospective first-person narrative. All told then, the main set runs to half a million words by thirty-two authors. The two independent samples run to another sixty thousand and *St. Ives* itself to one hundred and thirty-five thousand.

Using standardized word-frequencies in order to allow the other thirty authors equal play with the target-authors, I constructed a ranked list of the three hundred most frequent words of all. The top two hundred included few lexical words and were put to most use in my tests. Neither *St. Ives* itself nor the two independent samples participated in the formation of the word-list. Contrary to my former practice, I did not introduce tags to distinguish homographic forms from each other.

Using the software package *Excel*, a work-sheet for the statistical test I have called Delta[3] was then set up to compare *St. Ives* with the thirty-two members of the main set. It suffices for the moment to recall that, as used here, Delta scores register differences between a target-text and the several members of a group of genuine or notional candidates for its authorship. The lowest score in a set marks the least difference. When (as in the present case) the set is large enough, the scores can be converted into z-scores. These have a mean of zero and diverge from it in units of standard deviation. It follows that the strongest negative z-score in a set marks the least of all the differences. Scores ranging out below about –1.5 usually repay attention.

---

2   http://www.gutenberg.org/wiki/Main_Page [accessed 10/2/10].
3   The calculation and use of Delta scores and Delta z-scores have been shown elsewhere and their high but not unfailing reliability has been assessed. See Burrows (2002, 2003) and Hoover (2004). For a part-precursor, see Forsyth, Holmes, and Tse (1999, 393).

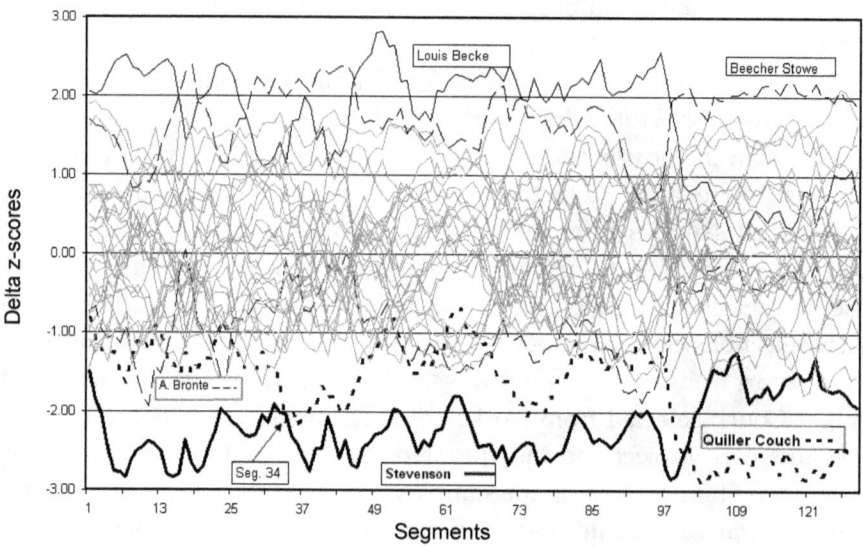

Figure 1. *St. Ives* and thirty-two authors.
Delta z-scores for 6000-word rolling segments, with 1000-word increments.

The two hundred most frequent words made the final set of variables. The target-text, *St. Ives*, was broken into successive 'rolling segments' of six thousand words, with increments of a thousand words. This allows us to model a reader's progress through the text while testing authorship at each step. It is as if we were to move through the calendar year, registering rainfall for successive six-month periods — January through June, February through July, March through August, and so on. In its 135,000 words, *St. Ives* offers 129 segments of this kind.

Figure 1 offers Delta z-scores for the differences, in each of 129 rolling segments of *St. Ives*, between that text and our thirty-two authors. The entries for Stevenson and Quiller Couch run across the foot of the chart, outside the cloud of other entries. One of the two leads the whole field in every one of the 129 results and his rival usually lies second. (Harriet Beecher Stowe and an Australian, Louis Becke, trail the field.) The only challenger worth naming is Anne Bronte, but even she barely impinges on the scores for the main pair. The strength of the result is emphasised by the fact that, at each step, the lowest z-score almost always lies below -2.0. Save for a lapse at Segment 34, Stevenson easily leads the whole field for the first ninety-eight segments. After that, the lead passes to Quiller Couch, who holds it without challenge. This pattern exactly matches what we know — that Stevenson wrote the first thirty chapters and Quiller Couch the rest.

The scores for Quiller Couch in both phases are worth more thought. Since he has no role whatever in the first thirty chapters of *St. Ives*, the fact that he often ranks next after Stevenson shows that his usual fictional style is much like that of *St. Ives*. And yet it is even more like our main sample of Stevenson, zigging where that zigs and zagging where it zags. *St. Ives* is least different from both writers in its passages of vigorous action. It differs less from others when dialogue supervenes. Segment 34, where it differs more from Stevenson than from Quiller Couch, is a long passage of reflection and description as the hero is travelling alone down the Great North Road. Much the same note is struck, as we shall see, in some of Stevenson's sombre, introspective tales. It is also to be heard now and then in his romances, as when Jim Hawkins first goes ashore on Treasure Island and when David Balfour thinks himself marooned. But the more characteristic passages in *St. Ives*, those where the Delta z-scores approximate to –3.00, are the prisoners' duel in Edinburgh Castle and some of the more perilous moments of the hero's travels. All this suggests that Quiller Couch was always a most appropriate author to carry on where Stevenson broke off. He certainly persisted in a mock-Stevensonian vein in later work like *Poison Island* (1912), where a sybaritic recluse lures treasure-hunters to their deaths on his private Caribbean island.

In the second phase of the novel, where Quiller Couch takes over, his Delta z-scores approach –3.00, receding slightly at the end. Those for Stevenson recede considerably but remain comparatively strong. Quiller Couch's *St. Ives*, in other words, remains very much his own. Yet it is a good enough imitation to stand nearer to Stevenson overall than to any of our other thirty writers.

The salient feature of Figure 1 is the sharp transition from Segment 98 on.

Our second case-study shows quite another pattern. Its subject is a novel called *The Boy in the Bush* (1924), which has an unusual history. The main outcome of D. H. Lawrence's visit to Australia in the early twenties was *Kangaroo* (1923), a powerful but turgid novel about a right-wing political movement of the day. But when he and his wife Frieda arrived, they met Mollie Skinner, a nurse in a convalescent home near Perth. A part-time novelist, she asked him to read a manuscript of hers. This was later to appear as *Black Swans* (1925). After reading it, he suggested that she try a new, less sentimental direction and agreed to help her bring the resulting work to publication. When her typescript reached him in America the next year, he not only began to tinker with the text but continued so vigorously that the novel is included in the Cambridge edition of his works as being by 'D. H. Lawrence and M. L. Skinner'. Its editor, Paul Eggert, shows that the decision is well founded. The question for us is not whether the work is collaborative but whether we can trace a more complex collaborative pattern than that presented by *St. Ives*. Nothing of Mollie Skinner's typescript is known to exist. But Eggert uses the evidence of the letters they exchanged, of Lawrence's autograph copy of the whole work, of two revised proof-copies, and of Lawrence's known habits of revision to claim it as 'a Lawrence novel' (Eggert 1990: liii). Eggert shows that, besides introducing an important change of direction towards the end, Lawrence added two closing chapters of which Mollie Skinner disapproved. Beyond this, he suggests that Lawrence made extensive changes throughout. The overall effect is to give a sort of colonial *Bildungsroman* a strong infusion of the idiosyncratic desert mysticism preoccupying Lawrence at that time.

Apart from the change of target-text, the only underlying difference between Figure 2 and Figure 1 is that long extracts from Lawrence's *Kangaroo* (61,125 words) and Skinner's *Black Swans* (51,014 words) take the place of Stevenson and Quiller Couch. The other thirty authors stand unchanged and the same word-list is used. Since both Lawrence and Mollie Skinner are of an age with the later-born members of the main set, the set fits them a little less well than it fitted Stevenson. But the advantage of close replication prevailed.

Partly, perhaps, for that reason the lowest range of Delta z-scores in Figure 2 runs out beyond -3.00. But Lawrence is always more idiosyncratic than most. In this work, moreover, there is much of the strong vernacular that colours *Black Swans* and *Kangaroo* and so draws them closer to it. This interpretation is supported by the fact that, of the other thirty authors, Emily Bronte is nearest to *The Boy in the Bush* while Edgar Allan Poe's high old-fashioned style stands at the opposite extreme.

Of the thirty-two authors studied, one or other of the two collaborators is least far from *The Boy in the Bush* in all 130 segments. That is as it should be. But, in a pattern quite different from Figure 1, the scores for the two of them keep criss-crossing and are often sharply opposed. Mollie Skinner has much of the running in the middle of the novel. Lawrence has the ascendancy not only in those later passages where he is known to have taken the initiative but also in the opening chapters. All this is in line with Paul Eggert's evidence and in close keeping with his conclusions.

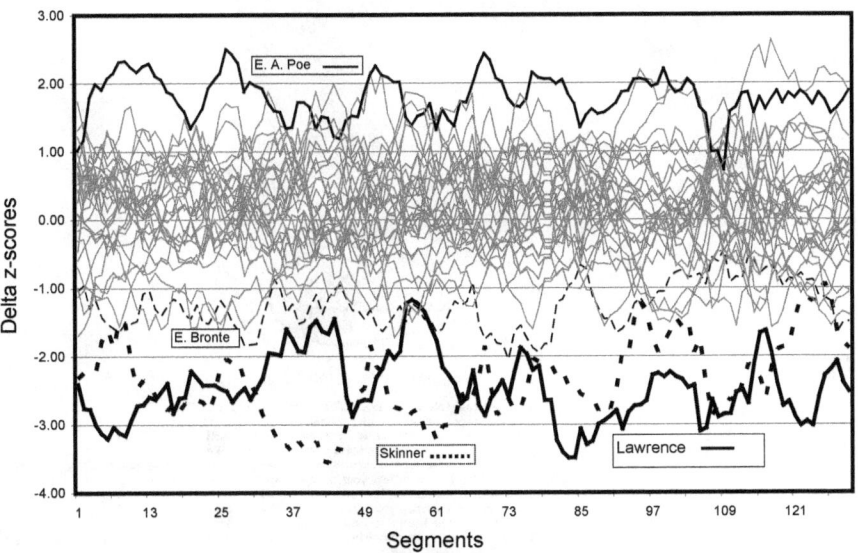

Figure 2. *The Boy in the Bush* and thirty-two authors.
Delta z-scores for 6000-word rolling segments, with 1000-word increments.

There are nevertheless some segments where the collaborators stand close to each other. This is the product, I suggest, of a particular level of revision where the changes are such that neither author's frequency-pattern is able to prevail over the other. At such moments, moreover, as around Segments 73, 95, and 119, the difference between our two known authors and Emily Brontë is at its least. If one composes artificial models, hybrid frequency-profiles, to which each collaborator contributes in designed proportions, the effect is to overlay the distinctive frequency-patterns of both authors. As the proportions are gradually altered to favour either author, the favoured one eventually prevails. But there can sometimes be transitional stages in which the two authors are not easy to distinguish from each other. At just such stages, quite other writers, with no claim at all to the authorship of the target-text, sometimes outscore them both.

The argument so far can be summed up in general terms. In ordinary single author works of sufficient length, the frequency patterns fluctuate from episode to episode or segment to segment as the text goes forward. Such fluctuations are governed by shifts of style as from action to description or from narrative to dialogue. Stevenson's part of *St. Ives*, as represented in Figure 1, is a fair specimen. It converges on and diverges from our main set of Stevenson's fiction but almost always stands nearer to Stevenson than to any of the other thirty-one authorial sets.

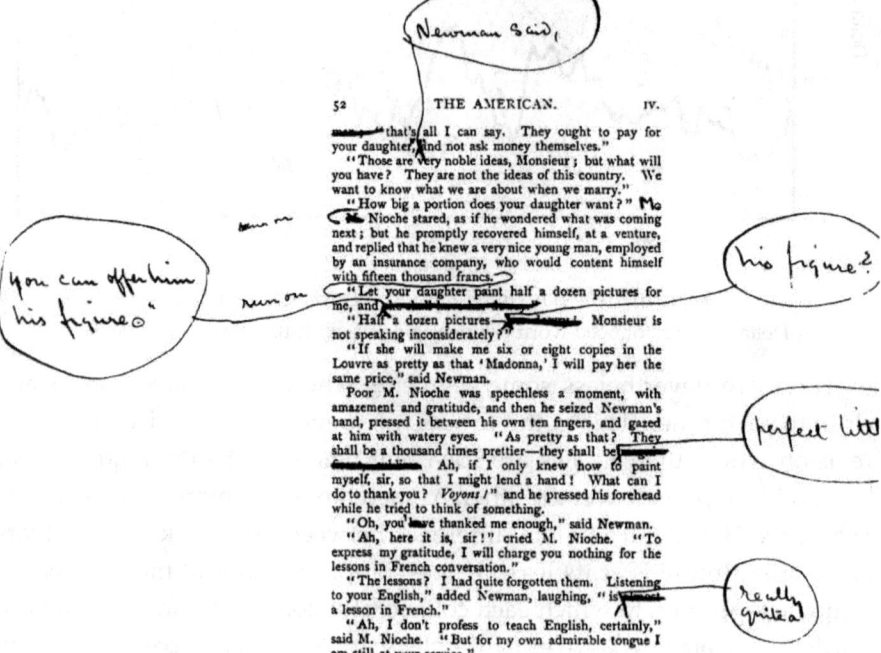

Plates 1 and 2 (opposite). Henry James, *The American* (1877).
Specimen of light revision (plate 1) and heavy revisions
(plate 2) for the New York edition (1907).

1. Never Say Always Again

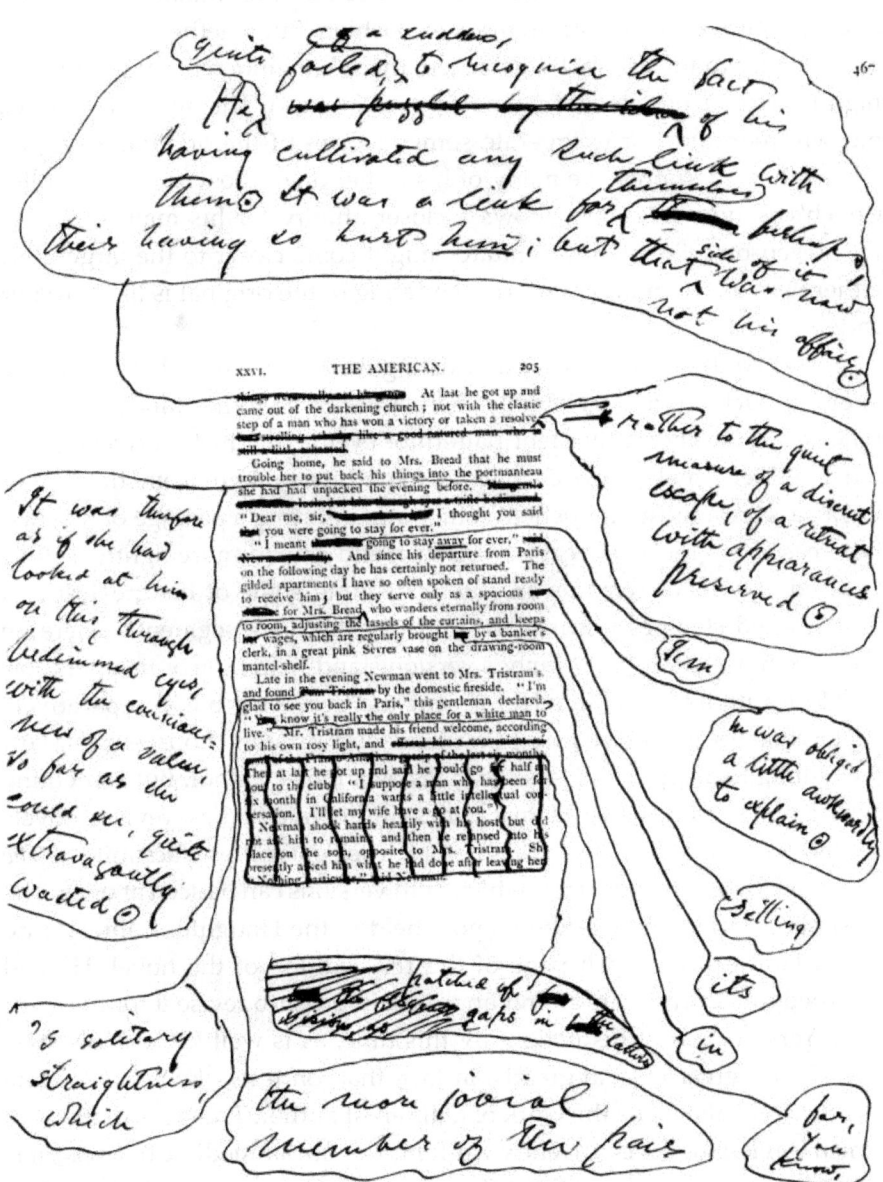

Texts of a second kind, where one author seeks to imitate another can also be expected to fluctuate in the same fashion. But whether or not a close resemblance to the original is achieved, there is no inherent reason for any high level of inconsistency as the text goes forward. The imitator's rendering will reproduce or exaggerate some features of the original, overlook some others, and preserve many of his or her own idiosyncrasies. Quiller Couch's section of *St. Ives* shows a closer affinity for his main text than for Stevenson's. Some other imitator might come closer to the target. But, either way, an essentially uniform rendering of the original is likely to pervade the whole.

Texts of a third kind, where an existing work is extensively revised, are likely to fluctuate more violently than either of the other kinds. Figure 2 reflects a typically inconsistent pattern of events in which Lawrence, like other revisers, makes few changes here and more there, sometimes leaving a passage almost untouched, sometimes inserting a passage of his own. Whereas many revisers weary of the task and emend more lightly as they proceed, Lawrence remains assiduous, making some of his greatest and best attested changes towards the end. Yet there are segments where he seems to have let Mollie Skinner's version stand with little or no alteration.

Most authors are obliged to accept the pervasive but comparatively slight changes introduced by publishers' and printers' house-styles. Few are willing to accept wholesale changes by another author. But something comparable occurs when Henry James, in his mid-sixties, revises novels he had written up to thirty years before. The Scolar Press facsimile of *The American* is a fine specimen, in which both versions can be seen at once. The facsimile is of a large workbook, now held in the Houghton Library, into which James pasted each page of the 1877 edition of the novel. He had returned to it thirty years after it appeared in order to revise it for the great New York edition of his fiction. By this time, as is well known, his style had altered greatly — so greatly, in fact, that, on tests like mine, his late novels could almost be the work of a different author. These are matters on which David Hoover is currently working. For our immediate purpose, it is enough to offer samples of the different levels of intervention that occurred as James worked through his old text in order to make it new. Plates 1 and 2 show the difference between lighter and heavier revision. In other places, pages of the original text are completely replaced by passages of manuscript or typescript. The varying levels of change observe no logic but that of the reviser's preference.

1. Never Say Always Again

Taking the preceding discussion as a framework, we can turn to our third case-study. The text in question is *The History of Ophelia* (1760), a novel that has always been attributed to Sarah Fielding, younger sister of Henry Fielding. The case for her authorship is not supported by the title-page, where 'by the author of *David Simple*', her usual phrase, gives way to 'published by the author of *David Simple*'. In her Advertisement, moreover, she actually disclaims authorship, saying that she found it in 'an old Buroe' and published it. The phrase used on the title-page has been treated as an inconsequential variation upon the expressions of anonymity expected of eighteenth-century women authors. The disclaimer in the Advertisement has been seen as an early example of a practice that was to become widespread, especially in ghost stories and other fictional extravagances. In both subject and treatment, there is much in the novel that anyone who knows her writings would accept as Sarah Fielding's. And yet, in the course of adding parts of this text to our set of Sarah Fielding's work, we quite unexpectedly came upon resemblances to the work of her famous brother. A series of different tests, some treating of very frequent words, some of much less frequent ones, have all supported the notion that Henry Fielding had a part in the composition of this work. If that is so, the only likely rationale is that Sarah Fielding drew upon some of his surviving papers but that her own contribution is far greater than she claimed.

Figure 3 employs the same procedures as those used above. The main set of texts has been replaced. The substitute, comprising almost 540,000 words, is made up of samples of first-person narrative by twenty novelists of the early and middle eighteenth century. The samples of the Fieldings' work comprise eight such narratives apiece, amounting to over 75,000 words each. All told, *The History of Ophelia* itself runs to almost 102,000 words.

The strongest z-scores in Figure 3 are in the positive register, where the bluff vernacular of Defoe and the breathless muddle of Mary ('Perdita') Robinson carry them far from all the rest. The effect of such strong 'outliers' is to drive other entries together. (The real differences in distance among a range of London suburbs are similarly made to seem smaller if Canterbury and Cambridge are shown on the same map.) It is evident, even so, that a majority of the strongest negative z-scores are Sarah Fielding's and that her brother is her principal rival. His ascendancy is strongest at the beginning but he also leads the field around Segments 40 and 70. Nowhere else in Sarah Fielding's writings, save for an acknowledged contribution to her

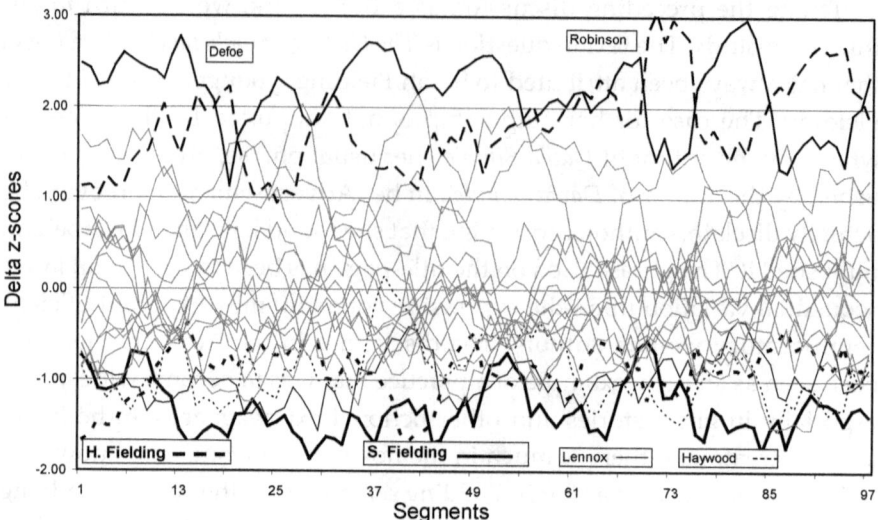

Figure 3. *The History of Ophelia* and twenty authors.
Delta z-scores for 6000-word rolling segments, with 1000-word increments.

Familiar Letters, does Henry Fielding score so strongly on tests like these. A range of other statistical tests, some treating of these frequent words, and some of the more unusual words, yield similar, often stronger, results. The most likely explanation is that, long after her brother's death, Sarah Fielding took up some of his manuscript fragments and wove them into a novel whose authorship she never claimed. The chapters dealing with the heroine's early life, her imprisonment in a country house, and her later visits to Bedlam and Tunbridge Wells are those where his hand is clearest.

Whenever the z-scores for the Fieldings diverge sharply from each other, the stronger of them leads the field of twenty authors. Whenever they converge, three other authors take a turn or two. In prose style (to speak simply as a reader), both Eliza Haywood and Charlotte Smith often show some resemblance to Sarah Fielding while Charlotte Lennox's more pointed style is not unlike that of Henry Fielding. Nowhere but in *The History of Ophelia*, however, has it proved difficult to distinguish any of them from either of the Fieldings. It appears likely that, as in *The Boy in the Bush*, some levels of revision blur the frequency-profiles and admit interlopers. On external evidence, none of those mentioned is a genuine candidate for the authorship of *The History of Ophelia*.

There is no need, however, to resort to external evidence. If each of these unlikely candidates is tested, in turn, against each of the Fieldings, one or other Fielding is the victor. The simpler discrimination of a head to head contest allows a much sharper focus.

One further possibility should be entertained. Sarah Fielding is known to have collaborated with a friend, Jane Collier, on *The Cry* (1757). Since Jane Collier's only independent work, *An Essay on the Art of Ingeniously Tormenting* (1753), is quite different in kind, it is misleading to include her in a direct comparison (where she scores badly). But a helpful inference is possible. Tests on *The Cry* show that it differs more from Henry Fielding than does Sarah Fielding's other work. A putative contribution by Jane Collier, therefore, is unlikely to account for those parts of *The History of Ophelia* where Henry prevails.

Together with Anthony Hassall, a Fielding scholar, I have written a more detailed study of this matter in which he takes up the historical and literary questions that arise (Burrows and Hassall 2006). After encountering some resistance from students of Sarah Fielding, this piece found an editor willing to publish a mildly controversial finding so that scholars can form their own opinions. It should be acknowledged that Peter Sabor, the most recent editor of *The History of Ophelia,* rejects our case and proposes that the stylistic anomalies of the novel may stem from its being written by Sarah Fielding intermittently over a period of years (Sabor 2004: 14-15). That, however, is not a difficult question to test. Sarah Fielding's style does indeed change over time. Nowhere else does it show so close a resemblance to her brother's work as in parts of this novel.

But my interest is not in arguing for victory. When the evidence is put before the scholarly community, our case will stand or fall on its merits. I raise it here because it is a suitable point of departure for a more general argument. Like any of us, literary scholars find it easy to preserve their equanimity in the face of evidence that favours their opinions. It is usually when the evidence runs the other way that we meet the pointed question: How much confidence should I place in a result like this? It is, as people say, a good question — a very good question indeed. The literary scholars who maintained their doubts in the matter of the *Elegy by W. S.* were ultimately vindicated. Such doubts as theirs are often held but they are not always justified by the evidence.

2. Questions of Confidence

2.1 Has Statistical Analysis a Place in Literary Studies?

On the face of it, literary texts offer an ideal arena for statistical analysis. They make up a vast range of specimens whose provenance and characteristics are well known and a further range where challenging questions arise on every side. By way of measurable variables, they incorporate large populations of phenomena, some frequent in occurrence, others extremely rare. Some behave according to straightforward rules, others are less predictable. Computers now make it possible to count, sort, and classify such phenomena with unprecedented speed and accuracy. As Paul Fortier, still much missed by many of us, would put it, the very nature of evidence in literary scholarship has changed. Whereas we would gather examples to illustrate a proposition and test it on our fellows, we can now gather all the relevant examples and put the case more firmly.

Among the many sorts of phenomena available, let us address ourselves to the study of words. Problems of definition declare themselves at once. Should *I'll* be taken as it stands or resolved into its constituents? In the latter case, should it be *I shall* or *I will*? Should word-types like *so* and *that*, which embrace several homographic forms, be left alone or given grammatical tags? Tagging brings an advantage in accuracy but, besides being laborious, it makes it too hard for others to replicate one's work. Much to Paul Fortier's satisfaction, I have come to believe that the text is usually best left as it stands.

Far subtler difficulties arise with truly polysemous words like *blue* where numerous literal meanings shade off into all sorts of metaphorical senses. Is it feasible to treat such diverse tokens as instances of a single word-type? In general, I believe, a given word-form can be seen as having one or more cores of meaning, populated by many almost synonymous instances and surrounded by a penumbra of increasingly unlike specimens. Especially in their outer, more sparsely populated reaches, different penumbra will sometimes overlap. At the very core, Shakespeare's *let* can mean either *hinder* or *permit*. But there will be few occasions on which *blue* means *red* or *chalk* means *cheese* or *romantic, classical*. There are several reasons for turning *I* into *we*, as in Margaret Thatcher's 'We are a grandmother'. But is it only in Australia that redheads used often to be addressed as 'Blue'? The virtue of a statistical approach is that a few exceptions are readily absorbed

1. Never Say Always Again

in any large population. This line of reasoning transcends the visible cases of difficulty and answers also to the more pervasive objection that every word-token is unique — that, as Robert Louis Stevenson put it, there are no true synonyms in English. But, I repeat, if each word-type is a cluster of near synonyms, it is usually a distinguishable cluster. At this point, the argument that words lose meaning when they are taken from their contexts can be seen as a version of a general objection to counting and classification. The idea that such procedures distort the very selfhood of unique living creatures (especially *moi*) can be either a rational complaint about unsuitable measures or a superstitious fancy. In either case, the questions arising are not peculiar to literary studies but bear on the ubiquitous presence of statistics in our lives.

In *The World We Have Lost*, Peter Laslett cites a survey of 1688 in which the population was divided almost equally into those 'Increasing the Wealth of the Kingdom' and those 'Decreasing the Wealth of the Kingdom' (Laslett 1971: 36). Economic rationalists may still be content to leave it at that. But Ian Hacking (1990) shows how such simple demographic records have broadened their range and increased their sophistication over the last two hundred years. His title, *The Taming of Chance*, is apt. Three main forms of statistics, I suggest, now pervade our lives. There are confidential surveys conducted, chiefly for exploitative purposes, by people like politicians and commercial entrepreneurs. Then there are scientific studies conducted, chiefly for the public good, by epidemiologists and others. And there is the unconscious or almost unconscious kind of statistical work that enables us all to live our daily lives. The first of these is of great influence but very little intellectual interest. Its principal effect is upon what we are allowed to buy, in the shops or at the ballot-box, and how it is packaged. The second can be a powerful force for the public good as, for example, when epidemiology led to a proper understanding of the malign effects of tobacco. It can also go a little awry when the statistics are incomplete or the results are misunderstood. Many people of my age benefited from being persuaded to turn from cigarettes to pipes. We now know that lung cancer was only part of the story and that pipe-smoking also did great harm. In another affair, one of the most effective drugs for osteoarthritis was withdrawn because it had some dangerous side-effects. It has emerged that the side-effects came from overdosage and that the media had misinterpreted and exaggerated the statistical evidence. But the drug remains unavailable. The third great branch of current statistics comprises those that we all use more or less unconsciously all the time. It embraces everything from planning the future or investing money to crossing busy roads, navigating roundabouts, and carrying raincoats — everything in which we assess risks and rely, often quite intuitively, on judgments of probability. In all three of these large areas, some measures best fit the case. Even the poignant cry, 'That traffic-light is always against me' can be stilled, if one cares to, by keeping an honest tally. The impetuous young motorist and the timid elderly one make different risk-assessments. Though both cause accidents, they are outmatched by the novice. No statistician he, he errs at random.

Like it or not, we cannot escape the use of numbers and the calculations of probability that beset us. We need to know all we can of the statistics imposed upon us. For those we ourselves employ, our best course is to seek appropriate measures, whether formal or merely rule of thumb, and to apply them with such rigour as seems due. All this considered, it is hard to see how literary studies could be exempt. On the positive side, let one immediate instance stand for many. The study of D. H. Lawrence must be advanced by fresh evidence bearing on the belief that he contributed extensively to *The Boy in the Bush* and identifying further passages as likely (or unlikely) to be his.

2.2 What Sorts of Measures Best Suit Literary Studies?[4]

When engineers use principal component analysis, I am told, they usually choose factors (such as velocity and mass) on which any group of specimens will record different scores. The chosen factors allow the scores to be arranged in ranked sequences (or vectors) showing how performance varies in the group. In literary applications of the method, we allow chosen specimens to distribute themselves according to their own dictates and then try to infer meanings for the main vectors that emerge. The top-down approach might bear, for example, on defining suitable limits of tolerance as specimens diverge from declared norms. Our bottom-up approach, however, has chiefly to do with classification — with the possibility that specimens of known proclivities may form interesting classes, with the relative importance of such classes, and with the affiliations displayed by specimens of doubtful or unknown provenance.

This simple difference is a watershed. On the one side lie categorical methods, like discriminant analysis and artificial neural networks, whose

---

4   For more information about the sorts of statistical method referred to in this section but not actually employed here, see Holmes (1994).

outcome is either Yes or No, either Accept or Reject. In cases of doubtful authorship, for example, these methods come into their own when only two candidates have any claim. On the other side lie more empirical methods, like cluster analysis and the 'bottom up' version of principal component analysis, whose outcome is more complex. The Delta procedure is of this more open kind. These are all better fitted for exploratory work in areas where that is requisite.

Authors themselves and the works they produce can be classified in many ways. Computational stylistics uses patterns of phenomena like word-frequency as part of that endeavour. We have mounting evidence that work by different authors, work in different genres, work of different eras, work in different national forms of English can all comprise statistically distinguishable groups. A further contrast, distinguishing between male and female authors, is coloured by differences of education in former times. But even the basic validity of such evidence is still contested. Partly because we are dealing with complex entities and partly because computational work in the humanities is still in its infancy, we do well to cultivate exploratory methods of analysis. For we have yet to find our Linnaeus: we have no agreed hierarchy of classes and no settled opinion as to whether our classes have strict boundaries or, as I suppose, more shadowy borderlands where monsters sometimes dwell.

Cluster analysis and principal component analysis both highlight whatever patterns of resemblance and difference emerge when a number of specimens are assessed in terms of their scores on a set of variables. When these methods are used in an exploratory way, any meaning attaching to a given pattern is a matter of inference. But, while they provide the genesis of many fruitful discoveries, such inferences must be tested sternly and persistently.

The last decade has seen an increasing attention to the need for more tests than one. More attention has been given to the use of replication and of suitable 'controls'. But we have been slower than we might to appreciate the need to make our tests as independent of each other as possible. The behavior of the language at different levels of word-frequency is so subtly interlocked that even the move from frequent words to rare ones does not yield complete independence.

In order to try a different tack, let us take a case where our results accord with the known truth. In the 129 rolling segments of *St. Ives*, all except one of the results are correct. By setting aside our outside knowledge, we may suppose that the test results need verification. The Delta test suggests, as we have seen, that Stevenson wrote most of *St. Ives* and that Quiller Couch contributed the closing chapters. But, taken alone, Figure 1 does not quite justify that conclusion because Delta is not an absolute test of authorship. It treats, in the present case, relative differences between successive segments of *St. Ives*, and thirty-two authorial samples of prose fiction. Since those by Stevenson and Quiller Couch are least unlike *St. Ives*, authorial inferences are obviously admissible. And yet, improbable as it may be, another author altogether might prove even less unlike *St. Ives* than any of these thirty-two. And, again, it is conceivable — though barely so — that our large samples of Stevenson and Quiller Couch stand apart for some non-authorial reason.

Student's t-test and the Mann-Whitney non-parametric test are used to determine which of many variables serve to differentiate two sets of specimens. To provide an adequate number of specimens, our main samples of Stevenson and Quiller Couch were each broken into thirty-six segments of two thousand words. The three hundred most frequent words of our thirty-two author corpus were taken as variables. Eighty-three of the three hundred words satisfied both tests at the 5% level of statistical significance or better. (The degrees of freedom usually exceeded sixty, and allowance was made for the 'two-tailed' character of the data.) A yield of eighty-three significant results out of three hundred, at a level where chance would admit a mere fifteen, shows that the two main sets of data come from genuinely distinct populations.

When these new data are employed on the original range of specimens, the outcome, not surprisingly, is even more clear-cut. At this point, however, the secondary sets of thirty thousand words apiece by Stevenson and Quiller Couch come into their own. These selections from their tales and stories are entirely independent of the previous sets. They were each broken into five successive segments — not rolling segments — of six thousand words. Stevenson's part of *St. Ives* was broken into seventeen segments of that size, of which five were chosen at random. Quiller Couch's part of *St. Ives* yielded five more. Word-counts for the eighty-three 'significant' variables were derived from each of these twenty segments. None of the twenty segments had any part in establishing the main list of three hundred words or in selecting eighty-three of them as differentiae.

1. Never Say Always Again

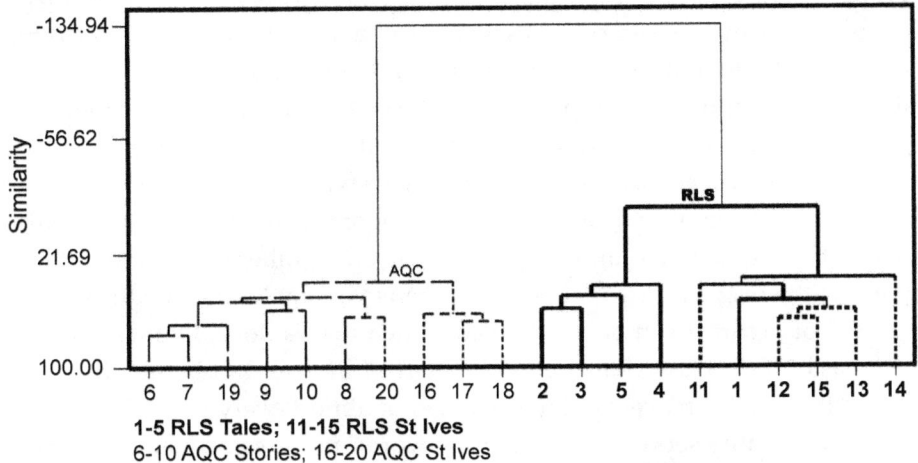

1-5 RLS Tales; 11-15 RLS St Ives
6-10 AQC Stories; 16-20 AQC St Ives

Figure 4. Cluster analysis of twenty 6000-word segments.
Analysis based on eighty-three Stevenson-Quiller Couch Differentiae.

Figure 4 is the outcome of a cluster analysis of these twenty specimens.[5] The division into two authorial families verifies our previous finding, justifies the belief that it was indeed authorial and helps to close the door on any putative interloper. The detail of Figure 4 also repays attention. On Stevenson's side, only one entry from the *Tales* intrudes into the sub-

---

[5] Cluster analysis compares the members of a set of specimens, each with every other, on the basis of their relative scores on a given set of variables. (In the present case, the specimens are texts, the variables are a range of words, and the scores are standardized word-counts) For each specimen in turn, its differences from every other are calculated and then squared to eliminate the negatives. The sum of these squared differences is extracted. The two specimens showing the smallest such difference are then united. The next smallest such difference either unites two other specimens or adds a third member to the first pair. The next smallest difference is introduced in the same way and the process continues until all specimens have been embraced. The outcome is then plotted in a dendrogram, an inverted tree-structure. As seen from the foot of the page, the y-axis shows a progressive departure from 100% similarity. The specimens are arrayed on the x-axis. The twigs of the inverted tree show which specimens united first, as being least different from each other. These pairs and trios unite in branchlets, lesser branches, greater branches, and so on until all are united in one trunk (usually at a low or even negative level of resemblance). Where specimens neighbouring each other on the x-axis do not unite, their proximity to each other is usually a reflection of the configuration of other unions.

The version of cluster analysis used here is part of the MINITAB package. The main options chosen embrace 'standardized variables,' 'Ward's linkages,' and 'squared Euclidean distances.' For an explanation of these terms, the MINITAB Help file refers the reader to Lance and Williams (1967).

group of entries for *St. Ives*. Like most long single works, *St. Ives* develops a 'note' of its own, as Henry James would say, and stands a little apart from a mixed sample of its author's writings. On Quiller Couch's side, the first three entries for *St. Ives* stand together. The last two lie in the sub-group of Quiller Couch's stories. Like most imitators, it may be, he gradually loses sight of his object and drifts towards his own style.

A sterner form of replication yields a supportive, though less powerful, result. If the two new samples by Stevenson and Quiller Couch are put in place of the original pair and no other change of any kind is made, a new version of Figure 1 can be established. When that is done, Quiller Couch still easily resists any challenge to his part of *St. Ives*. In his part, Stevenson still prevails on average but no longer at almost every point. The next step is to identify sets of 'discriminating words' in the same manner as the eighty-three described above. When that is done, the various challengers all fail in head to head contests with Stevenson. But because this further task must be undertaken iteratively, with each challenger in turn, the spectre of the unknown interloper can never quite be put to rest. A return to the texts explains why the new result is less clear-cut than the original. The original sample of Stevenson comprised selections from his romances. The new one draws on sombre, introspective tales like 'The Body Snatchers'. Both sets fall well within his stylistic repertoire but the former is more in keeping with *St. Ives*.

2.3 But is All this Really Scientific?

While this question deserves attention, I begin with reservations. I do not accept that scientists have a monopoly on serious heuristic methods. To call computational stylistics a science does not hallow it and may even misrepresent it. Nor, I believe, are scholars in our field much given to calling it a science. The suggestion is usually made by others, not always with a favourable intent. These reservations of mine are the product of long experience: but I know, only too well, that I am now moving on to ground where I am less at home.

Encouraged by Willard McCarty, I have done a little fresh reading about 'scientific method'. Putting it beside my shabby, old furniture is like putting a new bathroom into an old French hotel – one admires the facilities but wonders about the plumbing. At any rate, I take two examples. Sir Peter Medawar (1982) focuses on the central phase of experimental procedure.

Claude Bernard (1865), whom Medawar quotes approvingly, sets such procedures in a much broader heuristic framework.

Despite some differences of terminology, they are at one in an emphasis on the central experimental role of hypotheses as propositions susceptible of testing against fresh facts. Both of them regard unfalsifiable propositions as alien to the spirit of inquiry. They draw attention, albeit in different ways, to the asymmetry of proof: falsification is more conclusive than corroboration. In that light, they stress the need to persist unflaggingly in the task of disproof and they maintain that verification can never be more than dubitative or probationary. I can see nothing here that scholars in any field of rational inquiry would dispute.

Medawar's account of the genesis of hypotheses is narrower and, for me, less congenial than Bernard's. Perhaps because he is convinced that there is no such thing as an 'innocent eye', Medawar regards anything that precedes the formulation of a hypothesis as of little interest. It is inexplicable, an expression of mere 'idle wonder'. One may grant that the inquiring mind is no *tabula rasa*, but still share Bernard's belief that we often perceive important anomalies when our minds are not on duty. The response 'That's odd' rests upon an experience of what is normal but remains close to innocence. It is only when 'I wonder why' gives way to the truly pre-hypothetical 'I wonder if' that an experiment is in the making. But the ability to say 'That's odd' is fundamental. If the discovery of penicillin is the classic case, the example can readily be multiplied.

The ability to say 'That's odd' may be of particular value in fields like ours where theory does not — or does not yet — prevail. The many meanings attached to the word 'theory' cloud the question of whether empirical work like that of computational stylistics lacks a theoretic basis. (McCarty and Love write strongly on this topic from opposed standpoints. See McCarty, 2005, 139-55 and Love, 2002, ch. viii). From mere hobby-horses, through hypotheses (usually of some breadth), the word reaches out to include such general laws as Newton's and Einstein's. Let us cherish our hobby-horses but keep them in their stables. Let us welcome hypotheses and put them to the test. And let us stand firm against the suggestion that we can do nothing until we are ready, like Newton, Einstein, or Chomsky himself, to embrace the universe.

It is possible, nevertheless, to aspire to a modest generality. If language can be seen as a manifestation of cognitive behavior, it is only to be expected that the performance of any individual in this field, as in many others, should not only resemble but also diverge from the performances of other people. Ferdinand de Saussure brings this to a point in his distinction between *langue* and *parole*, between the set of linguistic resources available to us and the subset of choices we each make. Through a simple corollary, one may suppose that *parole* has a frequentative as well as a selective aspect. What else could give it an enduring shape of its own? One may also hope that a better understanding of computational classification will help to fill the ground between de Saussure and the various experiments we undertake. As matters stand at present, I have yet to see or hear of a text of any length whose patterns of word-frequency could not be distinguished from others of its kind or which failed to show meaningful affinities with others written by its author. To the extent that this tests his theory, de Saussure still holds his ground and serves us well.

In discussing what comes after the experimental phase of a scientific inquiry, Medawar and Bernard concur. Where an hypothesis is upheld, it still remains open to further inquiry. Failed hypotheses are to be rejected. (Medawar adds 'or modified' but says no more). Neither of them, unfortunately, sheds much light on the meaning of failure or on its sequel.

What are we to suppose? The strict position these eminent scientists take is a necessary response to human ingenuity. Most sets of data are susceptible of several hypothetical explanations. Any anomalies can usually be rationalized away. Why pretend to test hypotheses at all if one is determined to 'save' them when they falter? It is in this spirit, I suppose, that I have been reproached for explaining such anomalous specimens as Segment 34 of Figure 1. The question here is whether it is legitimate to try to diagnose the behavior of a single anomalous specimen in a field of 129. I do not believe that the objection to 'saving the hypothesis' should be carried so far. For if a single aberrant specimen spells failure, there is no place in science for the study of human behavior and no role for statistical analysis. Since that is patently absurd, we must think again.

An error in observation or calculation has no bearing on a hypothesis. When one is found, it should be rectified without ado. Such trivialities apart, it seems that scientists must distinguish between crucial, casual, and fruitful anomalies and between acceptable and unacceptable levels of tolerance. These will differ greatly in different fields of inquiry. But, in any field where 'zero tolerance' is not required, the value of statistical measures of significance and error is immense. It seems clear that we, too, must work along such lines and that we must persuade our traditionalist colleagues that it is right to do so.

And after a hypothesis is seen to fail? Dead end or new point of departure? That will depend upon the residual merits, if any, of the original hypothesis. Willard McCarty (2005: 286, s. v. 'failure') writes compellingly on the fruitfulness of failure. After a failure, to put it in my terms, there is likely to be a period of disappointment. But then 'I wonder why' comes back into its own, 'I wonder if' soon follows, and the game begins again. A new hypothesis emerges to transcend the old and is tested in its turn. If that is unscientific behavior, we must gladly draw our skirts aside and leave the scientists to their own ways.

3. How Much Confidence Should I Place in a Result Like This?

The question underlying this whole discussion sometimes reflects a desire for certainty. But successful scientific hypotheses remain dubitative. Statistical analysis deals only in levels of probability. Scholarship in the humanities is seldom regarded as definitive. Life itself is, in many ways, a game of chance. Should literary scholars ask us, as some do, for certainty? In its usual form, the suggestion is that, unless computational methods can offer certainty, they are more trouble than they are worth. A subtler version is latent in Joseph Rudman's demand (1998, 2000) for 'verifiably unique' authorial signatures. Many of his structures have been of great value. But here, as with his notion that it is time to settle upon a single agreed method of analysis, he, too verges on naivety.

We cannot offer certainty. But where there is an adequate body of material, computational stylistics usually offers strong evidence and is getting better at it. (For a somewhat more conservative assessment than mine, see Craig, 2004.) In my view, head to head contests are rarely difficult to resolve. In more open cases, the likely candidates can be identified. We cannot proceed with equal confidence in cases where an unknown interloper may be in the game. Even there, however, a weak set of results for known candidates may indicate that it is desirable to look elsewhere.

Our findings usually concur with the scholarly consensus because both parties are usually right. When there is no such consensus, our findings can be especially serviceable. And when our findings are seriously at odds with the consensus, *both* parties need to think again. The statistical evidence may not be valid and, when it is, it can still give rise to mistaken inferences. And even when, on the other side, a scholarly opinion is widely held and of long standing, it is open to correction.

2. Cybertextuality by the Numbers

Ian Lancashire

When we think in words, the thoughts come in grammatical form with subject, verb, object and modifying clauses falling into place without our having the slightest perception of how the sentence structure is produced (Lashley 1958).

I suppose that all of us have a primitive prompter or commentator within, who from our earliest years has been advising us, telling us what the real world is. There is such a commentator in me. I have to prepare the ground for him. From this source come words, phrases, syllables; sometimes only sounds, which I try to interpret, sometimes whole paragraphs, fully punctuated. When E. M. Forster said, 'How do I know what I think until I see what I say?' he was perhaps referring to his own prompter (Bellow 2006: 95).

1. Introduction

Readers who want to find the author in the text should not be too disheartened when they see only themselves. The New Criticism and Reader Response theory gave up trying, not unreasonably, because authoring takes place largely in the author's unconscious and resists being observed.[1] Cybertextuality,[2] the subject of this essay, theorizes the authorial process by

---

1 The works of Sigmund Freud make the acceptance of this simple truth much easier. As Karl Lashley says, we can recall the process of writing only in the act of writing (that is, language-making is a procedural memory; see Squire 1987: 152); we have no memory storage system that can save, for later retrieval, knowledge of the steps in which we create an utterance.
2 See Lancashire 2004b. Cybertextuality extends Espen Aarseth's term 'cybertext'

bringing together observations from four areas: Norbert Wiener's cybernetics, self-testimony by creative writers, cognitive psychology, and computer-assisted text-analysis. I first apply Wiener's communications theory to describe how authors craft sentences by subjecting their own chunk-sized phrases to mental cycles of uttering (messaging) and error-monitoring (self-feedback). Cybertextuality pays close attention to evidence for two hypothetical cognitive quantities, the cognitive chunk or phrasal word-packet, and the cognitive capacity or load. I then review what cognitive psychology knows of these numbers, and of our mental self-monitor.

I refer to chunk size as the alpha value. What constrains it is the capacity of the phonological loop of Alan Baddeley's model of working memory (Baddley 2000). This constraint comes with being human, although an author can appear to get around it by shuttling chunks rapidly in and out of working memory from the clusters or schemas that form, distinctively, in long-term memory networks and serve domains of knowledge in which the author has expertise. Computer text-analysis (stylistic counts and the repeating patterns in textual concordances) detects what even the author cannot perceive about himself: it reveals these chunks in the phrasal vocabularies of authors (Lancashire 2004a). Chunk size also limits the error-finding capacity of our mental self-monitor: mistakes that cross chunk boundaries normally escape notice. Authorial self-repairs in a holograph manuscript, such as Shakespeare's hand in *The Book of Sir Thomas More*, (1910) show this mental feedback at work. The second constraint is the omega value, the cognitive capacity or load for a thought. Virginia Woolf's holograph manuscript versions for *The Waves* (1976) reveal this size-constraint for her mind.

The alpha and omega values, these cybertextual numbers[3], inform the authoring process and help shape an author's idiolect. They do not change markedly from person to person. These two verbal capacities — of chunks, and of maximum text-size that chunks may combine to express a unified thought — also drive authors, both to invent language technologies that supplement their memory capacities and to empower conscious self-editing. These technologies act through the laws of copyright to replace the

---

(1997), which is first used in 1991 by the 'speculative fiction' poet Bruce Boston.
3   I call them alpha and omega because, in operating within their constraints, our minds approach as close to the Old Testament creative God as creatures of a post-Darwinian world can get. `I was in the spirit on the Lord's day, and heard behind me a great voice, as of a trumpet, Saying, I am Alpha and Omega, the first and the last: and, What thou seest, write in a book[...]' (Revelation 1:10-11).

concept of a creative author by that of an owner-author. The post-literate cyborgic author is a self-employed expert at expressing (not thinking) verbally (not conceptually) original texts that are always fixed in some medium. Fixation, when utterance takes an external form, is the critical step. It marks where the author-creator gives way to the author-owner, who may even be defined as someone who has never even read the authored text he owns.

2. Cybertextuality

Cybertextuality theorizes our authoring of speech and written text, in the context of what we know about language cognition and about the technologies by which we supplement that. Every language tool that we have made, from oral-formulaic metre to the digital workstation, speaks to our species' frustrations with native cognition in language production, that is, unassisted speaking, writing, and reading. Dissatisfied with how genes have designed us, we have built communications technologies that give us a flawlessly searchable and readable external long-term memory and an aid to working memory by which we can author error-free, carefully sculpted utterances, both brief and epic. The author uses a literary machine (this is Ted Nelson's term (1987), modified in Katherine Hayles' *Writing Machines* (2002)) as a cybernetic extension of her mind.

The cognitive mechanics of authoring need cybernetic concepts: both Espen Aarseth's book *Cybertext* (1997), which describes texts (such as interactive fictions) that ask readers to do physical work, and posthumanist Katherine Hayles (1999), stimulated theory to re-think Norbert Wiener's communications theory. The human-computer interface supplements and imitates cognitive language production by the inner Muse and her receiver, the inner Editor. We have even developed text-analysis software that facilitates the reading of texts. Such tools extend the human mind in uttering. By availing ourselves of them, we become cyborgic and partake of the character of a cybernetic organism. Authoring of texts is a recursive process in which hand-shakes cycle between a sender who utters something and a receiver who perceives the sent message and feeds back information about it to the sender. Unlike Wiener's cybernetics, cybertextuality asserts that the sender and the receiver are initially the same: we read ourselves before anyone else does. This is an old idea found in the speech-pathology research of Edward D. Mysak (1966). He argued that the 'speech system may be viewed as a closed, multiple-loop system containing feedforward and feedback internal and external loops' (1966: 17), that is, loops that take place wholly *within the mind*, as distinguished from Wienerian loops that involve the reactions of other listeners.[4] Cognitively, everyone utters speech, syllable by syllable, only after extensive self-monitoring for errors, and then self-adjusting for corrections.

Wiener coined the word *cybernetics* in the 1950s to name a theory of communication that has since morphed into information science and has influenced how everyone thinks (Wiener 1950/1967). The word comes from the Greek word for steersman, *kubernetes*. Cybernetics asserts the commonalties between how people communicate with people, how machines such as anti-aircraft guns and radar technology signal one another, and of course how people negotiate with machines like text-analysis tools. Wiener had the brilliant idea that communication is a hand-shaking exercise, a series of message-response transactions between sender and receiver. Each sent message prompts a response that enables the sender to correct the first message or to move on to something new. Wiener's five cybernetic modules are sender (author), receiver (reader), message (text), channel (medium), degrading noise (language and culture change, and more), and feedback (criticism). His 'theory of messages,' as he referred to it (Wiener 1950: 106; Masani 1990: 251-52), is that the sender steers or controls composition according to a receiver's incremental feedback because only after that response can the sender be certain that noise has not rendered the message unreadable. A message is thus an incomplete act of communication without its partnering feedback.

Biology has for a long time been influenced by cybernetics, and cognitive scientists frequently describe mental and neural processes as message-feedback in nature. Wiener's universal phenomenon, in cybertextuality theory, also embraces many aspects of literary research. For example, rhetoric and genre can be conceived as strategies of redundancy employed by authors who want to reduce reader misunderstanding that arises from

---

4   Mysak specified ten loops, two of them feedforward (ff) and five of them feedback (fb): thought propagation, word formation (ff), thought pattern-word pattern comparison (fb), word production (ff), actual word product-desired word product comparison (fb), word product-thought pattern comparison (fb), internal multiple-loop speech recycling, word product-listener comparison (fb), actual listener reaction-desired listener reaction comparison (fb), and internal and external multiple-loop speech recycling (19). Levelt's recent theory of lexical access in speech production (1999) uses the same terminology of feedforward and feedback in mapping cognitive processing.

cultural, gender, and social differences as well as from transmission errors often identified in textual criticism and scholarly editing. (Redundancy sacrifices cognitive message size to make messages immune to disruption by noise.) Reader-response theory internalizes the message-feedback partnership in the reader rather than the author. The scepticism that moves postmodern theorists to speak of the death of the author arises from their legitimate perception of how unconscious the author is of cognitive creative process, of how mysterious it is. We retreat into Michel Foucault's author-function (Foucault 1989/1969), that is, the owner-author in which law and capitalism trade.

From a cybertextual perspective, however, the author is partly alive in the work. Messaging and feedback cycles leave idiolectal and idiosyncratic traces that survive the author's replacement by the editor, the owner-author, the employer who asserts property rights on an authoring employee, the buyer, death itself, the deceased's estate manager, and especially the reader. Texts incorporate fossils of their own biological realization. Cybertextuality asks us to read texts in a new way, to discover within them the stigmata of authoring – the marks that distinguish its subjection to cognitive limitations. These are partly observed in uttering-feedback cycles as they create evanescent or frozen texts.

Of course, Norbert Wiener's five cybernetic modules do not map onto authoring as neatly as one might like.[5] The author is apparently unknowable, for the time being at least a see-through cellophane entity that we cannot perceive directly because we have no memory system to store (and thus consciously verbalize) what it is. The reader is the only part of the author whom we can see at work, subvocally as error-catching and inner speech, externally as what our writing and speaking tools utter back. Unlike

---

5   A researcher reading a blurred photocopy of an article, or someone listening to a friend's goodbyes on a cellphone losing power: cybernetics interprets these cases well. The article and the friend's goodbyes, however badly distorted by noise, are fixed and analyzable. The reader's and listener's puzzled reactions - *what's this? what did you say?* – are themselves also unambiguous. Everything here can be quantified. We can measure the percentage of loss in visual and acoustic signals and assign a value to them. That value would take into account the redundancy we build into language, unconsciously, to ensure that, despite plenty of interference, we can still understand what is being said. Given that fifty percent of alphabetic English is technically redundant, as Claude Shannon calculated (1948: 14-15; Pierce 1980: 75; cf. Reed and Durlach 1998), a great deal can be obscured without badly damaging the information in an utterance. For example, if a filter removes all sounds above or below 1500 Hz from speech, as A. B. Wood (1955) showed, there is only a 35 percent decrease in intelligibility.

Wiener's messages, both uttering and feedback are sent as phrasal fragments. Sometimes the sender fashions an utterance for two or more receivers and crafts the message so that they find different things in it. Messages are readable first, not externally, but in the sender's own working memory, a little living auditory and visual book that dynamically overwrites itself in seconds. Then they appear in iconic or echoic sensory memory for a brief time, unless machine-assisted. The channel for these cybertextual transactions is the mind's neural infrastructure, the brain, but the brain is not the simple left-to-right pipe by which Wiener's cybernetics represents the arena across which a message travels from sender to receiver. For one thing, as lesions prove, the channel can break down and generate the cybernetic noise that damages transmission. Uttering uses not a single channel but a crosshatch of dynamic and parallel processes operating and interacting simultaneously. Only when an utterance reaches our sincerest flattery of the brain, the computer, does it take a simpler path. The sources of noise that afflict cognitive messages in transmission – dementia among them – also resist easy explanation, although imaging devices, and biopsies and autopsies, have for a century gradually unveiled the havoc that cerebral lesions can wreak on cognitive functions.

Cybertextuality asks cognition patently awkward or impossible questions about an imprecise phenomenon, literary making. Scientific consensus abhors the quick answers we would like, and even science changes its mind sometimes. Cognitive-psychology experiments focus tightly on testing hypotheses advanced by previous experiments. Research runs counter to the grain of basic science when it treats governing theories, like Alan Baddeley's working memory, Willem Levelt's lexical access in speech production, and Walter Kintsch's construction-integration theory of text comprehension, as other than explanations that are consistent with cognitive affects and other experimental results. Not infrequently, an explanation for a well-attested empirical effect, accepted for some time, suddenly is controverted by a related experiment. Yet even cybertextuality theory, while speculative, anchors itself in an experimental science, text analysis. Here, the subjects of text-analysis experiments are Shakespeare's hand in the manuscript play of Sir Thomas More, and Virginia Woolf's method in creating *The Waves*.

3. Cognitive Authoring and the Chunk

Most of the human brain, topographically, is active at some point during an utterance.[6] The purpose, the plan, and the gist of a message originate in the pre-frontal cortex, like every other thing we intend to do. If we decide to read a sentence aloud, for example, processing begins once the visual cortex at the very back of the brain receives data from the eyes. The frontal cortex then sets in train an acoustic re-encoding of this visual data so that they assume the form they would have had if heard and passed on by the temporal auditory cortex. Next the brain must perceive semantically what is said. Wernicke's area in the left hemisphere in the brain of a right-handed person is associated with semantic comprehension. This assigns words (lemmas) to each sound from long-term memory. If Wernicke's area is damaged, the brain can produce word-salad sentences: they have a proper syntactic form but do not make sense. Whatever emotional (rather than logical and linguistic) content a sentence has is recognized by the right hemisphere of this right-handed person. Then the brain encodes the recognized word-train syntactically and phonologically: Broca's area, just forward of Wernicke's area, does this. A brain in which Broca's area is damaged utters semantically understandable sentence fragments lacking grammatical form. Activities at both sites tend to involve areas immediately under the cortex. Finally, the fully-encoded sentence moves to the motor cortex for pronouncing. Once the brain gives phonological form to an utterance, it can enter the catchment area of working memory as inner speech. After semantic and affective processing, we hear the sentence unfold subvocally and overtly aloud. It never occurs to many people that language production is unconscious because we experience its assured power immediately in uttering speech.

Functionally, this process takes one step after another, but it very probably happens all at the same time, each sub-process affecting every other. Different aspects of uttering take different paths through the brain. If we type an invented sentence, for example, the brain must re-encode the auditory data native to its language function into visual form and must issue instructions to the motor cortex on how to operate a keyboard. Localization of brain functions thus reveals the modularity of mental language processing. Certain activities take place in specific places in the brain, even though

---

6   See Geschwind (1979), a classical account of how the brain handles language; and Damasio (1994) and Lieberman (2000), for valuable correctives.

many activities are active simultaneously. Localization has proved especially meaningful in analyzing the writing of individuals who have been subject to medical testing.

Peter Garrard's research on novels by Iris Murdoch as she succumbed to Alzheimer's disease — an essay found elsewhere in this volume — is a uniquely important case study in that respect. A 'profound bilateral hippocampal shrinkage' that turned up at an autopsy after her death in 1999 affected the linking of her working memory to her long-term memory. *Jackson's Dilemma*, her final novel, exhibits lexical and semantic impoverishment, with a drop of twenty percent in vocabulary. This result was not unexpected: Alzheimer's Disease sufferers have a 'relative impairment in semantic processing' (Poore and others 2006). The medical tests and autopsy had turned up a medical condition – in effect, a growing deterioration in one location of the brain, something like a lesion – that coincided with a reduction in Murdoch's lexical store and in the information density of her prose. The link between Murdoch's body and mind in Garrard's case study was her working memory. The hippocampus, its gateway, must also be involved with the most important part of our mental life, where we directly and self-consciously hear and manipulate our language subvocally. When we hear ourselves think in the mind, we use working memory to do so. Sufferers of dementia gradually feel that space shrink. If there is any part of the complex cybertextual channel that we can access directly, that part is our working memory.

Alan Baddeley's sturdy model of working memory (formerly called short-term memory) has lasted nearly thirty years (Baddeley 1986). It has four functions: the phonological loop (where we hear subvocal mental language), the short-term visual sketchpad (where we summon up or store images, including written text), the episodic buffer (where we retrieve multimodal episodic memories), and an executive that manages these three slave systems. We use the executive to refresh what appears in either store, or to overwrite what is there with something else. Because our brain can only manage mental language if it is auditorily encoded, the visual sketchpad can keep a printed or a written sentence or page before our consciousness as an image, but before we can manipulate text cognitively as language we have to re-encode it phonetically (read it); thus we transfer it into the phonological loop. That loop, a kind of cognitive mobius strip, imposes big constraints on our linguistic self-awareness. The most important limit is on how much spoken language we can place in and retrieve from working memory. What can we say about its size in a healthy person? I refer to this size the alpha value because it characterizes where every utterance starts.

One of the best known quantities of working memory is George Miller's 'magical number' (1956): this is the maximum number of elements we can hold in active memory — seven, plus or minus two elements. Telephone numbers were allotted seven numbers for this reason half a century ago. Now that we have an area code as well, another three digits, we can only consciously keep a phone number in memory until we dial it by making several chunks represent two or more numbers. In 2000, Miller's 'magical number' was revised (on the basis of decades of experiments) by Nelson Cowan downwards to four chunks, plus or minus two chunks. Cowan estimates that the still uncertain size of each chunk is perhaps three or four items. Another variable is the Brown (1958) / Peterson (1959) duration rate for short-term memory items, which decreases markedly until it almost reaches nil at twenty seconds. An equation for a person's working-memory retrievability capacity, therefore, would have at least three variables: chunks, items (or subchunks), and their current duration, measured in seconds, within working memory. These quantities have been proposed by cognitive scientists after dozens of experiments with human subjects over half a century. Arranged in my simple model formula, they model one's retrievability capacity, the number of potentially retrievable items from Alan Baddeley's phonological loop, at any given point in time, as the alpha value.

The formula is $\alpha = (\beta * \gamma) * \delta$, where beta ($\beta$) is Cowan's chunk capacity, a number from two to six; gamma (γ) is Cowan's items per chunk, a number from three to four; and delta (δ) is the percentage of items still retrievable, measured by the seconds so far held in working memory since the last refresh or rehearsal, according to Brown and Peterson.[7] They estimate that memory loss increases, the longer the duration: nothing lost after no seconds, fifty percent remains after three seconds, forty percent after six seconds, twenty percent after nine seconds, twelve percent after twelve seconds, and so on. The range of alpha values goes from 0.6 items, for someone with the lowest chunk and item capacity near the end of maximum duration in working memory, to 2.8 items, for someone with a median chunk and item capacity in mid-duration, and to 24.0 items, for someone with the highest chunk and item capacity at the very point when everything is

---

[7] I hope that someone else, more qualified than myself, has devised or will devise a better formula.

planted or refreshed in working memory. Fernard Gobet and Gary Clarkson (2004) demonstrate that, for experts (those with the highest capacity), the number of chunks is fewer than three, but they are templates from long-term memory and the items they hold are go up to fifteen. The Gobet and Clarkson alpha value, then, for an expert with fresh working-memory content would be (2 * 15) * 1 = 30 items. The inner voice would have, if Cowan's experiments are definitive, half a word at the least, three words on average, and (at the most) two alexandrines or 12-syllable lines (or three pentameter lines, following Gobet and Clarkson).

The alpha value does not give *information calculated in bits*. That amount is less than the items represented by the alpha value because all human languages are redundant. Further, the alpha value is not an intelligence quotient, or a measure of long-term memory size, or a limit on what we can communicate to others. Almost all speech and thought-making take place in the unconscious mind and feed off a long-term memory store that we can probe but never read. Damage to phonological working-memory capacity does not impede sentence comprehension (Martin 1987). Alan Baddeley explains that, on the basis of experimental work with children and second-language learners, the phonological loop is the system that evolution has developed for the crucial task of language acquisition. Adults who have a disruption to this system do not have too many problems, provided they are not required to learn new languages (2004: 54).

We are aware of an intelligence working in the cognitive background as a gist of something we want to say. Although we can consciously schematize the process of thinking, we cannot recall *how* this gist emerges, that is, how we make a thought. Working memory thus limits the mastery of language, not thought. It is the mental function (other than immediate auditory or echoic memory) where we are conscious of what our mind generates or receives before vocalization and where we can do something about that awareness, such as commit it to long-term memory or to paper. Our unconscious continues to feed language effortlessly, spontaneously, into subvocal working memory in chunks that fit within the phonological loop.

The retrievability limit represented by the alpha value is unaltered by what enters our sensory stores, whether echoic or iconic. Both these immediate forms of sensory memory, echoic or auditory, iconic or visual, decay rapidly after 250 milliseconds or a quarter of a second and are gone utterly after half a second (Robinson-Riegler 2004: 104-5). The longer we continue to look at something, oddly, the more the iconic image decays (Robinson-

Riegler 2004: 106-07). We can deliberately store what we see in sensory experience in the visual sketchpad, but only after conversion to phonetic encoding can we manage it as language. As a result, we again appear to bump into the constraints of the phonological loop. What we hear from others as vocal speech overwrites some or all its contents. That is why it can be hard to finish a thought in words when someone suddenly breaks one's attention by talking to one. Our phonetic working memory has no shut-off valve, no filter, to save us from an incoming utterance in a natural language we know.

4. Cognitive Reading

It's unclear whether we actually edit what we say before we say it, but the fact that we edit what we have already said is not in doubt (Robinson-Reigler 2004: 421).

From time to time we catch ourselves in making a speech error. We stop what we are saying in mid-flow with an editing comment such as 'uh, that is' or 'um, I mean,' and we substitute a corrected word or phrase. These spontaneous self-repairs illustrate cybertextual cycling. (Comparable are the kinds of word-processing corrections that we make as we type a sentence.) Hesitations, pauses, or rests are another sign of message-feedback cycling. We may not know why we are hesitating after one phrase, and before the next, except that we are not ready to move on. In oral delivery, we nervously use fillers or paralanguage to keep the listeners' attention and signal that something else is on its way. If we time a lecturer's use of these fillers, one every few seconds, we can see chunking and cybertextual cycling at work.

Self-monitoring also occurs at the pre-vocal cognitive level when a mistake is interrupted in the middle of uttering it. Willem Levelt (1989: 467-8) proposes that, at different levels of utterance-processing (lexical, phonological, etc.), 'a watchful little homunculus' monitors, editor-like, 'the construction of the preverbal message, the appropriateness of lexical access, the well-formedness of syntax, or the flawlessness of phonological-form access.' His self-monitor intercepts or receives both inner (subvocal) and covert speech, checks it for errors, and reports back to what he calls the 'conceptualiser' so that it can reformulate the utterance (cf. Hartsuiker and others 2005: 4). As an example of an error caught subvocally, before articulation, Levelt gives the example, 'we can go straight to the ye-[...] to the orange dot,' and explains that 'To interrupt right after the first syllable [*ye*-], the error must already have been detected a bit earlier, probably before the onset of articulation' (1999: 33; and for additional evidence, see Hartsuiker and Kolk 2001). Another recent experimental finding, from magnetoencephalography, is that self-uttered speech takes about 100 milliseconds to activate the speaker's *own* auditory cortex (Curio and others 2000: 190). This suggests to me that self-monitoring of such errors occurs in prevocalic inner speech,[8] somewhat in advance of actual vocalization. Levelt believes that self-monitoring can only be effected by a cognitive process parallel to the one that authors an utterance. This process would read incremental stages of composed utterance and return feedback to the authoring process. Both processes would be simultaneously active and, at each exchange, would effect a cybertextual cycle.

There is already reason to believe that we cognitively model or construct what we hear and see, accepting our own model over the initial sensory data. Philip Lieberman (2000: 57, citing McGurk and MacDonald 1976), explains the well-known McGurk effect. When a person sees a video of the face of someone saying *ga* at the same time as the video sound system outputs *ba*, that person hears the intermediate sound *da*. If the person covers his eyes, however, he hears *ba*. Test subjects, faced with an inconsistency in the data (what might be termed noise), unselfconsciously hear only what they analyze as being said. The McGurk effect reveals that we use visual evidence to determine what a sound is, but it also demonstrates that we integrate, in a mandatory and spontaneous way, audiovisual speech syllables that disagree with one another and create a sound never made. Posner and Raichle report another instance of how a deep cognitive process emends sensory input: 'if one removes a phoneme from an auditory word and replaces it with white noise, what is often heard is the correct word with a burst of noise superimposed' (1994: 112). Semir Zeki agrees that 'One of the functions of the brain ... is to instill meaning into this world, into the signals that it receives,' but he cautions that often the mind must 'allow of several interpretations, all of equal validity.' (2006: 262). We experience these alternate meanings sequentially and do not feel obliged to select among them.

The brain betrays its cybertextual cycles in error recognition and recovery. Self-monitoring may extend to any cognitive language representation, whether in uttering or reading a word or syllable, where error or ambiguity

---

8   Baddeley suggests that the auditory imagery system, not working memory, may be responsible for inner speech that accompanies reading (2004: 49). If so, the distinction may be marginal because their capacities appear to be identical.

is perceived. For example, the remarkable N400 brain waves discovered in electroencephalographs (EEGs) of individuals reading semantically problematic or unexpected words show that the long-term memory store reads the message as it unfolds and comments on it using data that appear to be non-linguistic in nature. An N400, negative-voltage wave in the brain peaks 400 milliseconds after it encounters a semantically incongruous word (Robinson-Reigler 2004: 391; Federmeier and Kutas 1999). The N400 wave registers a channel-wide response to an unexpected mental utterance such as 'Experience is the mother of *despair*.' After formulating a message partially, the brain responds to it, occasionally with a N400 wave, other times with vocal self-repair. Because we cannot script our words haltingly in working memory before we say them, because we seldom know exactly what we are going to say until we actually say it subvocally or aloud (as E. M. Forster says), and because we hear ourselves speak and see ourselves write at almost the same time as a listener or a viewer does, we need an unselfconscious error-checking facility in place to catch mistakes.

Most speech errors caught by our cognitive self-monitoring involve a switching of word-onset consonants in small phrases (e.g. *phrall smases*). These are well within the alpha value for management in working memory. Larger errors in syntactical structure, such as subject-verb agreement in number, elude detection until we engage in close editing and proofreading or run an analysis by automatic style-checking software. The perceptual span in reading a text has a comparable capacity to the phonological loop. Our eyes traverse in successive fixations, saccades (left-to-right jumps), and regressions (reverse saccades). A saccade takes twenty milliseconds and traverses six to eight letters, and a fixation lasts 200-300 milliseconds,[9] unless it settles into a gaze, and encompasses about three characters to the right and fifteen to the left (or four to five words in length). College-level students move and fix their eyes 90 times for every 100 words, 25 percent of which saccades are regressive (Crowder 1992: table 2.1). The phrase, 'watchful little homunculus,' describes both the cognitive self-monitor and the reading eye. Both perceive mental speech segmented in comparable spans whose capacity may approximate also the alpha value.

Language self-consciousness appears to be a stream but, when examined closely, consists of staccato-like pulses in which a succession of chunks, proposed by a cognitive conceptualizer (which we experience as the gist of

---

9   We fixate more briefly on function words than on content words (Gleason and Ratner 1998: fig. 5.4).

what we intend to say), are monitored for correctness by a parallel process before being articulated. The Muse who brings texts piecemeal into being from darkness, and the Editor who announces corrections to those texts and knits them together from much the same obscurity, feedforward and feedback our utterances in cybertextual cycles. Messages are normally fragments. The phrasal size of caught speech errors, and the perceptual span in reading, both fall near the alpha value. Is this value, then, a broader cognitive storage limit? Although the brain has '10^{11} neurons connected by 10^{15} synapses' (Chklovskii and others 2004: 782), and the consensus is that our long-term memory capacity is limitless, working-memory capacity is conceded to filter and constrain information, especially language data, entering the long-term store. Is it possible, then, that there may be a maximum conceptual span, an upper limit on the extent of a cognitively manageable associative memory cluster?[10] Would it be so odd if all memory systems worked by the same numbers?

Gilgamesh, the Bible, *War and Peace,* and *La Divina Commedia* are not just phrasal sequences: these epic achievements have, camel-like, come through the eye of such needles as the alpha and omega values. It is unclear whether a faulty phonological loop would have prevented Dante, Tolstoy, and Shakespeare from writing. However, because language is always changing, language learning never stops. If evolution designed the phonological loop for language learning, then it is also, to a degree, the Procrustean bed of language. Has anyone in recent memory created a substantial utterance, novel-sized, simply with the unaided human memory system? Most of us cannot manage a list of groceries, even though we may well be able to use language well enough not to starve.

How have we overcome the limits of these values? We have externalized the Muse and the Editor. Writing, printing, and digital tools have exported much of our Muse, that is, our long-term memory and lexical production system (as Levelt calls it), into dictionaries, encyclopedias, and the world's vast libraries. Word processors operating on computer workstations with visual displays have imported some of the knowledge by which Willem Levelt's 'watchful little homunculus' corrects speech errors. Our workstation adds two additional dynamic systems to those which that our cognition calls its own. While the eyes are fixed on the page and on the screen, iconic memory maintains a much fuller copy of what we have uttered than working memory could ever have stored.

---

10   I discuss the omega value for this below.

5. Cognitive Capacity

What impact does a thought-capacity limit — the omega value — have on our uttered texts? Except for conversation, where the amount of text between turns is quite small, we do much better than generate phrases and paragraphs. The process by which we cobble our chunks into speeches, essays, and books uses two technologies, the more recent being external memory and processing systems from writing (which first unfettered length restrictions on sentences and paragraphs) to word processing, and a second, more ancient one in the *loci et imagines* method of artificial memory described in Frances Yates' *The Art of Memory* (1966). It asks the extemporaneous speaker to prepare by mapping the order of his sentences as stops on a walk through a public place like a forum or a mall, and the content of each of those sentences in an object placed, mentally, in each stop. As the author speaks, he guides himself by mentally taking his own guided tour through the place, pausing at each stop to pick up its object. (For example, if I memorized the structure of this essay by mapping it to my local retail park, I might think of artificial memory as the local Indigo bookstore and place a toy locomotive, symbolizing the *loci et imagines* method, at its front door.)

This method can be observed today in the behaviour of experts and mnemonists. Chess masters can rapidly move schemas (the templates in Gobet and Clarkson 2004), which are specially encoded and stored in long-term memory, in and out of working memory. They can expand the sub-parts of these schemas without losing track of where they are. This mental technique shuttles between the two memory systems, leading to a '10-fold increase in performance on tests of STM [Short Term Memory],' but only in their specific areas of expertise (Ericsson and Kintsch 1995: 211-12). Normally it takes between five and ten seconds to store a memory long-term and a second to retrieve it, but experts manage to make retrieval from long-term memory only 300 milliseconds longer than from working memory (1995: 215). This technique draws not on deductive logic but on stored memories of sequences of moves and positions on a chessboard. Experienced writers and readers have similar stocks of sentence and paragraph structures in long-term memory that can be applied at need. Writers like John Milton, Henry James, James Joyce, and Cormac McCarthy can produce very long sentences, extending well beyond page boundaries. Periodic styles like Milton's in *Paradise Lost*, composed mentally in daily segments while he was blind, and dictated to his daughters in the morning, must have grown from decades of expertise as a master of Latin, Greek, and Hebrew, and as Oliver Cromwell's Latin secretary. Milton and these other writers are as great experts in English composition as chess grand masters are in positional play. The making and exploitation of these schemas constitute individual traits, but they do not enlarge personal cognitive capacity. The expert learns to associate a more-or-less abstract analytic map in long-term memory with many small but fully-realized codes for that map in working memory.

That we cannot use an expert's mental technique *generally* suggests that some general cognitive capacity limit exists on our ability to comprehend thoughts as well as utterances. Edward Sapir and Benjamin Lee Whorf believe that we can only think in natural language – to them, there is no distinction between thought and language – while others believe that we think in non-linguistic concepts, often called mentalese, and then translate its output into language (Pinker 1994: 67-82). Language being a late evolutionary development, should we deny thought to so many other language-less species (including our own, not so long ago)? Insofar as language represents only a part of the content of our long-term memory, also, does it make sense that we do not think with the images, events, and sounds stored in it when so many testify otherwise? A non-linguistic mentalese offers a plausible foundation for the making of all languages from Swahili to symbolic logic and music, much as XML,[11] for example, enables us to devise a multitude of encoding languages. The inchoate gist we feel before saying something has not been shown to be natural language.

If languageless thought observes a cognitive capacity limit, does it exceed the alpha limit on speech in working memory? Well, of course who cannot comprehend instantly a sentence that takes longer than two seconds to utter? That granted, a limit manifests itself in many ways. When we artificially interfere with someone's working memory, as by giving a writer a second, simultaneous task, we know that his sentence length falls. We know that college students who had to hold in memory six digits concurrently even as they devised two-noun sentences wrote significantly shorter sentences (Kellogg 2004). The practice of professional writers is also telling. Average sentence length in 58 articles in *The Independent* newspaper is only 24.58 words (Hearle 2007), that is, about two alexandrines in length. Oxford

---

11   XML (Extensible Markup Language) is a set of rules for encoding documents electronically.

University Press recommends that sentences average 15-20 words. The most frequent length for sentences in the million-word Brown Corpus[12] is twelve words (Sigurd, and others 2004). Sentence length also turns out to be a factor in syntactic difficulty, as vocabulary length (in word-syllables, for example) is in semantic difficulty: together those lengths define readability measures like the Flesch-Kincaid (Kincaid and others 1975). If our minds did not have a cognitive capacity limit during reading, we would not have to develop readability measures that often exceed the phonological loop. These measures imply that a capacity limit exist for understanding outside working memory as well as for phonemes inside it. How big is this limit, and how do we even find the words and the measures to tell?

The omega value here names how large a language-mediated thought we can mentally grasp. This conceptual span is related to the gist with which authors begin in formulating an utterance. If we reverse the cognitive sentence-production process, translating sentences back into concepts, as readers do in text comprehension, we reduce an utterance with many parts (syntactic structures that build on phrases and words, supplemented by information on how to pronounce) to an originating, graspable thought. So far, we have not been able to measure how large this conceptually graspable entity may be, but several approaches look promising. Two appear in cognitive psychology: our ability to measure the psychological status of propositions; and the discovery that students who can solve a problem by using a worked-example fail — by exceeding their cognitive load — when asked to employ an ends-means technique. Others belong to the humanities. For example, self-imposed text-length restrictions plausibly register sensitivity to a general human cognitive capacity, so do the size limits of poetic forms. So far, little attention has been paid to text genres as evidence of cognitive capacity.

Propositions in cognitive psychology are subject-predicate units, concentrated to their ideational minimum, and their modifying elements. They differ from the three linked, unmodified propositions in a typical Aristotelian syllogism: the premises and the conclusion. The terms in logical propositions repeat in a set order, expressible symbolically as $A \to B$, $C \to A$, and $C \to B$.

---

12   The Brown Corpus is a carefully compiled selection of current American English, totalling about a million words drawn from a wide variety of sources. It was first compiled by Henry Kucera and W. Nelson Francis at Brown University, Providence, RI in 1963-64.

Here is an example:

Given that	1. Humans are mortal.	A → B
and given that	2. Socrates is human	C → A
it follows that	3. Socrates is mortal.	C → B

The first two propositions share a common term as a premise (human), and the last proposition joins the two unrelated terms in the preceding two premises (mortal, and Socrates). Propositional analysis in cognitive psychology, in contrast, concerns the mental status of any subject-predicate unit, simple or modified.

Walter Kintsch (1998: 69-73) describes half a dozen experiments about how test subjects mentally process propositions. One shows that we retrieve a proposition and its modifier differently. For example, if at some point test subjects are primed with a sample sentence, 'Socrates posed moral questions that never failed to annoy his wealthy students,' and later cued with the word 'questions,' these subjects would recall words from the core proposition (e.g., 'Socrates') better than ones from the modifier (e.g., 'students'). In another experiment, when subjects had to remember instructions, 'Doubling the number of propositions from two to four caused an increase in errors from 3% to 52%' (1998: 70), but doubling the number of words made no difference. Kintsch himself co-authored an experiment that showed that, for every proposition added to a text, reading time increased by 1.5 seconds. These results point to a capacity limit in maintaining in memory any proposition, that is, an utterance converted from natural language to its underlying conceptual meaning. Four terms in two propositions, read in three seconds, cause no trouble, but eight terms in four propositions, read in six seconds, cause cognitive breakdown. These numbers recall Cowan's two-second phonological memory capacity, 4 ± 2, yet they represent not sounded words but thought. Word-counts are not the right measure for cognitive capacity because readers often model (understand) text in terms of the propositions to which it can be reduced, and the word-count of an easily grasped proposition can well exceed the capacity of working memory. However, if we substitute propositional terms for words in Cowan's 'magic number,' the same formula seems to apply to cognitive capacity. Could it be 4 ± 2 propositional terms, if we keep in mind that, for an expert, a term may well point to a substantial schema in long-term memory?[13]

13 Cognitive load theory (Sweller 1988, 2006) shows that students often fail to solve a problem in mathematics or physics because they use means-ends analysis, which exhausts their cognitive capacity. However, students who use worked ex-

Do poetic forms offer corroborating evidence? Early verse forms such as the four-beat, two-part oral-formulaic Anglo-Saxon line link two short phrases by means of alliteration. In 1979 John B. Lord observed that Miller's 'magical number' constrains line-length in Anglo-Saxon verse, but the maximum number of lines that form a unified thought in Old English is hard to determine because no stanzaic forms existed then. However, we can measure the number of syllables in verse segments by poets such as Chaucer, after writing became common in England (a form of artificial memory). He used, not alliterating initial word-syllables, but nine- or ten-syllable lines bounded by terminal rhymes. If verse forms might be said to define a passage length, Chaucer's maximum-length verse unit was not the rhyming couplet in the *Canterbury Tales* but the rhyme-royal stanza found in *Troilus and Criseyde*: seven pentameter lines, mainly end-stopped, that rhyme *ababbcc* and have about seventy syllables or 56 words. A contemporary manuscript image shows Chaucer reading *Troilus* to a court audience, people with some education. He must have assumed that courtiers — who were not scholars — could hold and comprehend, as coherent thoughts, passages much longer than the capacity of working memory. Does Chaucer's rhyme royal conceivably mark an omega value, the cognitive capacity of a thought?

Let me convert the words in a popular hymn stanza to propositional form, Isaac Watts' 'Man Frail and God Eternal' (beginning 'Our God, our help in ages past'), written in common measure. Its eighth stanza has six different terms (*time, stream, bear everything away, sons, dream,* and *die at dawn*) in seven linked propositions.

> Time, like an ever-rolling stream,
> Bears all his sons away;
> They fly, forgotten, as a dream
> Dies at the op'ning day.

> 1. Time is like a stream.
> 2. A stream bears everything away.
> 3. Time bears everything away.
> 4. Time bears away his sons.
> 5. Time's sons are like a dream.
> 6. A dream dies at dawn.
> 7. Time's sons die at dawn.

amples (which help create schemas in long-term memory) can operate within their capacity and learn effectively. This expert technique does not increase the number of chunks but enlarges the scope of the terms in each chunk.

The fact that the word-count, 21, overflows average working-memory capacity seems to have had no effect on the ease with which ordinary people comprehend this stanza, but this sequence of seven propositional terms exceeds the 4 ± 2 capacity that the experiments of Kintsch and others suggest for cognitive capacity. Is the omega value larger?

I am guessing not. Most readers will not transform poetic text into logical form in order to comprehend it. They will likely process language as words, images, *and* episodes in a narrative: that is, they will simultaneously use two or more of the phonological loop, the visuospatial sketchpad, and the episodic buffer in working memory. Remembered images have the same 4±2 constraint (foci) as the phonological loop has for auditory speech (terms); possibly the episodic buffer may have some such limit as well. If so, and if we use the full resources of our working memory to be conscious of a verbalized thought, might it not expand to 12±6 elements in all? Watts' stanza has eight propositional terms (the subjects and objects *time, stream, sons, dream,* and *dawn,* and the verbs *be, bear away,* and *die*) and three images (time the river bearing sons away, sons flying forgotten, and a dream lost at dawn).

Our cognitive capacity could thus be a multiplier of the alpha value. If thought exists partly independently of the language in which it is expressed – and the behaviour of primates indicates that it does – we could understand the meaning of a sentence that is too large to fit, as auditory language, in working memory by activating the non-verbal slave systems of working memory. Cognitive capacity, the phonological loop, the visuospatial sketchpad, the episodic buffer, and the visual reading span might all be defined in terms of a single comparable constraint.

6. Reading Authorial Process

How can we determine an author's cognitive capacity? A reading method — not for meaning but for process — cannot be expected to mature quickly because it waits on scientific research of brain function. Yet, I have stumbled over some heuristic techniques. The extent of text that an author can write *before repeating himself* might well signal his omega value. Shakespeare's appears to have been about as long as a 14-line sonnet (Lancashire 1999). The output of a blind author, someone who could not store his utterances in writing or by dictating to a machine, might establish a limit: in creating *Paradise Lost* when blind, Milton reputedly could create and hold 20-30 decasyllabic lines a night before uttering them to an amanuensis. Or, when an author edits a written version of a text, the average size of his interpolations — newly-minted and inserted passages — might represent a cognitive limit.

Alpha and omega values may not themselves be stylistic markers but they point to what we should be looking for. Although chunk size is universal, the lexical combinations that comprise an author's chunks will be idiolectally distinctive. Cognitive capacity does not vary from one person to another, but the schemata that authors, as experts, expand to use that capacity and can rapidly shuttle in and out of working memory reflect individual expertise. (A critic must work hard not to impose his own schemas in interpreting an author's schemas.) Authorship attribution might also conceivably develop measures for how authors express propositional content. We might use the ratio of a proposition's length in terms and modifiers, to the word-count of the corresponding text into which that proposition is translated, as a stylistic marker. Francis Bacon's *Essays* are as renowned for their Tacitean concision as Sir Philip Sidney's prose is for its Ciceronian amplitude. On average, it seems likely that Sidney will take more words, Bacon fewer, to declare the same proposition or thought.

If authors sometimes leave traces behind in rare written drafts and audio recordings, once we learn to read a text for authorial processing, we can detect these traces. Examples are everywhere, but I will discuss only two, the spontaneous flow of Shakespeare's Addition II in *The Book of Sir Thomas More* (1910), and Virginia Woolf's calculated recraftings of passages in *The Waves* (1976, 2006).

The Book of Sir Thomas More

Hand D in this unpublished play, found over one hundred years ago in British Library MS Harley 7368, is now accepted by most scholars as Shakespeare's, from about 1594-95. This offers an opportunity to test cybertextuality. G. Blakemore Evans (1974) describes the 147 lines of Addition II by Hand D as 'an authorial first draft, with vague and carelessly used speech-prefixes and with deletions and insertions made in the process of composition' (1974: 1684). Figure 1, below, a facsimile of folio 9r (part of this Addition), shows 52 lines of text, with 446 word-tokens, of which 243 are word-types, for a type-token frequency of 0.41, a fairly high rate of repeti-

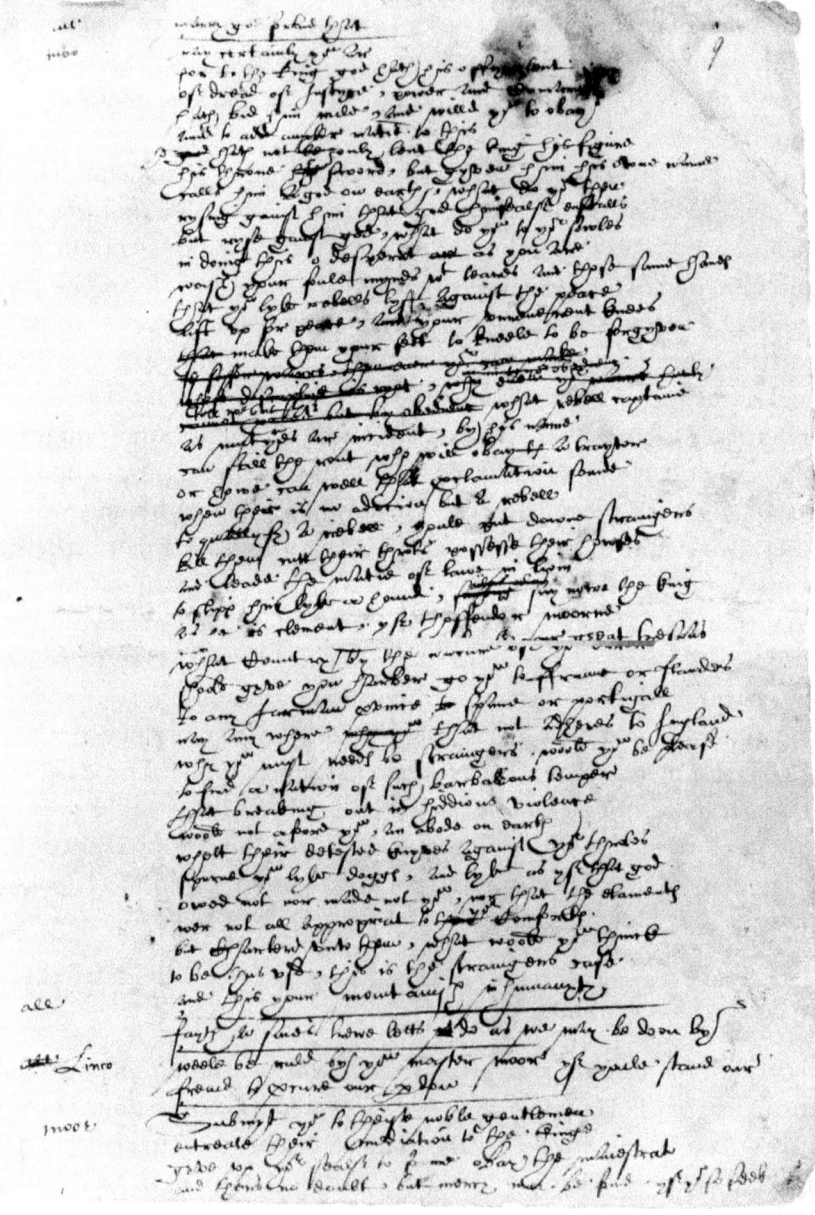

Figure 1: fol. 9r, British Library Harley MS 7368 (Croft 1973: I, 23).

tion. The secretary hand has some odd features, like the so-called spurred *a* (*hath* in line 7).

Table 1, below, is a transcription of this page. Two numbers precede each chunk, its line number, and then the number of its syllables. It segments Shakespeare's chunks according to three boundaries, the verse-line end, mid-line punctuation, and the points of error-repair. Shakespeare's composition took place in chunks that correspond in phrasal length to the alpha value, self-repaired speech errors, and reading span. Pairs of passages, the first pair in italic, the second in boldface, and so forth, show Shakespeare repeating himself: evidence for chunk-segmentation, as well as of feedback from reading what he had just penned. Marked, in small capitals, are several passages where Shakespeare's composition slowed down considerably, to judge from letter spacing, word-size, and writing out of a word normally abbreviated. These hesitations conceivably mark moments where his cognitive Editor was at work.

Blank-verse lines, written so as to be 10-11 syllables in length, are conceptual units for playwrights of this period. Shakespeare shaped his words so as to fit them in these 10-11 syllable sequences, but he often broke lines at mid-point: here, in 24 of the 52 lines. These caesural pauses are marked plainly by a comma or a period, and occasionally by a long space, encoded here as ◇. Shakespeare does not routinely use full-stops in his writing. For example, lines 18-19, 'why euen yor hurly / cannot proceed but by obedienc what rebell captaine / as mutynes ar incident, by his name / can still the rout,' have no sentence-ending period or comma after 'obedienc'? Or lines 24-25 go unpunctuated despite their stream of verbs: 'youle put downe straingers / kill them cutt their throts possesse their howses.' Rather, Shakespeare appears to use a full-stop as a pause while he waited for the next phrasal unit to emerge. The two dozen set-off 5/6-syllable half-lines show a regular constraint at work, suggesting that Shakespeare composed in phrasal chunks.

The ten errors that Shakespeare makes reveal his mind in the act of emending them as he wrote. Six of these self-repairs exhibit cybertextual feedback and unveil aspects of his language cognition.

1. In line 7, after writing *god hath not le* (7), and regretting the repetition of both *god* and *lent* from line 3, Shakespeare crosses out *god* and adds *he* just to the left of it and decides to qualify the verb by *only* (and so he excises the first syllable of *lent*).

Line	Syllables	Text
1	6	ALL MARRY GOD FORBID THAT
2	6	MOO NAY CERTAINLY YOU AR
3	10	FOR TO THE *KING GOD HATH HIS OFFYCE LENT*
4	5	of dread of Iustyce,
4	5	power and Comaund
5	4	hath bid him rule,
5	6	and willd you to obay
6	10	and to add ampler matie . to this
7	3	*he god hath not ~~te~~*
7	8	*only lent the king* his figure
8	4	his throne ~~his~~ & sword,
8	7	but gyven him his owne name
9	6	calls him <> a god on earth,
9	4	what do you then
10	10	**rysing gainst him** <> that god himsealf enstalls
11	4	but <> **ryse gainst god**,
11	6	what <> do you to yor sowles
12	7	in doing this <> o desperat ~~ar~~
12	3	as you are .
13	10	WASH YOUR FOULE MYNDS WT TEARES <> AND THOSE SAME HANDS
14	10	that you lyke *rebells lyft* against the *peace*
15	4	**LIFT** <> **VP FOR PEACE**,
15	6	**AND YOUR VNREUERENT KNEES**
16	10	**~~THAT~~ MAKE THEM YOUR FEET** <> to **kneele** to be <> **forgyven**
17	4	is safer **warrs**,
17	6	then euer you can **make**
18	7	**whose discipline is ryot,**
18	4	**why euen yor ~~warrs~~ hurly**
19	14	cannot proceed but by obedienc what rebell captaine
20	7	as mutynes ar incident,
20	3	by his name
21	11	can still the rout who will obay ~~th~~ a traytor
22	10	or howe can well that proclamation sounde
23	11	when ther is no adicion but a rebell
24	7	to quallyfy a rebell,
24	5	youle put downe *straingers*
25	10	kill them cutt their throts possesse their howses
26	10	and leade the matie of lawe in liom
27	6	*to slipp him lyke a hound,*

2. Cybertextuality by the Numbers

Line	Syllables	Text
27	8	~~sayeng~~ alas alas say nowe the king
28	5	as he is clement,
28	5	yf thoffendor moorne
29	11	shoold so much com to short of your great trespas
30	6	as but to banysh you,
30	5	whether woold you go.
31	11	what Country by the nature of yor error
32	12	shoold gyve you harber go you to ffraunc or flanders
33	6	to any Iarman province,
33	5	to spane or portigall
34	4	nay any where ~~why you~~
34	7	that not adheres to Ingland
35	7	why you must ◇ needs be _straingers_ .
35	4	woold you be pleasd
36	11	to find a nation of such barbarbous temper
37	11	that breaking ◇ out in hiddious violence
38	5	woold not afoord you,
38	5	_an abode on earth_
39	10	_whett their detested knyves against yor throtes_
40	4	_spurne you lyke doggs,_
40	6	and lyke as yf that god
41	6	owed not nor made not you,
41	6	nor that the elaments
42	11	wer not all appropriat to ~~ther~~ yor Comforts .
43	6	but Charterd vnto them,
43	4	what woold you thinck
44	4	to be thus vsd,
44	6	this is the straingers case
45	11	~~all~~ AND THIS YOUR ◇ MOMTANISH ◇ IN HUMANYTY
46	13	fayth a saies trewe letts vs do as we may be doon by
47	12	~~all~~ Linco weele be ruld by you master moor ◇ yf youle stand our
48	7	freind to procure our pardon
49	10	moor Submyt you to theise noble gentlemen
50	10	entreate their ◇ mediation to the kinge
51	12	gyve vp yor sealf to forme obay the maiestrate
52	4	and thers no doubt,
52	6	but mercy may be found. ◇
52	5	yf you so seek it

Table 1. Transcript of fol. 9r, British Library Harley MS 7368

The two self-repairs occur within a four-word span. The first error interruption occurs in mid-syllable at *le*. This indicates the short strokes in which the cognitive engine pumps out utterances, as well as shows that the inner Editor is pre-conscious, seeing a problem at a point preceding vocalization.

One more error occurs because Shakespeare recognizes that he is repeating himself.

2. Another hand, belonging to a professional scribe (and thus irrelevant for our purposes), crosses out everything in lines 17-19 and adds two replacement clauses, 'in in to yor obedienc' and 'tell me but this' above the lines.[14] Shakespeare's only deletion here is to cross out *warrs* (line 18) and write *hurly* afterwards. He appears to have recognized an unwise repetition of the word from the previous line. When he corrected this is unclear.

The first occurrence of *warrs* takes place 12 words before the error halts Shakespeare. This result could have been prompted either by a regressive saccade or by a conceptual trace or by active iconic memory as he was looking at the page on which he was writing.

Four self-repairs arise from a last-moment change in immediate syntax that does not affect the preceding text.

3. In line 12, Shakespeare deletes the eighth syllable, *ar*, just after he had written it, evidently because he realized that it would be hard to fill out the line to 10-11 syllables: he then adds the needed three syllables, *as you are*. The motive for this self-repair is a problem in metrical line length.

4. At the start of line 16, a change in syntax dictates the deletion of *that*: Shakespeare remakes a subordinate clause modifying *feet* into an imperative clause. The deletion must have been made immediately.

5. In line 27, Shakespeare deletes *sayeng* and replaces it by *say* to introduce an imperative clause. (The addition of *alas alas* above, an extrametrical four syllables, is harder to understand: the scribe later deleted these words.)

6. At line 34, Shakespeare deletes *why yo^u* to introduce a seven-syllable subordinate clause rather than immediately give the seven-syllable exclamation, 'why yo^u must needs be straingers,' that he instead postpones to the next line.

All these self-repairs[15] signal cognitive feedback to the author's own

---

14 Scribal changes are not included in the transcription.
15 There are four other self-corrections. (1) A worry about repeating *his* three times leads him to cross out the second *his* in line 8 and overwrite it with an ampersand. Because it does not follow the offending *his*, Shakespeare could have corrected it in re-reading the finished speech. (2). In line 21, he deletes *th* and follows imme-

2. Cybertextuality by the Numbers

emerging speech. Note how Shakespeare often makes syntactical changes at phrasal boundaries: only then can his Editor perceive how his unconscious mind is tying a phrase to its successor. Another way of putting this is: Shakespeare fought his own unconscious maker at its weakest, which was in forging long units (sentences) from sequences of short ones (phrases).

In this page, Shakespeare was affected by what he had just uttered on six occasions when he repeats, with variation, word-clusters or semantic groupings that occurred earlier. One (we have already seen) elicited a conscious error check: the repetition of *god*, *lent*, and *king* (3, 7). Caroline Spurgeon found this semantic combination also in *Richard II* (1930: 265-66). Three other clusters have repetitions following one another closely: the cluster *rise*, *gainst*, and *god* (at lines 10 and 11), the cluster *lift* and *peace* (at lines 14 and 15), and the cluster *wars*, *discipline / obedienc*, and *riot / rout* (at lines 17-18 and 18-21). These occur inside spans that fit into working memory. Two others, however, activate only after a long interval, eleven and eight lines later. The first is the cluster *obay / obedience*, *king / rebell*, and *name* (at lines 5-8 and 19-21). The second is the cluster *straingers*, *cutt / knyves*, *throts / throtes*, *howses / abode*, and *hound / doggs* (at lines 24-27 and 35-40). Spurgeon finds these clusters in half a dozen plays as 'peculiarly characteristic of Shakespeare' (1930: 269). Here they look like feedback from persistence of vision, the effect of iconic sensory memory as Shakespeare kept his eyes on the page; or, from time to time, when at a pause, he let them shift upwards in a recursive saccade. All illustrate cybertextual cycles at work.

The last evidence of self-monitoring occurs when Shakespeare's hand slows down, the writing equivalent to hesitation in speech. A combination of traits in letter spacing, word-size, and expansion of a normally abbreviated word identify three passages as written more slowly than the rest. They are (a) lines 1-3, (b) lines 13, 15, and the first half of 16, and (c) line 45. The two telltale orthographic signals of delay in lines 1-3 are the separation of initial *fo* from the rest of the word in *fo rbid* (1) and *fo r* (3), and the whole or partial isolation of initial or medial *t* from the rest of the word in *cer t ainly* (2) and *t o* (3).[16] Note also the separation of *g* from the rest of the word *g od*

---

diately with *a traytour*: the indefinite article does not suggest a specific individual. (This also characterizes Shakespeare's usage later at lines 23-24 where he writes *a rebell*.) He catches this error right away. (3) At line 33, Shakespeare deletes the *to* in ~~to~~ *spane or portigall*, presumably for metrical reasons. (4) At some point, Shakespeare corrects a spelling mistake, the second *r* to *b* in the word *barbarous* in line 36.

16   Later, at lines 16 (*forgyven*), 38 (*afoord*), and 51-52 (*forme* and *found*), this separation disappears. Normally, initial *t* in *to* is unseparated (see lines 5-6, 11, the second half of 16, 24, 27, etc.).

(1), and the isolation of *r* in *ce r t ainly* (2). Line 13 has both separated initial *fo* (in *fo ule*) and the first occurrence, on this page, of expanded *your*. Shakespeare normally uses abbreviated *yo*', the sign of a rapid hand at work, as in lines 11, 18, 31, 39, 42, and 51. Lines 13, 15, and 16 (each slowly penned), however, each has expanded *your*. The third passage, line 45, exhibits three features of slow penmanship: unabbreviated *your*, the isolation of *t* in the odd word *momtanish*, and the separation of the prefix *in* (in *humanyty*).[17]

Each delay in writing coincides with a cognitive problem. Lines 1-3 reveal Shakespeare pausing to work out what More's speech to the mob will be. Delays at lines 13 and 15-16 appear related to Shakespeare's repair of errors at the end of line 12, and the beginning of line 16. Line 45 is especially interesting. Shakespeare originally intended this line to be the crowd's (as the speech prefix *all* shows), but after he penned the prefix he decided that it would be More's crowning indictment of the mob. The first content word in this insult, 'momtanish,' is unrecorded elsewhere in English: whatever it means, Shakespeare invented it, and to this day it must elicit an N400 wave on reading.[18]

Virginia Woolf's *The Waves* (1931)

Woolf's most experimental novel is streams of consciousness by half a dozen characters, but it was her own unconscious that initiated those streams. Separated by interludes that describe the sea, her chapters reveal stages in a lifetime. *The Waves* once existed in two holograph manuscript drafts, three typescripts, and a final printed text dating from September 1929 to mid-1931. None of the typescripts has survived, but the first and second holographs have (Woolf 1976: 30). She typed in the afternoon what she wrote in longhand each morning, but usually without changing anything. Leonard Woolf observed that during typing her 'conscious critical intellect was in control and the tension was less' (1976: 38). One manuscript-typescript pair thus represents each of a version A (1929-30) and B (1930-31), and she used the former as a basis for the latter. Because versions A and B have deletions and marginal additions, the two holographs actually reveal

---

17 The presence of several large spaces separating words, occurring at lines 11, 16, and 45, may be a fourth trait of hesitation.
18 It may be a portmanteau word, `mome+tan+ish`, i.e. tanned or sunburned like a common mome or fool. See OED `tan` v., and `mome` n. 2. Wentersdorf (2006) suggests that `momtanish` is `a contraction of mahometanish` but if so the word is still a poser because the OED recognizes only the different word-form, `Mahometish.`

2. Cybertextuality by the Numbers

four versions, initial and revised A, and initial and revised B. In each version, Woolf also sometimes rewrote the same passage several times (1976: 40). She stored her composed utterances as text in order to work on them and trusted her editor more than her muse.

One passage in the published novel (2006: 72) concerns a late-night experience by Jinny, one of her six main characters. It appears once in both versions A and B (1976: 190, 505). Version A, in 69 words, describes Jinny walking down a dark street under windows behind which people had undressed and gone to sleep. Then a taxi turns a corner and casts a white light on her. Version B, in 122 words, is written in the first person, from Jinny's point-of-view, rather than in the third person. Interpolated in materials from version A is Jinny's meditation of body-parts she feels — her knee, feet, neck, and head — in 45 additional words. Woolf transforms a narration of successive events in version A into a singular, present experience in version B. The final printed version, in 169 words, adds a further passage, found in the middle of the thoughts and experiences of the first two versions, that describes the street in terms of the burning of street lamps, the rush of pedestrians, and some standing policemen. This has about 48 words. Table 2 holds an encoded transcription of A, B, and the final printed text.

Chunk size (measured by punctuation) increases over the three versions from 1-3 to 1-7 words, and average sentence-length from 4.9 to 6.3 words. The longer in time that the text survives in external memory, on paper, the longer its length grows. Gradually Woolf's use of external-memory tools relax the constraints of the alpha value in working memory. Each version also becomes progressively longer by the addition of one more thought or experience. A single thought (in 69 words) becomes two (in 139 words) and then three (in 169 words). Woolf rearranges the material of the previous version, deleting some words, expanding others, but she also injects a new passage into the centre of the old.

The text grows incrementally. Words deleted in the holographs decrease from 14.8 percent to 12.2 percent, and words passed on from A to B, and from A and B to the final print copy, increase from 34.8 percent to 68.9 percent. Storing the text where it is visually accessible normally stabilizes an author's text, but Woolf's working habits show that, although she likely reread Version A in starting Version B, she carried forward only chunk-size phrases from it and she recast the sentences entirely. For example, version A uses the past tense and the third-person, but version B the present tense and the first-person. A says 'everybody <u>*must*</u> have ... <u>*gone to bed*</u> ... which

Version A: MS Draft

[underlining: words carried forward to Version B; //: left margin addition]

It was all _dark_. Indeed, just before the cab turned the corner, one might have been in _the street_ was so _dark_ that everybody _must_ have been _asleep_, & _undress_ed _gone to bed_, a_sleep_ already; _undressed, undress_ed – which was incredible to _Jinny_: For she was _pass_ing beneath their windows // in silver, in _white_; pointed, her body // so different; in a state, that this _momentary dark_ness affected her solemnly; like _the dark_ness _before light_; like the hush ¬_music begins_ the violins.

Version B: MS Draft

[underlining: words carried forward from Version A; bold: words carried forward to Version C;//: left margin addition]

// & **the dark** chimney pots & the blue [width?] as I _pass_ shuttered shops; as I _pass_ the _bed_ rooms // '**How strange** that they should have **gone to bed**' said Jinny. **There are no lights in any of these houses. The street** is almost **dark**. They _must_ be _undress_ing; they _must_ be **go**ing **to sleep**; while I sit why the **night is** just **beginning. I feel white**; I feel shining. Silk is on my knee. My feet feel the pinch of shoes. the stones my hands a necklace lie cold on my throat; my head is smooth; I can sit bolt upright, arrayed prepared; I wait for the so as **not to touch** my head. // **I am arrayed, prepared** // **This is the** _momentary_ **pause**; the prelude; _the_ **dark moment before** the **light** pours flares; over me. the _music begins_.

Version C: Printed

[underscored: words carried forward from Version A; bold: words carried forward from Version B]

'**How strange**,' said _Jinny_, 'that people should _sleep_, that people should put out the **lights** and **go** upstairs. They have taken off their **dress**es, they have put on **white** night-gowns. **There are no lights in any of these houses.** There is a line of **chimney pots** against the sky; and a **street** lamp or two burning, as lamps burn when nobody needs them. The only people in **the streets** are poor people hurrying. There is no one coming or going in this **street**; the day is over. A few policemen stand at the corners. Yet **night is beginning. I feel** myself **shining** in the _dark_. **Silk is on my knee. My** silk legs rub smoothly together. **The stones of a necklace lie cold on my throat. My feet feel the pinch of shoes. I sit bolt upright** so that my hair may **not touch** the back of the seat. **I am arrayed, I am prepared. This is the** _momentary_ **pause;** the _dark_ **moment**. The fiddlers have lifted their bows.

Table 2: Three versions of a passage from _The Waves_

was incredible to *Jinny*,' whereas B inverts that structure, '**How strange that they should have gone to bed.**' She thus appears to have started over completely, returning to her muse and its long-term-memory stemmata to regenerate the utterance. The image or word-cluster in long-term memory, strengthened by the afternoon typing, would have held *dark*, *moment*, *street*, and *light*, *Jinny* and *white*, and *undressed* and *sleep*, eight items occurring 14 times. Woolf's authorial process from version B to the final copy was different. Some ten sentences from version B recur in the final copy almost verbatim. Much more editing from the page was going on than re-uttering.

The three versions show how chunks structure successive revisionings of a passage in *The Waves*, but they also define Woolf's omega value. She does not allow repetition to mark her omega limit, but the two interpolations in the last two versions have a like size. They extend to 45 and 48 words in length and amplify two images or ideas in the original, Jinny's whiteness and the street. In version A, verbal repetitions of *dark*, *darkness*, and *undressed*, three consecutive events (the undressed going to bed, followed by Jinny's walking, ending with the cab's turning the corner), and two images (dark and light – the undressed sleeping and the street in dark, Jinny in sudden light) seem manageable in the three slave systems of working memory. The single added thought includes four images in visuospatial working memory (Jinny's knee, feet, throat, and head), and the repeated words *feel* or *touch*, and *silk*, look to be manageable. Because everything happens in the present, the episodic working memory slave system appears inactive. Last, the 45-word addition in the printed copy presents three visual foci: street lamps burning, rushing pedestrians, and standing policemen.

In these examples, we observe two authorial processes, Shakespearean flow and Woolfian inflation. Shakespeare creates spontaneously and corrects only in mid-flow. Once he reaches his cognitive capacity, he sometimes repeats, with variations, what he has just uttered. Woolf spontaneously utters a passage in writing and reads it back into her long-term memory by typing it out. She then either regenerates the same thought in a new flow or she edits the typed copy down on paper. In both instances, she typically interpolates a new, spontaneously uttered thought. She inflates her text from within. From my inadequate samples, Shakespeare's cognitive load appears to be larger, about 70-75 words to Woolf's 45-50 words.

7. Conclusion

Cybertextuality draws on cybernetics, computer text analysis, and cognitive psychology to illuminate authors in the texts that survive them. Readers do not constrain an author's works; the author's cognitivity does. Without an author's desire to say something, without personal emotional drives associated by Antonio Damasio with the pre-frontal cortex (1994), there would be no work. The author fashions its propositions, images, and episodes from his unique associational long-term memory and private, pre-linguistic thought. When he unselfconsciously formulates the language for these declarations, he faces mental constraints that have only become obvious in the past century. He cannot directly observe the cognitive process of uttering until the very end. The capacity of his working memory limits, to under two seconds, the amount of language he can consciously work with, and then it has to take phonological form as inner speech. If what an author wants to say lies outside his long-honed expertise, it cannot be shuttled in and out of working memory rapidly and will overflow cognitive capacity. What fits within it emerges, pulse-like, pre-phonologically as unspeakable chunks or phrases, sometimes with errors. To exert some control over this opaque, maddening-at-worst, inspiring-at-best creative process, the author relies on cybernetic feedback from his mind's equally hidden cognitive monitor. It tracks phrases and halts him in mid-stride when it finds an error. His uttering happens, interrupted regularly by hesitations, paralanguage, and self-corrections. Often it is only the feedback of questions by those who are listening that enable the author to define what he intends to say, and to say it.

Texts (manuscripts, printed books, digitalia) mark significant victories by both their authors and our species over these limitations. We have unrelentingly developed both cognitive and mechanical technologies consciously so as to gain control of our *making*. Both these mental and external technologies create feedback mechanisms and give rise to cybertextual cycles. An expert writer pre-builds propositions in long-term memory as maps or schemas, and assembles an utterance by linking two of his memory systems in a collaboration that is cybernetic. Writing, the first external technology, made explicit the contents of a collective long-term memory and offered a visible space that supplements working memory. Then came the computer. Its outliners[19] map symbolic concepts to the ampler language

---

19   An outliner is a particular type of digital text editor that allows the grouping

in which texts must be expressed. Digital technology, however, goes well beyond storage to create agents that can interrupt, interrogate, and gloss a writer's work *currente calamo*. Text-analysis tools, readability software, and spell-and-grammar checkers offer feedback on features of writing.

If authorial process can be read, if we can detect how the author operates within alpha and omega cognitive limits, the maker is not entirely inaccessible in the text. We need not capitulate to capitalism, which turns a literary creator into an owner, the bearer of copyright. How we are to read authorial process is of course much disputed ground. I can suggest heuristics only at this time. Repeated phrases (isolated and clustered), shifts in the cursiveness of handwriting, in-process authorial corrections, the extent of editorial interpolations, and other stylistic measures (e.g. changes in vocabulary richness) signal mental habits that comprise the cognitive base of a literary work. When Christians search for the Logos in the texts of the Bible, and today when we use, in a revealing metonymy, an author's name for his collected works, we anthropomorphize an alien neurological entity that we also have within us but of which we are all, nonetheless, largely unconscious. Cybertextuality does not deny the loss of the creator with a photographed face and a pronounceable name but finds in all texts an anonymous entity. We need authorship attribution methods that can analyse more works than are orphaned in copyright limbo.

---

of text in sections that are organized in a tree (or hierarchy) of concepts, an outline.

3. Textual Pathology
Peter Garrard

1. Introduction

In very broad terms, the theme of this chapter is disruption of brain function and its effects on higher order linguistic structure. More specifically, I will outline the changes caused by a particular species of neurodegenerative pathology — Alzheimer's disease — on the physical apparatus of the brain, the impact of these changes on the brain's ability to execute the cognitive tasks involved in the production and comprehension of language, and the extent to which this functional disturbance is evident in the products of a particular form of linguistic output, namely the production of a literary text. If literary aesthetics is the study of sensory, emotional and intellectual beauty in literature, and neuroscience the study of how the brain does what it does, then here I open a backdoor on the question with which this volume is occupied by considering physical causes for defects of such beauty where we would most expect to find it.

I shall begin by providing a few brief, orienting explanations of brain structure in health and disease before moving on to the infinitely more complex and controversial subject of how this inchoate mass of axons, dendrites, synapses and neurotransmitters instantiates a level of organisation that we perceive and experience as cognitive activity.

Although a treatise on battlefield surgery, including detailed macroscopic descriptions of the cranial cavity and cerebral cortex, survives in a 17th century BC papyrus, and although Claudius Galenus of Pergamum (129-200 AD), experimented on the nervous systems of a number of different mammals, it is nonetheless neat, comforting, and if nothing else memorable, to consider the origins of modern neurology as synonymous with two Englishmen: Head and Brain. Sir Henry Head's (1861-1940) experiments on cutaneous sensation were largely conducted on himself and a cadre of dedicated colleagues (patients' subjective reports were considered too unreliable as a basis for scientific theorising). His legacy was taken up by Sir Walter Russell (later Lord) Brain (1895-1966), who wrote a textbook of neurology (*Brain's Diseases of the Nervous System*) that is now in its eleventh edition (Donaghy 2001) and for many years edited the journal that might as well have been named after him. Sadly, this line of descent did not continue in the manner of little Lord Tangent (the only son of Lord and Lady Circumference in Evelyn Waugh's *Decline and Fall*) with Viscount Lobe, and the Hon. Mrs. Sarah Bellum. Happily though, it also escaped that fictional family's painful and ignominious extinction.

2. The Brain

When removed from its protective bony casing, the brain of an adult human appears as a multi-lobed organ with a furrowed surface and has a volume of about 1.4 litres. It weighs around a kilogram and a half, which is on averag approximately two percent of total body weight. The brain is a paired organ, consisting of two mirror-identical hemispheres. Slice through one of these hemispheres, and it becomes apparent that it consists of a surface layer (or cortex), overlying a deeper material (known as white matter), and that the ridges and furrows on the surface are a result of a large outer surface folding in order to fit within the rigid confines of the containing skull. In general, as you move away from the cortex into the deeper structures of the brain – midbrain, cerebellum, brainstem – you encounter structures critical to reflexive rather than ratiocinative activity: the cerebellum for maintaining balance and coordination; the upper brainstem for ensuring that eye movements are yoked together; the lower mediating involuntary protective or vegetative phenomena such as blinking, coughing and breathing. It is when these structures are disconnected from higher centres, that one encounters the clinically ambiguous and philosophically difficult states such as brainstem death (in which all cognitive, reflexive and vegetative activity has ceased while the body lives on), the 'vegetative state' (where there are brainstem reflexes without apparent cortical activity), or the 'locked in state', in which cognitive activity is present but invisible because of complete muscular paralysis.

3. Textual Pathology

Magnify up and you find that both white matter and cortex are composed predominantly of nerve cells (neurons), with a characteristic if variable morphology consisting of a cell body, from where the cell's growth, metabolism and behaviour is controlled, a narrow process or axon, which makes contact with other neurons, and a complex of extensions known tautologously as the dendritic tree, with which the axons of other neurons make contact.

In contrast to this structural complexity a single neuron is, in functional terms, a rather boring entity, being limited to only two states (active or inactive), two effects (excitation or inhibition), and one property (which I will call unit memory). When it is inactive, the inside and outside of a neuron are maintained in a state of electrical equilibrium, with the interior slightly negatively charged relative to the exterior. When activated, the direction of polarity rapidly changes; this change is propagated along the length of the cell until it reaches the axon terminus, which makes contact (synapses) with a dendrite of a neighbouring cell. At this point, the cell's depolarised state causes the release of a protein (neurotransmitter), which acts at the membrane of the neighbouring neuron. This chemical signal may be either excitatory (encouraging the neighbour into an activated state), or inhibitory (making the neighbour more resistant to activation). Any individual neuron will be subject to inputs from many thousands of axon termini, some of them sending excitatory signals, others inhibitory; and whether or not the second neuron becomes active or not therefore depends on the numerical sum of large numbers of positive excitatory or negative inhibitory signals received.

The unit memory of an individual neuron, which enables it to alter in response to previous activity – such that it becomes permanently more or less likely to respond to similar stimuli in the future – is a property with a biological basis that can be demonstrated in laboratory preparations, and is known as 'long term potentiation', or LTP (Bliss and Lomo 1973). LTP is also assumed to be the biological basis for the learning that we experience at the psychological level, which is held to depend on this sort of plasticity taking place in large-scale neural assemblies. Donald Hebb predicted all this in 1949, long before its biological basis was worked out:

> When an axon of cell A is near enough to excite cell B and repeatedly or persistently takes part in firing it, some growth process or metabolic change takes place in one or both cells such that A's efficiency, as one of the cells firing B, is increased. (Hebb, 2002/1949)

These days, Hebb's insight is usually summarised by the more memorable phrase 'cells that wire together fire together'.

Interspersed with neurons are a large number of other cells, collectively referred to as glia. Glia outnumber neurons by a factor of ten to one, and subserve a diverse range of functions: some simply act as structural support for neurons, some regulate the chemical balance of the internal environment, and others form components of the brain's immune system. A particularly important species of glial cell ensheathes the axons of neurons in the deep white matter of the brain, forming a membrane that enhances transmission of electrochemical activity, as well as insulating it from interfering activity in its neighbours. Thus, the cells of the white matter are able to carry out their primary function: forming channels of communication between geographically distant brain regions. Cortical neurons are devoid of this insulating sheath, hence the colour difference on the cut slice; in the cortex, therefore, informational units combine, at both short and long range, to produce a complex system with an effectively limitless number of states.

3. Cognition and the Brain

Unless we commit ourselves to the implausible doctrines of dualism (Popper and Eccles 1977), and claim that mental activity is different *in kind* from the physical changes that are occurring, from millisecond to millisecond, inside the brain, we are left with the question of how all this neurochemical activity gives rise to what we experience and see as cognitive activity and its products. There has been no serious scientific attempt to support the dualist position for over two decades, and it now seems clear that dualism is not so much a solution, as a reversal and a postponement of the problem: for if neural activity is not the basis of mental activity, then what is it for? To cool the blood, as Aristotle speculated? And if mental activity has a different basis, then why does it seem so difficult even to begin scientifically to characterise it?

David Marr, the visual neurophysiologist, was the first to articulate the idea that the brain, or for that matter any informational system, is susceptible to description at different levels (Marr 1982). He identified these as, at the highest level, the goals of the system, followed by the methods used to achieve the goal, and the material means by which such a method is implemented. We might think of a digital clock, a clockwork timer and an hourglass as sharing a common goal (the division of time into equal portions), while exploiting the physical properties of a range of materials in order to achieve it. When applied to the brain, the top level clearly maps on to psychological constructs (memory, decision making, communication), while neural structures represent the means. To articulate description of the brain's method — its algorithms — is a challenge that is synonymous with the modern discipline of cognitive neuroscience.

To claim that the brain is a computer still prompts a sharp intake of breath from those with an aversion to over-simplistic analogies. Clearly the danger of any analogy is to take it too far and too literally, leaving room for the inevitable *reductio ad absurdum* ('if the brain is a computer, then where is the keyboard?'). Of course, for those who appreciate the power of analogy, even this imaginary piece of chicanery invites a very simple answer: a keyboard is a device for inputting information to a desktop computer, and therefore maps neatly on to the brain's sense organs. That such an explanation is unlikely to be considered a satisfactory response by the analogy-phobic is hard to comprehend: I have never heard anybody object to the assertion that the heart is 'a pump' or the kidney 'a filter'. The unexceptionable claim of cognitive neuroscience, however, is not so much that the brain is 'a computer', or even '*like* a computer' but that a computer and a brain (and their physical components) are examples of the same general kind of thing; both are devices for representing, storing and manipulating information. The analogy-averse are perhaps responding, over-sensitively, to the equally self-evident fact that one is infinitely more advanced, complex, powerful and versatile at accomplishing these goals than the other.

So if we accept that the brain is implementing its goals in the matrix of billions of boring, interconnected single units that I began by describing, then the next questions to arise are, first, what sort of work does it do, and secondly, how does that work result in the goals being accomplished? A series of constraints, moral and technical, mean that we can only investigate these fundamental questions scientifically in an indirect manner, though there are experimental approaches, some of which exploit techniques for *in vivo* visualisation of brain activity while it works towards different cognitive goals. The best known of these techniques is functional magnetic resonance imaging, or fMRI, which produces maps of regional changes in blood flow (a surrogate marker of local neural activity) during performance of a well-defined cognitive task. Another approach is to rely on the occurrence, through accident or disease, of distortions in cognitive activity following damage or disruption to brain function, and then to try to correlate the physical properties of the damaged region with the details of the functional deficit (cognitive neuropsychology).

A third approach is to try to simulate the achievement of a goal using computational units with similar properties to those employed by the brain. This endeavour is referred to by a variety of different names, including 'connectionist modelling', 'parallel distributed processing' and 'neural network theory': all excellently descriptive names for the same simple idea. Take an informational unit which, like a neuron, can be either active or inactive, and allow it to influence, in a positive or negative way, any number of similar units on to which its activity extends. Set the resulting network in motion, and watch activation propagate through it. Make the connections between units modifiable, such that those that are subjected to large amounts of activation become more sensitive to similar activation in the future, and vice versa. Leave such a network alone, and it will eventually settle into an unchanging steady state. However, it can also be provided with a target state to achieve, and provided with regular feedback on whether it is getting closer to or further from this target. If this feedback process is accompanied by small incremental changes in the responsivity of its units, then the target state will eventually be reached.

To appreciate that a similar incremental process may underpin some forms of biological learning, think of the process of learning to throw a basketball through a hoop: if the ball falls short, or overshoots, we adjust our technique accordingly, and after many such sessions we find our initial throws more accurate than they were when we started out. Thus, learning (a task or skill) is at least one goal that can be instantiated in a network of simple units with modifiable connections.

What about more complex and abstract cognitive activity, such as the ability to generalise or draw inferences? We can think of this in terms of the essential cognitive goal of forming generic concepts from experience of only specific instances. For instance, seeing Rex, Rover, and Snowy in the park, hearing them referred to as 'dogs', and then correctly deciding that Lassie (whom we have never seen before) is a member of the same category. There are various ways of accomplishing such a goal: one would be to learn, in addition to the defining characteristics of Rex, Rover and Snowy, the necessary and sufficient conditions for membership of the class of things to which they belong. Another is to store descriptive representations of each example, and to look for similarities between the stored representations

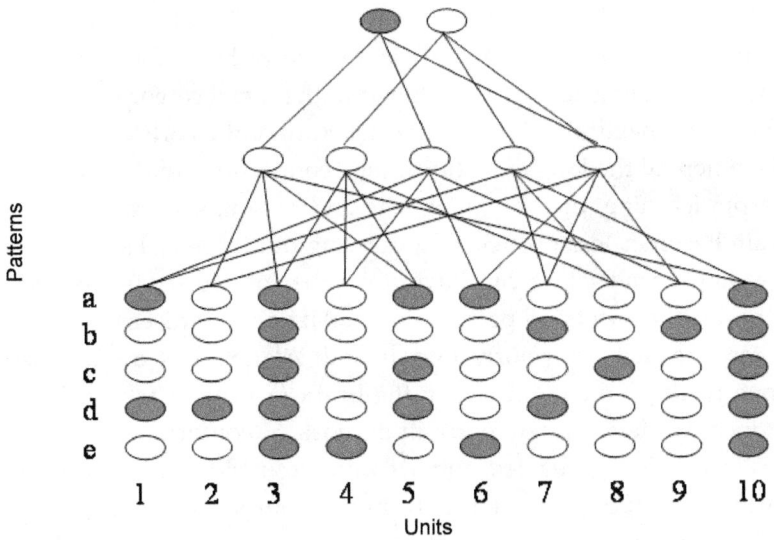

Figure 1: Simplified connectionist network consisting of three layers of active (filled) or inactive (unfilled) units, and weighted connections. By modifying its weights in response to error, the network can 'learn' to associate each of the input patterns (a-e) with activity in either of the two units in the output layer: a form of categorisation task.

and anything novel. It should be self-evident that the first of these two strategies is not employed in this instance (though it is in others, such as the ability to distinguish between a square and a rectangle): for any set of necessary and sufficient characteristics of a dog that you might give me (fur, legs, ears, a bark, etc.) I could provide an example of a dog that was missing at least one of them, but which you would be forced to concede was still a dog. The second strategy is undoubtedly more flexible, though also risks giving rise to widely differing definitions.

The problem can be modelled in a network of simple units, in which the task to be learned is the assignment of a series of inputs to one of two categories (see Figure 1). It turns out that what the network comes to represent is an average, or prototype, of these various patterns; patterns close to the prototype (whether or not the network has been trained on them) are assigned; those that do not reach this threshold are rejected. So the network not only learns, it *generalises* to new materials. Better still, if a similar task is given to human subjects, most will claim to recognise a prototype as familiar even if they had never previously been exposed to it (Whittlesea 2002).

4. Neurodegeneration

The point of the above was to provide a sense of how cognitive activity might be thought of as being instantiated in the intact cerebral cortex. It is not difficult to imagine that, when the structure of the cortex becomes disrupted – when all the long and short range connections that have built up to underpin learning, memory, language and reason, start to break down – the brain becomes less proficient at carrying out these tasks. This loss of structure and organisation can have a number of causes, but by far the commonest is the onset and progression of Alzheimer's disease.

For reasons that are poorly understood, Alzheimer's disease begins when one of the proteins made by the brain (a protein whose function is still incompletely understood) undergoes a conformational change, becomes insoluble, aggregates, and accumulates inside and between cortical neurons, disrupting function both in the neuron itself and at the synapse. In common with many complex systems, a degree of redundancy is

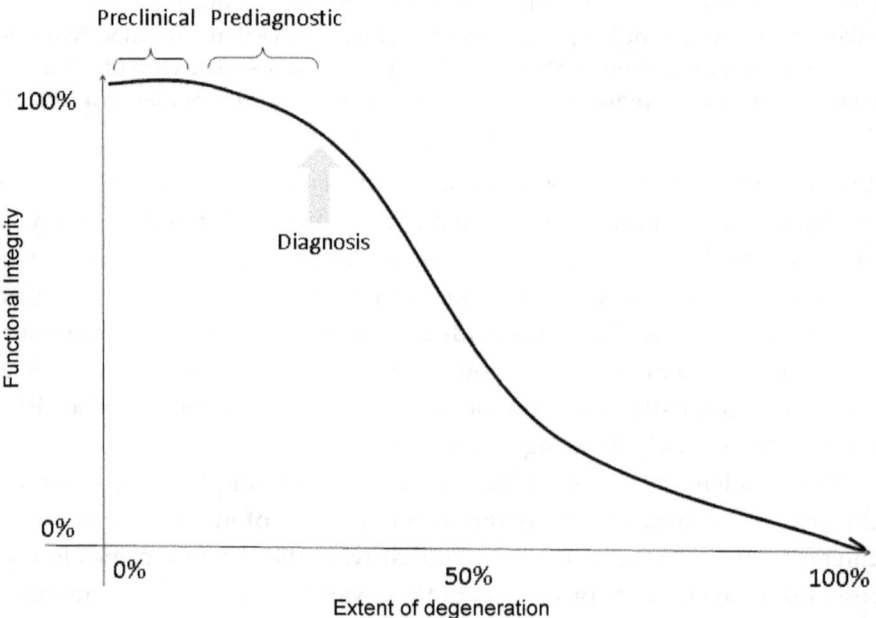

Figure 2: Hypothetical relationship between neuronal loss (x-axis) and cognitive function (y-axis), in a neurodegenerative disorder such as AD. Cognitive function remains intact in the face of early degeneration (preclinical phase), and undetectably deficient thereafter (prediagnostic phase) until sufficiently obvious to allow a diagnosis to be made.

built into the high-level organisation of the brain, enabling it to function as normal even when a proportion of its structural components have become damaged or lost. There follows a further phase, during which functional disruption takes place but is so mild that the patient and his/her associates are unaware of its true nature. These phases are illustrated in Figure 2 and can usefully be referred to as the preclinical and prediagnostic. The length of the prediagnostic phase depends on a number of variables, including the sufferer's willingness to seek help, and the diagnostic capabilities of the doctor, but typically lasts between six and twelve months. The length of the preclinical phase is more difficult to determine, though it has been argued to extend for many years or even decades (Ohm et al. 1995). I will return to this graph and this point towards the end of the chapter.

5. Effects of Neurodegenerative Pathology on Language

Once a diagnosis of Alzheimer's disease has been established there is (at present) no way back, and accumulating damage brings about increasing disruption to various cognitive abilities. In Alzheimer's disease the first ability to suffer is usually the acquisition and retention of new information (usually referred to as 'episodic memory'). As more and more of the brain succumbs, however, the neural circuits required for maintenance of attention, visual discrimination, and language also begin to undergo degeneration, resulting in progressive functional decline in all these abilities. Since language is the theme of this chapter, let us look briefly at how these difficulties manifest themselves.

One of the earliest difficulties encountered by patients with Alzheimer's disease is one of word-finding (an inability to call to mind the correct word to describe a concept one wishes to convey). This is a familiar — it might even be claimed universal — experience, and it almost certainly becomes commoner with increasing age. There is not, as far as I am aware, empirical data to support the latter assertion, and even if there were, it would not necessarily imply that incipient degenerative change was responsible, since there are both demand and supply side changes to cognitive activity at different stages of life. By way of a personal anecdote, I was recently asked to give my opinion on a patient in front of an audience of clinical colleagues, and was forced to stop in mid-sentence by a sudden inability to

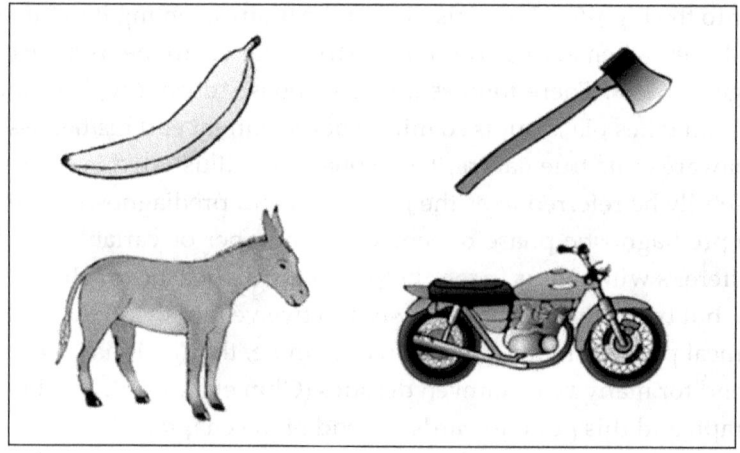

Figure 3: Sample stimuli used in a naming test.
This straightforward technique may detect difficulties with word retrieval and verbal output difficulties early in the course of dementia.

produce the word 'confabulate,' despite having used it in an aside to a colleague five minutes earlier. I am sure that this experience has been shared by many, if not all, readers.

Everyone is familiar with the so-called 'tip-of-the-tongue' phenomenon. In fact it is so widespread that scientists, including a group at University College London, have used 'tip-of-the-tongue induction' as a technique for examining the brain's word production system (Vigliocco et al. 1997). The subject is provided with definitions of low-frequency words, and asked to produce the term thus defined. For example: [what is the word for] 'a bittersweet longing for things, persons, or situations of the past'; and 'a navigational instrument for measuring the angular elevation of the sun or a star above the horizon'. This seemingly easy task becomes far from straightforward when the subject is put under time pressure, leading to the frequent 'tip-of-the-tongue' states for words such as *nostalgia* and *sextant*.

I mention this here principally to sharpen the contrast between normal, everyday word production difficulties and the profound, clearly pathological problems that are seen in patients with Alzheimer's disease and other forms of dementia. For such patients retrieval of even simple vocabulary items becomes a daily and progressive problem. Even in the early stages, patients will exhibit marked difficulty producing common, concrete nominal terms in response to pictures such as those in Figure 3. Later, they may

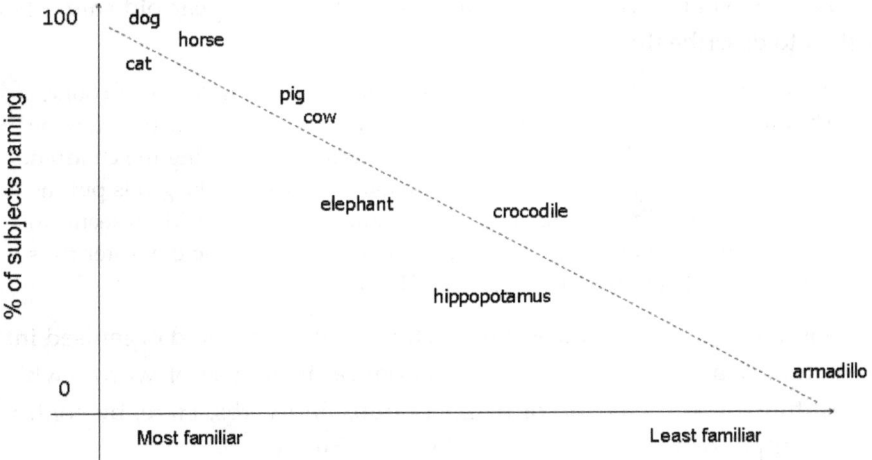

Figure 4: Percentage of subjects successfully naming various items. Subjects' ability to name pictures of items is strongly influenced by how familiar they are with the to-be-named item.

even fail in the considerably simpler task of selecting the correct referent from an array when the item is spoken by the experimenter.

Moreover, there is typically a complete overlap between items that cannot be visually matched in this way and those that cannot be named. There is also a clear and graded relationship between the quality of the naming response (i.e. how close the subject came to producing the correct word), and the same subject's ability to produce a list of the item's features (Garrard et al. 2005). Also, if we arrange the test items in terms of how frequent or familiar they are likely to have been in the lives of an average 60 or 70 year old, it is those at the more unfamiliar end of the spectrum that present the greatest difficulty. See Figure 4.

A somewhat more naturalistic technique for studying the phenomenon of language breakdown systematically is to give the subject a task that requires the production of continuous speech: this could be the recounting of a familiar story (the story of Cinderella is typically employed), or a story implicit in a picture. For historical reasons, the picture that is most often used is the 'cookie theft scene' from the Boston Diagnostic Aphasia examination, first published by Harold Goodglass and Edith Kaplan in 1972 (Goodglass 2001). The picture shows a kitchen scene with various evolving events represented, such as an overflowing sink, a daydreaming housewife, and a boy falling off a stool as he reaches into a jar labeled 'cookies' behind her back.

Here is what a typical cognitively normal 60 or 70 year old said when asked to describe this scene:

> It looks like a very chaotic situation. Children are trying to pinch cookies. They are pinching them but he is falling off a stool. The sink is overflowing whilst mummy is drying the dishes. She seems to be ignoring the children. Looks like a very tidy kitchen. There is a garden outside. The girl is putting her finger to her lips saying Shh! so that mum will not hear. Mum seems to be absorbed in something else while she is at the sink while the water runs over. Very difficult to understand that. Her foot is in water.

This is a fluently produced account, narrative in intent, and organised into structurally acceptable sentences, economical in its use of words, which constitute a good selection of distinct nouns and verbs. Here, by contrast, is the output of a patient with established dementia:

> The little girl is looking up to her brother. She holds up her left hand and puts her other hand into her mouth to help him. The boy has picked up…a cookie or something…. says so on the jar. Going to give it to the girl balancing in a way. The girl is just holding a plate and various pieces of …well… something useful. Standing at a window. Whether the window is open is not quite clear to me. The thing where the water is running out. The girl doesn't bother. The window is open. Plate and two cups. House outside changed it movement.

Note that this subject utters roughly the same number of words. Despite one or two pauses the rate of production is similar. There is a hint of syntactic disintegration (subtly in 'looking up *to* her brother', more obviously in the fragmentary final sentence). What is perhaps most striking, however, is the impoverished variety of vocabulary used: both daughter and mother are referred to as 'the girl;' the word 'tap' is replaced by a circumlocution; the sentence structure is shorter and simpler; there is little sense of narrative – only of piecemeal description.

Most neuropsychologists working in the field of language breakdown in Alzheimer's disease have come to the conclusion that these data imply a breakdown in the representation of word and object meaning in the degenerating brain: in neuropsychological terms this would be referred to as a disintegration of 'semantic memory' (Garrard et al. 1997). It is assumed further that this faculty forms part of a long-term memory system accrued over a lifetime of experience with the world and its contents, and represented in the brain in the form of a distributed network of information.

6. The Iris Murdoch Project

The patient who produced the second of the two 'Cookie Theft' descriptions was Iris Murdoch, one of the most acclaimed writers of the twentieth century. Between 1952 and 1995 she published 26 novels, as well as several volumes of poetry and (mainly philosophical) non-fiction. She died in 1999, with a much-publicised diagnosis of Alzheimer's disease, a diagnosis which was later proven at *post mortem*. She wrote her final novel *Jackson's Dilemma* (Murdoch 1995) a year or two before the diagnosis was made, but during this time, subtle evidence of cognitive difficulty was beginning to emerge. It seems clear, in other words, that *Jackson's Dilemma* was written during the prediagnostic period (see Figure 2, above).

Henry James's famous comment that a writer is '[...] present on every page of every book from which he sought so assiduously to eliminate himself', is reflected in the critics' assessments. Of her debut novel, *Under the Net*, published in 1954, Kingsley Amis wrote that it revealed a 'brilliant talent'. Praise was lavished on her eighteenth novel *The Sea, the Sea* when it came out in 1978, and was later endorsed by the award of the Booker Prize in the following year. But the reception, in 1995, of her final work of fiction was altogether different. Many critics tried to hide their lack of enthusiasm under a cloak of respect. Others were little short of insulting, including one who compared the book to the work of 'a thirteen year-old schoolgirl who doesn't get out enough' (Quoted in Porlock, 1995).

An obvious and inescapable question, therefore, is whether the distinctive quality of *Jackson's Dilemma* reflected the effects that incipient Alzheimer's disease was exerting on its author's linguistic — and *a fortiori* literary — abilities. The reasons why such a question may be both possible and interesting to answer are worth spelling out: first, it is rare indeed to have the opportunity to examine cognitive processes in any detail during this intriguing prediagnostic phase; it is rarer still to be able to do so retrospectively, enabling the products of cognition to be examined while the subject is still blithely unaware of any problems. Moreover, the existence of twenty-five previous similar works provides a within-patient control sample of exceptional size and quality. Add to this what is known about Iris Murdoch's highly individual approach to writing: she would carefully work out characters and plots for up to eight months before spending six months writing out the book in longhand (she never used a typewriter, let alone a wordprocessor). There is no evidence that she agonised over choice of words, indulged in repeated revisions of passages, or made extensive use of a dictionary or thesaurus (in fact she neither needed nor owned such aids[1]). Work in progress would occupy the pages of a large pad, which she carried around and added to whenever and wherever she found herself unoccupied (for instance, while waiting for a train, or visiting her husband in hospital where he was recovering from a broken leg) (Bayley 1999). Her publishers would be sent longhand manuscripts (and often complained that they could not read her handwriting), but she eschewed any editorial interference (Wilson 2003). In other words, what we get from the published texts represents only a minimal change from the words that were first committed to paper during the initial act of creation.

A second, more speculative question might be to ask what the study of texts produced under conditions of cognitive impairment can reveal about the process of literary creativity. The idea that there may be a 'neuroscience of literature' is likely to sound at best far-fetched, at worst heretical. Yet there is a burgeoning scientific literature on the effects of frontal lobe damage on creative potential in the visual arts (Miller and Hou 2004). In addition the stylistic changes in the output of Willem de Kooning, whose paintings became diminishingly abstract with the progress of the more advanced stages of Alzheimer's disease are well documented (Espinel 1996). Such observations of the effects of brain damage on creativity in the visual sphere have given rise to hypotheses about the roles (both positive and negative) of specific cognitive processes — such as self-monitoring, inhibition, emotional regulation, and abstract ideation — in creative expression. Similar observation in the literary domain would lend justification to more generalised theoretical models, and perhaps also to an empirical approach to the neural basis of the artistic temperament.

There is an opposing line of argument that the distinctive quality of *Jackson's Dilemma* is the result, not of prediagnostic Alzheimer's disease, but of a deliberate and ground-breaking experimentation with novelistic form: that the apparent lapses in maintaining a consistent authorial point of view that we see in *Jackson's Dilemma* are deliberate and subtle artistic touches; the strangely inverse relationship between Jackson's prominence in the narrative and his importance to the advancement of the plot, the lack of anything in his fictional life that can genuinely be termed a dilemma, and his relative anonymity as a character, all reflect a deliberate decision on the part of the author to 'privilege the peripheral over the central' (Todd 2001). But in the

---

1 John Bayley (personal communication).

best traditions of getting one's retaliation in first, I would point out that, in respect of the work on which I now report, the book was analysed at the linguistic rather than stylistic level, on the basis of *a priori* hypotheses derived from two decades of study of language breakdown in Alzheimer's disease.

True, Iris Murdoch may conceivably have set out to write in a stylistically innovative fashion, but it seems scarcely plausible to suppose that the end point of this exploration should map on to language breakdown in Alzheimer's disease across a range of different dimensions. Alternatively, just suppose that Murdoch had, with tragic foresight, set out to write *as if* she was suffering from Alzheimer's disease, turning *Jackson's Dilemma* into the dementia analogue of Mark Haddon's *The Curious Incident of the Dog in the Night Time* (2003), whose fictional narrator carries a diagnosis of Asperger's syndrome. Although the latter has been praised in the literary world for its credibility as well as originality, such enthusiasm was not shared by those with special insight into the mind of autistic individuals.[2] For these reasons it will be fascinating, if or when an Alzheimer's disease equivalent does appear, to compare its linguistic characteristics to those which Karalyn Patterson, John Hodges and I discovered when we subjected the text of *Jackson's Dilemma* to a series of systematic analyses (Garrard 2005).

We began, naturally enough, by selecting the works for comparison with *Jackson's Dilemma*, and decided to use one from the early period, together with a further work from the 1970s, which was the most prolific and highly acclaimed period of Murdoch's writing career. *Under the Net* (1954), *The Sea, The Sea* (1978), and *Jackson's Dilemma* (1995) are stylistically diverse works: the early work is energetically comic, while the middle and late novels rarely stray into light-hearted territory; *Under the Net* and *The Sea, The Sea* are both written as first person narratives, while *Jackson's Dilemma* is written (most of the time) from the point of view of an independent and omniscient narrator. *Jackson's Dilemma* and *Under the Net* are both approximately half the length of *The Sea, The Sea*, though the latter is divided into significantly fewer chapters (8, compared with 20 for *Under the Net* and 13 for *Jackson's Dilemma*). Clearly, these variables do not correlate with one another across this particular subset of books; nor, more importantly, do they vary in any systematic way across Murdoch's works as a whole.

Next, dialogue was eliminated from the text to be analysed. The rationale behind this decision was that the choice of vocabulary in such passages

---

2 http://iautistic.com/autism-myths-the-curious-incident-of-the-dog-in-the-night-time.php [accessed 10/12/09].

is likely to vary, and may be atypical, depending on the character portrayed. The resulting data were converted to word lists and frequency counts using Rob Watt's 'Concordance' software.[3]

What about the hypotheses? We saw from the examples given above that word production, albeit in the somewhat unnatural context of picture naming, correlates strongly with the frequency and familiarity of the word to be produced. Moreover, in a large scale regression analysis of such naming responses given by Alzheimer's patients, lexical frequency (the number of times-per-million that a given word typically enters spoken or written language) is strongly predictive of success, while word length has no such effect: few patients were able to produce the name 'elk' appropriately, but most could recognise and name an elephant.

Using the Medical Research Council's online psycholinguistic database[4] we were able to match up to 80% of the vocabulary used in all three books with recorded values of written frequency. Word length was obviously obtainable for all words. Comparing mean word length across the three novels, there was a wide range of values in all three works, and considerable overlap between them. In contrast, when we compared lexical frequency, there was a clear and consistent pattern of difference, indicating a higher mean frequency in *Jackson's Dilemma* than in either of the two earlier works; the precise analogue of the frequency effect in naming (high frequency items preserved, low frequency items lost) that we had predicted (see Figure 5).

As I noted when discussing the Cookie Theft picture description earlier, deficiencies in spontaneous speech production are much more notable for their lexical and semantic than their syntactic properties. It is much more difficult to quantify syntactic integrity, and there is huge variation within the cognitively normal population. Moreover, even if we believe Pinker's notion that the ability to use syntax is some kind of linguistic universal, whose possession may even be genetically determined (Pinker 1994), derangement of syntax can manifest in a rich variety of ways. One can look, for instance, at the relative use of different common parts of speech: in our study, the proportions of these did not vary, using a chi-square test, between the three books, when either word tokens or unique word types were considered. Other measures, such as grammatical complexity, cannot reliably be automated and are therefore not suitable for large-scale enterprises such

---

3   www.concordancesoftware.co.uk
4   www.psy.uwa.edu.au/mrcdatabase/uwa_mrc.htm [accessed 10/12/09].

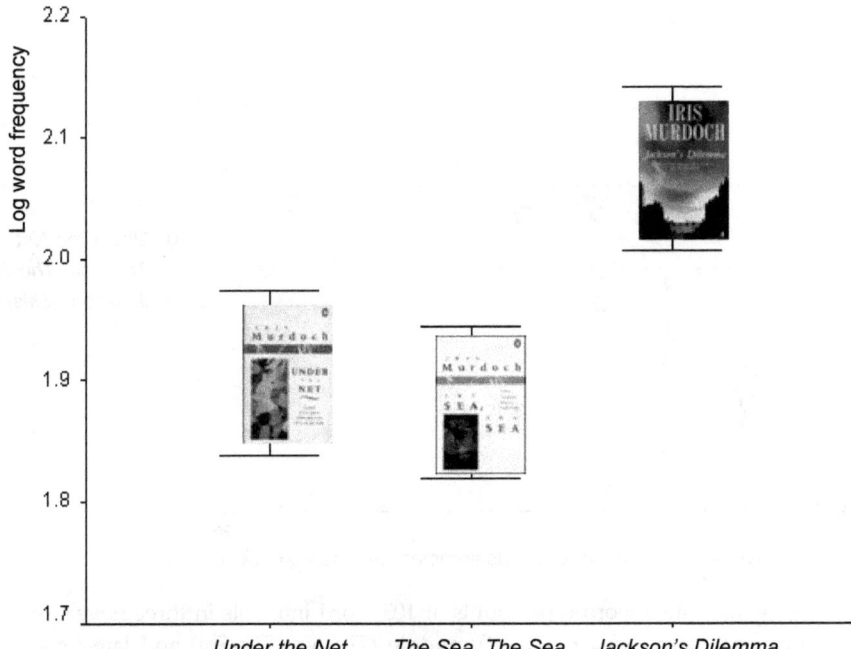

Figure 5: Comparative mean word frequency (usages per million words).

as this, though sentence length correlates strongly with complexity, and is often taken as a surrogate measure of it. Here we saw a hint of a change not only in the form of a slight shortening of the mean sentence length in *Jackson's Dilemma* compared with *The Sea, The Sea*, but also in a change in the opposite direction between the first and mid-career novels.

So far so good, but my instinct is that, to exponents of digital stylometrics at any rate, I might be taken to task for relying too heavily on top-down approaches. So it is heartening to mention that perhaps the most striking finding of the study came from a more data-driven analysis.

At intervals of 10,000 word tokens, we plotted the cumulative numbers of different word types. Figure 6, below, provides a graphic illustration of the rate of introduction of novel word forms as the three works progress. Writing in English, a language with over a quarter of a million words, and possessing a wide repertoire of foreign and technical usages, we would not expect an author such as Iris Murdoch easily to exhaust her vocabulary in the course of a 100,000 word novel. These slopes suggest that *Under the Net* is characterised by a dynamic use of vocabulary from beginning to end, and that this quality is even more prominent in *The Sea, The Sea* (the effect,

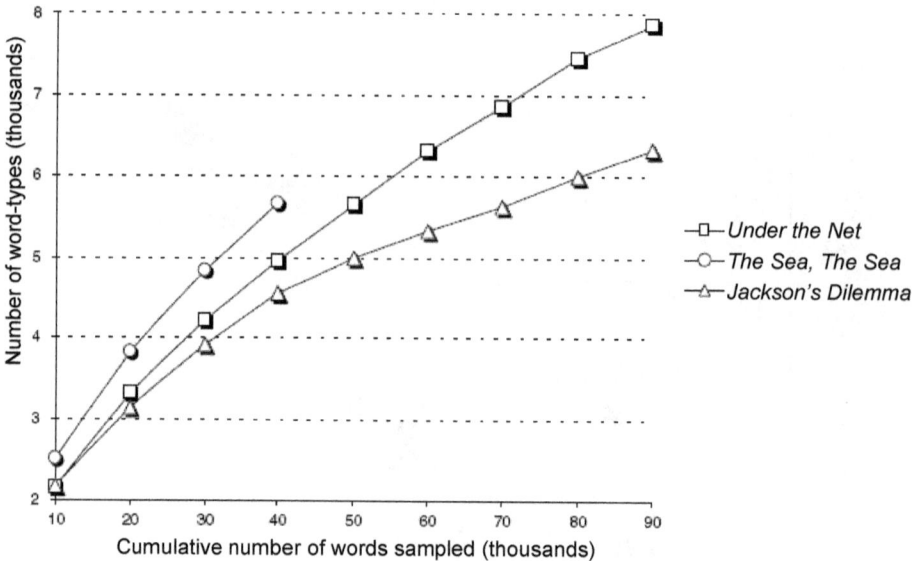

Figure 6: Cumulative word-type counts at 103 word intervals in three novels of Iris Murdoch, from early (*Under the Net*), middle (*The Sea, The Sea*) and late (*Jackson's Dilemma*) periods. The flattened rate of increase in the late book implies increased recycling of previously used words, presumably due to a restricted available vocabulary.

one assumes, of twenty-five years' experience of creative writing). Compare the slope plotted for *Jackson's Dilemma*, with its gentler take-off, and earlier and more pronounced flattening out, suggesting a much lower limit to the vocabulary remaining available for use.

What we do not yet know is whether these three observations, consistent though they are, indicate a chaotically fluctuating range of values, or a consistent trend towards greater stylistic and grammatical sophistication, towards a wider and lower frequency vocabulary, the trend propelled forward by maturity, experience, confidence and success, and then backwards by Alzheimer's disease into decline. We both suspect and hope that the latter is the case, because if it turns out to be so, then the timing of this decline will provide a unique window on that elusive preclinical phase of Alzheimer's disease.

Iris Murdoch's steady and prolific literary output over four and a half decades presents a unique opportunity to try to answer these questions, though the enterprise will be vast and time-consuming. However, thanks to the patience and dedication of a series of students and assistants who

3. Textual Pathology

have been associated with my research group,[5] we are beginning to make inroads, and I would like to spend the remainder of this chapter presenting some preliminary data from these further (unpublished) analyses.

Starting out as we did with three novels, we felt it an acceptable investment of time to acquire fully digitised versions of each. The acquisition period also gave us time to think about what methods of analysis would be appropriate to the dataset. But a longer wait, while the remaining twenty-three books were scanned and proof-read could not be justified. So Arnab Majumdar and I decided to concentrate on the final two decades of Iris Murdoch's career; that is to say, on the eight novels that she wrote from 1978 to 1995: *The Sea, The Sea* (1978) *Nuns and Soldiers* (1980); *The Philosopher's Pupil* (1983); *The Good Apprentice* (1985); *The Book and the Brotherhood* (1988); *The Message to the Planet* (Murdoch 1990); *The Green Knight* (1994); and *Jackson's Dilemma* (1995). Our aim was to trace back the changes that had been found in the three book comparisons, looking for a point at which this change first began to emerge. If such a point could be shown to exist it would be reasonable to suppose that it represents the earliest changes of Alzheimer's disease, and perhaps even a marker for the elusive preclinical phase of the disease. Alternatively, a continuous trend may be identified from the time *The Sea, The Sea* was written, suggesting that the preclinical phase of the disease stretched back over many decades.

Since the findings of the three book comparison were, in most cases, statistically very robust, we felt justified in using a random sampling approach to save time. We therefore used sequential random numbers to select pages, lines, and words in each text for further analysis. Two hundred words were sampled from each text using this method, and psycholinguistic variables examined as before. We looked first at the ratios of content to function words (which can be considered a hybrid measure of a lexical and syntactic character). This ratio remained at a level of around 0.5 throughout this late creative period. A flat line also characterised the imageability scores (i.e. how concrete or abstract the words tended to be – another powerful predictor of word retrieval in dementia (Bird et al. 2000)). Yet there was no indication at all that Iris Murdoch's vocabulary became more concrete towards the end of her life. In fact it was, once again, only with lexical frequency that we found any convincing evidence of change. As illustrated in Figure 7, the mean lexical frequency of the random word sample remained at a

---

[5] For the record: Lisa Maloney, Dr. Arnab Majumdar, Helen Gould and Thurza Honey.

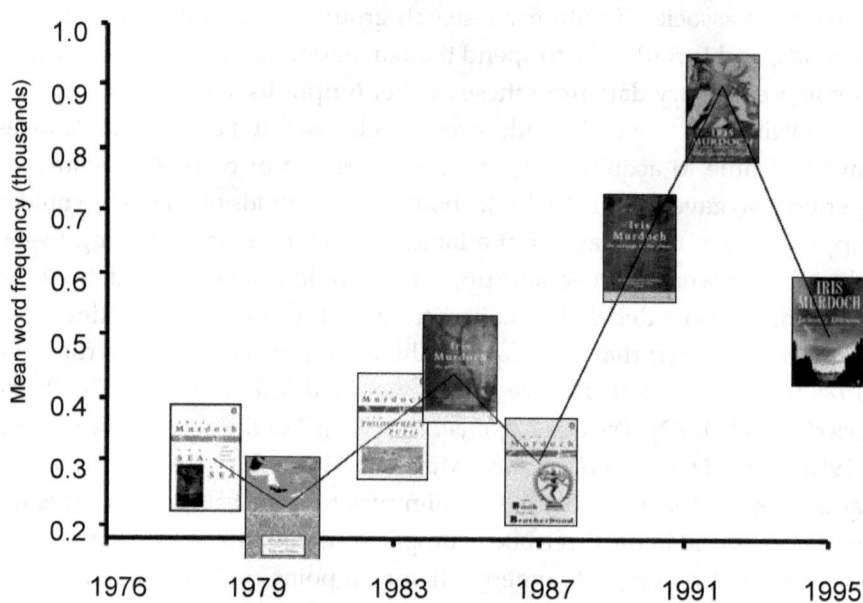

Figure 7: Mean values of lexical frequency for randomly sampled text taken from all of IM's novels written between 1978 and 1995.

consistent level until the publication of *The Book and the Brotherhood* in 1990. At this point, there is a marked increase in the mean lexical familiarity of the sampled words, a trend that continues to be reflected in the penultimate novel. Between *The Green Knight* and *Jackson's Dilemma* however, the trend shows a partial reversal.

What might be the significance of this time series? The most uninteresting explanation might be that the differences between books simply reflect the range of variability to be expected from random samples of 200 words, a possibility that we were not able to rule out on the basis of tests of statistical significance. Further, similar analyses are therefore warranted, based either on entire novels or on larger random samples. From the pattern of change, however (i.e. an Alzheimer's disease-like marked increase in frequency beginning at a plausible time-frame relative to the author's eventual illness) it seems likely that the data are highly informative. If genuine, the observed differences index the onset of Alzheimer-like cognitive changes between ten and thirteen years before death. Attribution of the components of this lead-time to preclinical and prediagnostic stages is a more speculative enterprise, but it is interesting to note that the sharp reversal in the trend towards a higher frequency vocabulary associated with *Jackson's Dilemma* appears roughly to coincide with the emergence of what were later recognised as early signs of dysfunction and may therefore represent a compensatory effort on the author's part. It may be that compensatory behaviour — particularly if unconscious and automatic — marks the onset of this stage of disease progression in other patients, and/or across other cognitive domains.

7. Hypotheses, Methods and Future Directions

Where to go next with this text corpus, and more generally with this investigative enterprise? One of the most rewarding aspects of the media blitz that followed the appearance of our work online in December 2004 was the interest that it aroused in other research fields. Through contact with the Centre for Iris Murdoch Studies at Kingston University I have since discovered a wealth of written material — letters, annotations, notebooks — spanning the period of cognitive decline, which simply cry out to be systematically evaluated. Contact with the Centre for Computing in the Humanities at King's College London opened my eyes to the thoroughly data-driven analyses which John Burrows (2007) among others have used in authorship studies. Now that a digital archive of the majority of the Murdoch novels is available, I hope to be able to implement these techniques with a number of aims, including replication of our findings from the original study, and focusing in on the elusive preclinical period and the temporal locus of change. Consistent and statistically robust patterns of change from these analyses would raise the possibility of finding similar effects in other bodies of text, such as letters and diary entries, whose timing can be pinpointed more accurately. Equally important to this enterprise will be other writers and historical figures who suffered from dementing illnesses late in life, analysis of whose work may yield results of importance to literary history and authorship, as well as to the understanding of the cognitive effects of Alzheimer's disease. One body of work in particular — the *verbatim* transcriptions of Commons and Lords debates (Hansard) — may well turn out to demonstrate linguistic changes referable to the presymptomatic and preclinical periods of the Alzheimer's disease that was eventually diagnosed in one of the most fascinating and enigmatic political figures of our times. If so, then one of the most enduring mysteries of British political history (the reasons behind Wilson's sudden and unforeseen departure from the office of Prime Minister) may come a step closer to being solved.

4. The Human Presence in Digital Artefacts[1]

Alan Galey

1. What Lies Beneath

> The reader wanders at leisure over smiling fields; he plays and runs and never stumbles; and he never gives a thought to the time and tedium it has cost me to battle with the thorns and briars, while I was clearing the land for his benefit. He does not reckon […] how great the discomforts that secured his comfort, how much tedium was the price of his finding nothing tedious.
>
> Erasmus, letter to William Warham, Archbishop of Canterbury (1976 [1514-6]: 262)

This essay considers the tensions between the surface orderliness of scholarly resources and the stubborn irregularity of textual materials. Textual scholarship stands to contribute two key ideas to the digital humanities: first, that there is more to electronic forms than what reaches the screen; and second, that the relationship of form to content is complex and sometimes beyond exhaustive modelling. These two points may seem commonsensical enough within a book-history context, but much of the hypertext theory that dominated the previous decade gives little impression they could matter. Part of the burden of digital textual studies must be to counter the influence of those hypertext theorists who rushed to essentialize computing, the Internet, and digital textuality. More recent work by Katharine Hayles, Matthew Kirschen-

---

[1] The work presented here was supported by the Social Sciences and Humanities Research Council of Canada. Different parts of this article were presented at the conferences of the Society for Textual Scholarship and the Society for Digital Humanities / Société pour l'étude des médias interactifs, the University of Toronto's Faculty of Information Studies, and Texas A&M University. I am grateful to those audiences for their questions and comments and especially to Willard McCarty, Richard Cunningham, Christopher Moore, and Stan Ruecker for their comments on early drafts. Any remaining errors are mine.

baum, Lev Manovich, Alan Liu, and others associated with media-specific analysis and new software studies has shown what technically informed perspectives can bring to the study of digital textuality.[2] Kirschenbaum describes their approach as one that 'cultivates granular, material readings of the inevitable cultural and ideological biases encoded by particular applications and interfaces' (2004a: 533). Such modes of reading expose continuities with past textual practices that some versions of hypertext theory were predisposed not to see — yet such 'granular, material readings' render new textual practices and technologies no less exciting for all that. This essay argues that it should be disquieting to see a deepening separation of material form from idealized content in our tools at the very moment when literary critics have established the materiality of texts to be indispensable to interpretation. As digital textual studies takes shape as a field, it finds itself caught between these divergent trends in computational practice and literary theory.

Textual scholarship has long been driven by an anxious desire to know what lies beneath the perceptual surface — the authorial consciousness embedded in written language; the original of multiple versions; the moments of live inscription held within inert physical artefacts. If the object of textual work is to delve beneath surfaces, the subjects who carry out that work find themselves at the threshold, negotiating between the dead past and living present. In Gary Taylor's oft-quoted formulation, 'Editing is a ritual we perform over the corpus of an author who has passed away' (1988: 50), and all such rituals exist for the sake of the living. Digital textual scholars might well sympathize with Erasmus (quoted in the epigraph above) as he laments the conditions of his editorial labours on the Vulgate of St Jerome. Erasmus's words capture the double-vision that texts demand of us with regard to their mediation of surfaces and depths. It is the same with our tools, digital and otherwise. Beneath any smoothly functioning computer interface such as a Web browser, the source code may harbour the 'thorns and briars' (in Erasmus's words) of half-solved bugs, lingering after the 'battle' with materials and deadlines to build the digital artefact. In a similar manner, the monuments of textual, philological, and historical scholarship are often associated with what Erasmus calls 'discomfort' and 'tedium' in their production, as is the fictional Edward Casaubon's miserable *Key to All Mythologies* in *Middlemarch*, or sometimes even spring from terrible trauma and loss, as in the case of Alfred Pollard's 'punishing work schedule' (Maguire 1996: 28) while he grieved the deaths of his sons in

---

2 On media-specific analysis, see Hayles 2004.

World War I. Battlefield or cleared land: both metaphors for the edited text are present in Erasmus's picture of textual labour, positing a substratum of textual remains beneath the reader's feet.[3] What then is 'the price', as Erasmus puts it, to be paid for the illusion of digital texts and environments as 'smiling fields' where the user never stumbles? The following discussion approaches that question by examining some theoretical assumptions that shape the digital tools of Erasmus's inheritors.

As Erasmus implies, we cannot detach technical concerns from the aesthetic, symbolic, and hermeneutic dimensions of textual work, and his preoccupation with unseen complexity takes visual form in Figure 1. This image shows what lies beneath the main reading room in the New York Public Library's Central Building at 5th Avenue and 42nd Street, an icon of cultural heritage. The illustration comes from the cover of an issue of *Scientific American* published five days after the new building opened to the public in 1911. The genre should be familiar — a representation of the inner workings of an interface between readers and a massive collection of texts, using a visualization technique (the cutaway view) to make the unseen mechanism intelligible to non-specialists. In the reading room at the top, patrons and librarians use a system of catalogues, request slips, and pneumatic tubes to order books housed in the stacks below. The books, once located, ascend to the reading room via mini-elevator. We can also read a foreshadowing of the digital humanities' open-access ethos here, too, since this union of aesthetics and machinery serves a public library.

But *Scientific American*'s tribute to *fin de siècle* design and engineering also illuminates anxieties about what lies beneath it. The image embodies the kind of metaphor for archiving that Thomas Richards uses to describe the symbolic importance of the British Museum at the data-collecting height of the British Empire, and especially its basement as a chaotic space that was symptomatic of the material pressures of data overload (Richards 1993: 4-16). The stacks beneath the New York Public Library reading room emphasize a volume of information that, as a totality, goes unseen by its users. As in Richards' metaphor, there is even a basement at the very bottom of the New York Public Library's stacks, where boxes appear in disordered contrast to the stacks and retrieval system above. Such are the pressures felt by structures that must be at once monument and infrastructure.

---

3   On textual scholarship in *Middlemarch*, see Lerer 2002. On Pollard, see Maguire 1996: 28, and Taylor 1988: 50-1.

Figure 1. A Sectional View of the New York Public Library, Central Building, Main Reading Room. Cover issue of *Scientific American*, 27 May 1911 (Picture collection, The New York Public Library, Astor, Lenox and Tilden Foundations).

The image also displays a fixation with human presence in the form of the tiny figures that populate the stacks (forty-seven of them). Where Erasmus claimed to feel alone in his task of textual management, no such isolation seems possible in this system. One could imagine this image without the figures, as a strictly technical blueprint, but the purposeful distribution of humans throughout makes this a representation not just of mechanical automation but also of human labour. The book is a text on a human scale,

4. The Human Presence in Digital Artefacts

and this image goes out of its way at least forty-seven times to reassert a human presence in a system that holds books, readers, and machines within its compass. Yet none of the humans or books are individuated anywhere in the image; we are shown neither individual readers nor recognizable books that matter in their specificity. As the accompanying article states approvingly, the system 'distribute[s] the reader rather than the volumes which he reads', and 'automatically [...] divides the thousands of readers who wish to consult the books into the intellectual classes in which they belong' (Anon. 1911: 527). Even with the focus on the scale of 'thousands of readers' and their intellectual subclasses, this representation of the library seems to forget roughly half of the library's potential users: only male readers are represented. The living moments of encounter between individual readers and texts, in all their diversity and idiosyncrasy, remain deferred in this representation, implicit in the image but inscrutable to our eyes. The logic of the image, then, is as much temporal as spatial: celebrate resource-building now; understand the particularities of material later.

This large-scale mode of representing reading stands in contrast to humanist depictions of individual reading and writing in Erasmus's time. That instinctive humanist desire to draw closer, like Tantalus, to some idealized but elusive textual encounter finds powerful expression in Vittore Carpaccio's 1502-3 painting *The Vision of Saint Augustine* (Figure 2, below).

Carpaccio's painting depicts Augustine penning a letter to Jerome at the precise moment of the latter's death, as the ghostly presence of the letter's addressee fills the room. In Carpaccio's probable source, a 1485 Venetian edition of the life of Jerome, Augustine in his cell at Hippo is attempting to quantify the joy of souls in the presence of God, and is just putting pen to paper to ask Jerome in Bethlehem for his thoughts.[4] The information Augustine seeks comes to him in a moment of miraculously instant communication that accords more with our present than with the epistolary of the ancient world. Jerome, the archetype of textual scholars, rebukes Augustine's reduction of knowledge to human numbers: 'Augustine, Augustine, what are you seeking? Do you think that you can put the whole sea in a little vase? [...] Will your eye see what the eye of no man can see? [...] By what measure will you measure the immense?' (quoted in Roberts 1959: 292).[5]

---

4   On the painting's probable source and the misidentification of the painting as a depiction of Jerome himself, see Roberts 1959.
5   The translation is Roberts's from *Hieronymus. Vita et transitus*, Venice 1485 (Huntington Library, transcribed by Eugene Brunelle): 'Augustine, Augustine, quid queris: putasne brevi immittere vasculo mare totum [...] Que oculus nullus hom-

Figure 2. Vittore Carpaccio (1455-1525), *Vision of Saint Augustine* (Alinari/Art Resource, New York).

Human text gives way to divine voice, and the letter to Jerome becomes the perfect interface, instantly receding before an unmediated presence. Where the *Scientific American* image shows a perfectly synchronic system, outside of time and history, Carpaccio shows us an instant of collaborative intellectual work deeply embedded in history. In Alexander Nagel and Christopher S. Wood's reading, 'The fluttering pages of the open codices, the fall of shadows, the alerted dog, the poised pen all suggest the momentariness of that moment, the evening hour of compline, as Augustine tells us. This is secular time, the time of lived experience, whose each moment repeats but differs from the previous moment' (2005: 403).[6] Most importantly, *The Vision of Saint Augustine* is not our vision, and the miraculous text Augustine receives from Jerome lies beyond the limits of human representation.

Both of these scenes depict technologies for managing multiple texts — Carpaccio places numerous writing implements, books, and a horizontal reading wheel in Augustine's study — but his painting meditates on the partialness of human knowledge, while the *Scientific American* image celebrates the abstraction of a mechanical system. Both use encounters with

---

inum videre potuit tuus videbit? [...] Immensa, qua mensura metieris?' (Roberts 1959: 297).
6 On Carpaccio's depiction of temporality and its relation to the history and nature of reading, see Bringhurst 2006.

4. The Human Presence in Digital Artefacts 99

documents to reflect on orders of experience that exceed human capacities. Reflecting on a copy of the Carpaccio painting given to him as a student, K. Anthony Appiah comments that 'the shelf of books behind the saint — his library — contained most of the works he would have thought worth reading'; 'he would almost certainly have read all of them' (2005: 45).[7] Today, Appiah notes, more is printed in a single city in a week than Augustine or Jerome could have read in their lifetimes: 'we are, in short, drowning in the particulars we humanists study'. In essence, the *Scientific American* image is 1911's answer to Appiah's fears, and to the question posed in the title of a colloquium and article by Gregory Crane: 'What Do You Do with a Million Books?' (2006).[8] One could read the Carpaccio and *Scientific American* images' differences as emblematic of the digital humanities in its present state, which emphasizes abstract, large-scale approaches such as linguistic corpora and data mining, the social-science version of literary history practiced by Franco Moretti (so-called distant reading), and text analysis techniques that derive patterns from multitudinous low-level observations rather than situated acts of subjective interpretation.[9] These approaches represent a movement away from the humanities' traditionally idiographic tendency (to seek local knowledge about specific cases) and toward the natural and social sciences' nomothetic tendency (to seek abstract patterns and general laws).[10] These approaches also share something in common with the *Scientific American* image in that they place the viewer or critic in a superhuman position, showing systems of words and texts from a perspective that no single human could occupy in real space and time. Moretti stresses that distance can be 'a condition of knowledge' (2000: 57; emphasis

---

7   Appiah actually refers to 'one of Carpaccio's great murals of Saint Jerome' but it is more likely that he has the Augustine image in mind. Carpaccio's other paintings of Jerome do not feature libraries, and this image was often mistaken as a depiction of Jerome (see note 4 above).
8   The colloquium was co-sponsored by the University of Chicago and the Illinois Institute of Technology; see Crane 2006 and the Million Books Project, a collaboration between Carnegie Mellon University Libraries and the Internet Archive: http://www.archive.org/details/millionbooks [accessed 19/10/2008].
9   For an early, influential critique of quantitative methods in literary studies, see Stanley Fish's 'What Is Stylistics and Why Are They Saying Such Terrible Things About It?' (1980/1973). The term ' distant reading' comes from Moretti 2000: 56-8; the opening to his more recent book, *Graphs, Maps, Trees*, suggests a movement beyond this term (Moretti 2005: 1).
10   The terms *idiographic* and *nomothetic* originate with the neo-Kantian philosopher Wilhelm Windelband (1998/1894: 13), and today see more frequent use in anthropology and psychology than in literary studies. On the tradition of thought about the distinction they name, including Max Weber, see Manicas 1998.

removed), but *The Vision of Saint Augustine* complicates the metaphors we use to represent distance, proximity, and the quantifiable. The viewer of that painting remains all too human. Carpaccio invites his viewers just to the threshold of human experience, inviting us to cast our eyes, like Augustine in the painting, beyond the frame of human perception even as we accept its limits. The scale of the human is the preoccupation of both images.

Such is the power of tools and representations alike: to shape thinking, both through the conclusions they enable and the metaphors they deploy. The concerns this essay advances have tended to remain tacit in the digital humanities, a field whose sustaining progress narratives and investments in fundable projects foster a sense of itself as an onward march into the future — an *avant garde* that was the first to embrace computing as a tool for humanities scholarship. Yet the tool-building enterprise risks falling into a binary in which digital tools represent innovation, dynamism, and provocative instability, while the materials they operate upon — very often literary texts — represent availability, continuity, and unproblematic stability. This binary makes it easy to forget textual work always has an interpretive dimension that depends upon the complexity of humanities materials, especially after bibliographically aware literary scholarship in the wake of D.F. McKenzie and Jerome McGann has established the value of joining interpretation with the materiality of texts. Our understanding of that relationship has become intertwined with another, less obvious one: the tension between tools and materials in the digital humanities.

2. Digital Textual Scholarship

> Every tool is a weapon,
> If you hold it right.
>
> Ani DiFranco, 'My IQ' (2002)

Whenever we ask what new technology can do for textual scholars, we must not lose sight of a deeper question: what is at stake in the work textual scholarship does, digitally and otherwise? What makes this work worth doing? Progress narratives almost always leave something important behind, and information culture itself has been accused of systematically forgetting its own history (Day 2001: 3), and of succumbing to a 'rhetoric of newness' and 'rhetoric of amnesia' (Rabinovitz and Geil 2004: 2). Indeed, we have been here before. The digital humanities now occupy much the same position that W.W. Greg and the other New Bibliographers did in the era when the New York Public Library's Central Building first opened its doors. At that time, the cultural pressures that went with social and technological change required the assimilation of vast amounts of technical knowledge about the transmission of texts — and by extension, the seemingly transmissible parts of culture itself — into a coherent progress narrative. This narrative had to account not only for the literary documents that had survived, but also for the practical means by which culture could be preserved and disseminated into the future through editing (and through the related activities of historical bibliography and bibliographic appraisal, enumeration, and preservation). Like digital humanists today, the New Bibliographers lived in a time of new media and information technology; they had to articulate their work to a changing academy that often did not understand it; they were obliged by their material to command a detailed knowledge of how texts, humans, and machines interact; and they had to respond to the often-contradictory imperatives of explaining and making.

Today, textual studies stands not only as a beneficiary of new tools to solve old problems — and, let us hope, to find new problems — but also as a well-developed perspective on new kinds of cultural artefacts. Throughout this essay, the term *artefact* encompasses products of human artifice that can be studied for interpretative purposes, like books, but also what McKenzie somewhat awkwardly called 'non-book texts'.[11] (*Digital artefact* can also mean an instance of visual noise in a digital image, but that usage does not enter this discussion.) The terminological challenge is to find a noun that includes books as easily as cultural productions like video games, films, and paintings, but avoids the scientific and programming connotations of the term *object*. Anthropologists and archaeologists have also thought about this problem. For example, Anders Andrén makes a distinction between artefacts and texts, though not a rigid one (1998: 146-53), and Karin Barber takes *text* to include artefacts and verbal performances (2007: 1-29). Book historian Matthew Brown helps to focus the concept by describing *artefact* as 'a term which suggests an authentic, extant source, not a copied, transcribed, and edited version' (2004: 702-3). However, Brown's description becomes complicated when we consider whether a copy of a video game can be an artefact, since there are no instances of, say, the

---

11   See McKenzie 1999/1985: 13, as well as his chapter on 'The Broken Phial: Non-Book Texts' (31-53).

game *Myst* in the world that are not copies — or can such cultural works never attain artefactual status? What then of a copy of the Shakespeare First Folio, itself an edited text created in part from scribal transcriptions, but which advertises itself as 'Published according to the True Originall Copies' (Blayney 1996: 3)? A thorough definition of *artefact* is beyond the scope of this essay; instead, it may be more useful to consider the intellectual contexts in which we define a term like *digital artefact*.

On its present course, digital textual scholarship may well turn out to be a continuation of the project of D.F. McKenzie. By the time of his death in 1999, his work and influence had gone a long way toward disentangling the field from the orthodoxies of the New Bibliography, and had reintroduced historical and interpretive perspectives into editorial theory, which predecessors such as W.W. Greg had tended to regard as a closed system of transmissible texts, human agents, and mechanical constraints.[12] This essay takes its title from a phrase of McKenzie's, for whom bibliography's great virtue was that it could 'show the human presence in any recorded text' (1999/1985: 29). These are words to conjure with: the phrase '*any* recorded text' opens the scope of textual scholarship's materials to all manner of what McKenzie called 'non-book texts', including 'films, recorded sound, static images, computer-generated files, and even oral texts' (1999/1985: 4), to which we could add software, born-digital fiction and poetry, and now blogs, wikis, and social networking websites — the kinds of intensely socialized digital texts whose existence in a Web 2.0 world would likely have fascinated McKenzie had he lived to see it.[13] It is worth noting that he tended not to describe computers simply as new tools for the textual scholar's toolbox, but rather as a welcome challenge in a continuing professional obligation to account for new forms of communication. As McKenzie suggested in his centenary lecture for the Bibliographical Society in 1992,

---

12 These currents run throughout most of McKenzie's work, but see in particular his chapter 'The Book as an Expressive Form' (1999/1985: 9-30). For an overview of responses to McKenzie's position see van der Weel 2005; the most pointed criticisms may be found in Tanselle 1991.

13 See also McKenzie 1999/1985: 13 and 39. This broad scope has proven easier to embrace in theory than in critical practice. For example, David Greetham's review of Burnard, O'Brien O'Keeffe, and Unsworth (2006) highlights several problems with the collection's overall conception, particularly that 'the absence of painting, dance, film, television, video games, music (about all of which there has been some very challenging discussion of late) makes the collection almost relentlessly text- (or linguistics-) based' (2007: 135).

4. The Human Presence in Digital Artefacts 103

> That obligation has acquired a new urgency with the arrival of computer-generated texts. The demands made of bibliography and textual criticism by the evolution of texts in such forms, the speed with which versions are displaced one by another, and the question of their authority, are no less compelling than those we accept for printed books. By the logic of our discipline, we're equally committed to acknowledge that these textual artefacts also embody the conditions of their construction. (McKenzie 2002/1992: 272-3)

This is a remarkable statement for being both progressive and conservative at once. In the progressive sense, McKenzie naturalizes the expansion of textual scholarship's circle of knowledge to encompass the digital, such that the modifier *digital* becomes redundant in *digital textual studies*. By his logic, to reject inquiry into digital artefacts is to reject the very essence of textual scholarship. But this vision of textual studies also conservatively extends the traditional concerns of print and manuscript bibliography to digital artefacts, with McKenzie's first thoughts tending toward the enumeration of versions and the establishment of authority among them.

Does digital textual scholarship then consist of applying existing descriptive and analytic methods to digital artefacts? To an extent, this conservative approach works, and the single most edifying example so far may be Kirschenbaum's article 'Editing the Interface: Textual Studies and First Generation Electronic Objects'.[14] Taking as his subject canonical electronic literature such as Michael Joyce's *afternoon* Kirschenbaum deftly applies a McGannian awareness of bibliographic codes in reading the material nuances of born-digital objects. This mode of reading raises a question the field is still working to answer: 'what if a textual scholar, well-versed in theories of textual editing, were [...] to be given the task of preserving the original text of *afternoon* in some stable and standardized electronic format for the sake of the scholarly record? How would our scholar go about it?' (Kirschenbaum 2002: 33). This is the kind of question that should keep textual scholars awake at night, not to mention librarians, archivists, and literary scholars.

Two ways of approaching the answer emerge: first through interpretation, by showing how interface elements such as icons and windows in different operating systems and versions may affect how we understand the work; and second through description, adding to our vocabulary terms such

---

14   When it appeared in 2002, this article had a catalyzing effect on many textual scholars, especially those of the generation that had grown up with personal computers in the home. Its importance was recognized with the Society for Textual Scholarship's prestigious Fredson Bowers Memorial Prize in 2003. The ideas presented in the article were developed in Kirschenbaum 2008.

as *layer, version, release, object, state, instance,* and *copy*. These terms bridge the formalized languages of programming and descriptive bibliography, two worlds that make remarkably similar investments in precise language and meaningful distinctions. The bibliographical edge to Kirschenbaum's approach allows him to delve beneath the surfaces of digital artefacts, illuminating the facets of material construction and software design that many literary hypertext enthusiasts and cyberculturalists have tended to pass over or 'mystify' (Kirschenbaum's word) with weak, off-the-shelf interpretations of poststructuralist theory (2002: 25). Searching for an exemplar of digital textual scholarship, Kirschenbaum's article hearkens back to two recognizable strengths of the past century's bibliographical tradition, one being McGann's materialist hermeneutics, and the other, the New Bibliography's rigour in accounting for the physical features of books.[15]

Yet for all its innovation, this early example of digital textual scholarship also relies upon a conservative view of scholarly editing as fundamentally preservational — an updated version of Greg's 1932 dictum that 'Books are of value in proportion as they preserve the past' (1998/1932: 136). As textual scholarship extends its scope to include digital artefacts, it must do so while itself changing from within. In seeking to avoid the weak version of poststructural criticism, with its ill-informed descriptions of digital texts as inherently unstable and non-physical, Kirschenbaum's analysis risks jettisoning what we might call strong poststructuralism, whose influence on textual studies has prompted resistance to the idea of stable origins, interest in texts as mediators of power and not just as bearers of aesthetic worth, questioning of the construction and uses of canons, and valuing of multiple authority as richness.[16] If hypertext theory in the nineties failed to understand how digital texts work beneath the surface, the computing humanists who did understand tended to underestimate poststructuralism's abiding influence. Susan Hockey, for example, mischaracterizes the relationship between textual studies and electronic editing: 'the major difference between a printed and an electronic edition is that a fairly standard and well-documented model has developed for a printed edition, but no such thing exists for an electronic edition' (2000: 133). Even eight years later this remains an insightful statement about electronic editions, but it overlooks the profound changes the print 'model' underwent in the wake of the

---

15 The appendix to Kirschenbaum's article, titled 'Towards Some Principles of Computational Description', is a deliberate echo of Fredson Bowers's landmark 1949 book, *Principles of Bibliographical Description*.
16 The phrase 'multiple authority is richness' comes from McLeod 1982: 421.

New Bibliography's dethroning through the eighties and nineties, which drew force from the influx of poststructuralist theory in literary studies. Although textual scholarship often presents itself in a conservative light as a conduit of tradition and guardian of cultural heritage, its own future depends upon recognizing, *pace* Greg, that all recorded texts are also of value in proportion as they provoke thought and change in the present.

3. Interface and the Stakes of Design

> Long-term preservation of digital heritage begins with the design of reliable systems and procedures which will produce authentic and stable digital objects.
>
> UNESCO Charter on the Preservation of Digital Heritage, article 5

Tensions between tools and materials in the digital humanities manifest themselves in both the design and analysis of digital artefacts. In particular, the preservation imperative described above brings cultural pressures to bear upon all textual scholarship, digital and otherwise, such that Greg uses loaded words when he speaks of books as a 'precious inheritance' (1988/1932: 136). Digital texts lack the same symbolic status as documents like the Magna Carta, Shakespeare First Folio, or United States Declaration of Independence, each of which confers a sense of material origin upon master narratives. We can see tensions at work in some of these documents' digital counterparts on the Web, specifically by reading their URLs for connotations of stability and authenticity. Here are two examples:

> Universal Declaration of Human Rights
> www.un.org/Overview/rights.html
>
> Canadian Charter of Rights and Freedoms
> laws.justice.gc.ca/en/charter/

In both cases, human-readability coincides with machine-readability in the form of the Web address, which in turn confirms the stability of the content of these foundational documents. Future stability of such digital artefacts is the concern of UNESCO's Charter on Preservation of the Digital Heritage, which states that 'The purpose of preserving the digital heritage is to ensure that it remains accessible to the public' (article 2). But contrast that document's own URL with the ones above:

> UNESCO Charter on Preservation of the Digital Heritage
> portal.unesco.org/ci/en/ev.php-URL_ID=13367&URL_DO=DO_TOPIC&URL_SECTION=201.html

Although it is possible to find a slightly simpler URL that brings us to a PDF version of the document (UNESCO 2003), this unwieldy chunk of code is the closest thing we have to a stable address for the Charter in the native format of the Web. As a digital document, the Charter says one thing but does another, creating a contradiction between its content and form: the aspirations of cultural heritage pull in one direction while the design of the code pulls in another.

These tensions become visible in digital objects through the double-vision that characterizes textual scholarship: to see at once both the signifying surface and what lies beneath. By nature textual scholarship resists the fallacy of *screen essentialism*, the tendency to essentialize digital text as 'easily erasable pixels of light flickering on the screen', as Marie-Laure Ryan does in one of the canonical articles of hypertext theory (1999: 95). In Kirschenbaum's definition, screen essentialism depends upon 'the bias towards monitors and display devices in new media studies, where the vast preponderance of critical attention has been focused on what happens on the windowed panes of the looking glass' (2004b: 95). The term comes from Nick Montfort's critique of certain biases in new media studies:

> When scholars consider electronic literature, the screen is often portrayed as an essential aspect of all creative and communicative computing — a fixture, perhaps even a basis, for new media. The screen is relatively new on the scene, however. Early interaction with computers happened largely on paper: on paper tape, on punchcards, and on print terminals and teletypewriters, with their scroll-like supplies of continuous paper for printing output and input both. (Montfort 2004: [n.p.])

Under such conditions there was a more consequential distinction between input and output processes than we generally experience with PCs, sometimes involving a gap of days between the submission of input and the receipt of output from a large, shared mainframe. This is not to suggest that screens are unimportant, but rather that critics need to balance their attention to computers as objects with an understanding of computing as process, in which the screen is but one layer of interface. To see the algo-

4. The Human Presence in Digital Artefacts 107

rithm within the UNESCO document's cumbersome URL is to understand the contextualizing system, just as the *Scientific American* illustration makes a point of revealing the system that humans normally cannot see (at least without a wrecking ball). When reading digital artefacts, textual scholars might question the conventional wisdom that the only good interface is a transparent one.

If textual scholars tend to position themselves at the threshold between the surfaces of texts and their mysterious depths — between Erasmus's 'smiling fields' and the New York Public Library's buried stacks — then digital materials may lead them to new kinds of thresholds. As in bibliography, questions about preserving and reading digital artefacts lead inevitably to the topic of their design. Reading the human presence in a digital artefact requires knowledge of markup, encoding, and even programming, raising the problem of negotiating multiple fields: on the one hand, textual scholarship (which some take to include book history, or at least to overlap substantially with it); and on the other, *interface design* as a catch-all term for a practice that brings together human-computer interaction, information design, usability studies, and programming. Textual scholarship's close ties with book history significantly complicate its relationship with design — though such complexity can be productive.

The greatest conceptual difference between book history and interface design lies in their temporal orientations. If textual scholarship remains focused on the past, interface design is naturally oriented toward the future. Interface design is all about how things *should* be, how to improve the deliverable yet to be delivered. This temporal orientation manifests itself rhetorically. Design gurus like Jakob Neilsen and Bruce Tognazzini tend to intone their advice in the imperative, often synthesizing vast amounts of data into PowerPoint bullets. For example, Neilsen offers the sensible dictum that 'Error messages should be expressed in plain language (no codes), precisely indicate the problem, and constructively suggest a solution'.[17] In this sentence Neilson implicitly looks forward to a time when error messages make sense, when cryptic '404: not found' errors in web browsers no longer lead novice users to wonder if there were really at least 403 other mistakes they could have made. This orientation spans the continuum from professional to academic writing on design, including work that is not overtly part of the 'how-to' genre.[18]

---

17 Jakob Neilsen, 'Ten Usability Heuristics', UseIt.com http://www.useit.com/papers/heuristic/heuristic_list.html (2005) [accessed 19/10/2008].
18 For example, see Dillon 2004 and any of Tufte's books, such as *Visual Explana-*

By contrast, book history is just that: *history*. It looks back to how things were, even in the very recent past, and how they came to be as they are. To those ends, its chief products are narratives in the form of scholarly books and articles. Increasingly though, the term *history of the book* is expanding into *history and future of the book*, generally a positive development but by no means a straightforward one, since the future is not available for study in the same way as the past. The digital humanities' most productive response to this difficulty has been to ask 'why speculate when we can prototype?'; that is, to regard the future of the book as something we create, not just observe and comment upon.

This difference in temporal dispositions does, however, lead to trade-offs. If traditional textual scholarship can seem too historical, with its preservation imperative acting as a brake on any experimental tradition from within, then so too can interface design be accused of not being historical enough, sometimes uncritically assuming a synchronic view of readers and texts that ignores cultural, historical, and political contexts. This is not to suggest that design lacks an historical discourse of its own; quite the contrary. For example, the history of design is a core component of most degree programs in the field, and Edward Tufte's books on information design exemplify a breadth of historical and cultural materials that most textual scholars would admire. However, a substantial part of computer interface design has nonetheless developed in a way that disregards historical understanding as central to the knowledge it produces. Similarly, Tufte himself draws on the work of book historians to offer his insightful readings of 'visual confections' in seventeenth-century English books (1997: 122-5, 134-6), and Andrew Dillon begins a chapter on reader studies with an epigraph from Bacon's essays (2004: 3), but neither really contextualizes his argument within the specific concerns of the seventeenth century, the way a literary critic or cultural historian would. History here is not even background, let alone context; it is only a source of materials. Writing like a cultural historian is not Tufte's nor Dillon's purpose, since the epistemological context for their approaches is not history but cognitive science, just as it is with the interface design coming from computer science. That is by no means a weakness — both of their works cited here are excellent introductions to their topics — but it is a difference that must be acknowledged.

For digital textual scholars the problem is not that the humanities and (social) sciences are different, but that a psychological or historical

---

tions (1997).

4. The Human Presence in Digital Artefacts

perspective may present itself as the only valid one. This essay sides with the historical perspective mainly because it has been neglected in interface design, which looks instead to cognitive science for its epistemological framework. Ronald Day suggests that the origin of this trade-off between disciplines was the constitution of information studies in response to corporate and military needs in postwar America, resulting in

> willful ignorance of Marxist, nonquantitative, non-'practical', and, largely, non-American analyses of information — analyses of information and society and culture have almost totally been given over to so-called information specialists and public policy planners, mainly from computer science, business and business schools, the government, and the quantitative social sciences. (Day 2001: 5)

The consequence for related fields such as human-computer interaction has been what Day calls a problematic 'focus on quantitative methods of analysis, a neglect of critical modes and vocabularies for analysis, a dependence on naive historiographical forms [...], and a neglect of art and culture outside of conceptions of historical transmission (that is, "*cultural heritage*")' (2001: 5; emphasis added). Tufte's work deftly bridges the cognitive and the qualitative, but the overall disciplinary trade-off Day describes may well account for blind spots such as the design of the UNESCO Charter as a digital artefact, as well as problems in other digital projects that lock their materials in a conceptual box labelled *cultural heritage*. Many of the literary texts which bear that label — *Hamlet*, *Ulysses*, *The Canterbury Tales*, *The Prelude* — have complex histories of transmission intertwined with interpretive concerns, and textual scholars may receive new kinds of illumination from the material histories of films, audio recordings, graphic novels, and video games. The humanities' investment in the inner complexity of materials productively complicates the task, as McGann describes it, 'of re-editing — of representing — in digital form the entirety of our received textual and documentary archive' (McGann 2001: 194). Digital textual scholars have found themselves charged with building a new humanities archive using someone else's tools.[19]

---

19   This sentence paraphrases McDayter 2005. McGann makes a similar argument in several places; see 2001: 169-70, 2004a: 409-10, and 2005a: 114. For an analogous critique of the related field of archival studies, see Brothman 1999: 67-8.

4. Religious Issues: Form and Content

> The sonnets of Shakespeare remain the sonnets of Shakespeare even in the most abominable edition. Nor can the finest printing improve their quality.
> Aldous Huxley, Introduction to *Printing of To-Day* (1928: 1)

With a few exceptions, accounts of the intellectual and institutional transformations of the digital humanities often overlook the tension that results from using other disciplines' tools: pulling in one direction, computational practices mandate the abstraction of content from the details of its presentation; pulling in the other direction, literary studies now values those very presentational details as integral to the interpretation of texts. Many of the software tools computing humanists use today embody the design principle of treating form and content as not only distinguishable (as literary critics do in order to talk about them), but also as divisible into components like XML (eXtensible Markup Language) files and stylesheets. Such matters reach beyond pragmatics; as Alan Liu argues, the 'cardinal needs of transformability, autonomous mobility, and automation resolve at a more general level into what may be identified as [a] governing *ideology* [...]: the separation of content from material instantiation or formal presentation' (2004: 58; emphasis changed from original). Liu names this 'governing ideology' *transcendental data*, in which the separability of data from their presentation via technologies like XML means that 'our interfaces today are ever more transparently just [...] skins or, put technically, templates, schemas, style sheets, and so on, designed to *be* extricable [from content]' (2004: 62; emphasis in original). This ideological formation, when manifested in pragmatic terms, confronts digital textual scholars with the kind of dilemma known as a 'religious issue' in programming jargon: is it desirable, let alone possible, to divide the content of a text from its material form for the purposes of machine-readability and large-scale computation?[20]

It may be helpful to consider first a related question: how did this problem overtake digital textual scholarship? The answer lies in how the theoretical and practical conversations about digital texts have unfolded in the humanities. The topic of interface arose late in the critical discourse, arriving only after others like hypertext and multi-linear narrative had asserted their centrality. A case in point is the final paragraph of McGann's influential 'Rationale of Hypertext' (2001, itself a gesture back to Greg's 'Rationale

---
20   On religious issue and related terms, see the *Jargon Lexicon*, http://www.jargon.net/jargonfile/r/religiousissues.html [accessed 19/10/2008].

4. The Human Presence in Digital Artefacts 111

of Copy Text'). In his conclusion, McGann points to something missing:

> this discussion of the decentered text has left out of account the actual implementation of the theoretical design. It has left out of the account the *user interface* that organizes and delivers the logical design of the archive to specific persons. [...] A major part of our future work with these new electronic environments will be the search for ways to implement, at the interface level, the full dynamic — and decentering — capabilities of these new tools. (McGann 2001: 74; emphasis in original)

This frank admission is belated in more ways than one, since the paragraph exists only in the latest published version of McGann's 'Rationale' in *Radiant Textuality* (2001), not in the earlier versions published in the journal *TEXT* (1996a) and the book collection *Electronic Text: Investigations in Method and Theory* (1997). The textual history of McGann's own 'Rationale', one of the most influential critical examinations of hypertext, thus stands as a synecdoche for the critical discourse as a whole.

No less significant, however, is that McGann ends on the word 'tools', a term that marks the borderline between the older hypertext theory and newer digital humanities. Hypertext theorists observe the effects of digital technologies; digital humanists actively develop them, embodying the design ethos of *thinking through making*. (Some, like McGann, do both.) Yet the no-nonsense pragmatism of digital humanists has not insulated them from repeating the mistakes of their predecessors. The late arrival of interface to the theoretical conversation has replicated itself in the lateness of interface design tools native to the humanities.

Although the belatedness of interface has not received due attention, neither has it gone unremarked.[21] Kirschenbaum notes two dangers of deferred interface design in a digital humanities project: first, that a hasty, under-resourced design phase is disproportionate to the influence of that design in the reader's experience; and second, that deferring the interface assumes content is distinct from, and precedes, form (2004a: 524-5). Presently, the first of these two dangers is diminishing as textual projects like digital scholarly editions incorporate the lessons of usability studies from fields like human-computer interaction (HCI).[22] The more insidious danger

---

21 For example, McGann brings up interface as a way of grounding a recent exchange about databases and archives (2007: 1588). From within archival studies, Hedstrom (2002) offers one of the best explorations of the links between interfaces, archives, and digital resources.

22 An example is the Electronic New Variorum Shakespeare (described in Werstine 2008), whose prototype interface was the subject of a Killam Trust-funded usability study in 2007-8 (Moore, Galey, and Ruecker 2008). See also the Orlando

is the methodological creep toward the separation of form and content, which runs counter to the humanist tendency to see the two as distinguishable but fundamentally indivisible. For example, McGann points to Steven DeRose's proposition that a book is the same regardless of variables such as format (quarto versus octavo) and font (Garamond 24-point versus Times 12-point): 'So far as I can see, nearly all the leading design models for the scholarly treatment of imaginative works operate from a naive distinction between a text's "form" and "content"' (McGann 2001: 185).[23] Kirschenbaum elaborates on why McGann's word 'naïve' might be warranted:

> the weight of established wisdom in a field like interface design rests on a fundamental disconnect with the prevailing intellectual assumptions of most humanists — that an 'interface', whether the windows and icons of a website or the placement of a poem on a page, can somehow be ontologically decoupled from whatever 'content' it happens to embody. (Kirschenbaum 2004a: 524)

However, what McGann and Kirschenbaum describe here is not merely loose thinking on the part of designers, nor a matter of critical inattention to discipline-specific theoretical discourses, but a basic conflict of values between the text-oriented humanities and other, data-oriented disciplines. Methodology reflects epistemology, and tools can invisibly import assumptions from other fields into the humanities.

What makes the 'religious issue' of form and content so fraught is that non-textual scholars like DeRose have only been repeating what had become conventional wisdom in their knowledge domains.[24] That con-

---

Project's usability research in Brown et al. 2006: 17-21.
23   McGann cites DeRose in a presentation titled ' Structured Information: Navigation, Access, and Control,' given at a 1995 conference and available at http://sunsite.berkeley.edu/FindingAids/EAD/derose.html [accessed 18/10/2008]. For a more thorough explanation of DeRose's position, see DeRose et al. 1990, one of the opening salvos in the OHCO debate (see note 23 below).
24   Specifically, DeRose invokes the idea that all texts have an essential structure in the form of an Ordered Hierarchy of Content Objects (OHCO), a tree structure of non-overlapping nodes that conveniently matches the structure of all XML documents. The debate over the OHCO theory of text divided critics along the question of the materiality of texts — though some participants might characterize the debate differently — with DeRose, Allen Renear, and their co-authors on the pro-OHCO side, and opposing them McGann, Hayles, and others with links to textual scholarship. From a textual studies perspective, the OHCO thesis lost in theory but won in practice. The materialist hermeneutics and media-specific analysis of McGann and Hayles, respectively, have lost no ground in literary and textual studies, but the OHCO model is everywhere in our digital tools, from the structure of XML documents, to the historical core of the TEI guidelines (see http://www.tei-c.org/

4. The Human Presence in Digital Artefacts 113

ventional wisdom has made its way into the humanities, for example in James Cummings's explanation of XML's usefulness to the Records of Early English Drama project: 'The increasing separation of content from presentational aspects has been fundamental for the interoperability and flexibility that makes XML so valuable' (2006: 181). But how do we determine value? Practically, such separation is a welcome convenience; intellectually, its value is suspect since it impairs textual scholars' ability to use text encoding to model the complexity latent in their materials. Although Cummings accurately describes XML's advantages over HTML for the encoding of born-digital documents like academic articles, his description becomes deeply problematic when applied to the encoding of non-digital materials like manuscript poems (he takes many of his examples from Chaucer). Cummings's explanation overlooks the crucial distinction between prescribing presentational details and recording them — a non-trivial distinction in textual scholarship, which searches for the human traces left upon material artefacts.[25]

The seductiveness of form-content abstraction derives from its ability to simplify the task of encoding, even for those trained to appreciate complexity in texts. We can see the different temporal orientations of design and book history mirrored here, as the conventional wisdom governing the design of new digital documents extends, anachronistically, to the reading of textual materials from the past. Cummings and DeRose represent a tradition which, in the spirit of the Huxley epigraph above, regards content as literally that — meaning contained in the language of a text. (Tom Davis, in a tongue-in-cheek paraphrase of Karl Popper, terms this attitude toward information as the 'bucket theory' of communication [1998: 106].)[26] On the other side of the doctrinal divide, McKenzie's simple dictum stands in contrast: 'forms effect meaning' (1999/1985: 13).[27]

Guidelines/ [accessed 11/2/2010]), to the Document Object Model that underpins browsers and other Web technologies. See Schreibman 2002 for a balanced overview of the positions; for key entries in the debate, see DeRose et al. 1990; Renear 1997; Renear, McGann, and Hockey 1999; McGann 2001, as cited elsewhere here; Hayles's chapter on 'Translating Media' (2005); and Robinson 2009a.

25   Peter Robinson, for example, argues for the value of encoding the minutest details of presentational information in Chaucer's manuscripts (1996a). The problem is not that Cummings is unaware of editorial theory; evidence to the contrary may be found in Cummings 2007.

26   The history of the term *information* is also relevant here; see Nunberg 1996 and Capurro and Hjørland 2003. For a discussion of the concept of information within the context of theorizing tools, see McCarty 2002: 382-3 and 2005: 110.

27   As if to prove McKenzie's point by accident, a recent book history anthology

Paradoxically, the digital humanities have produced valuable practical venues for thinking through such religious issues (for example, the Text Encoding Initiative), but also communities of practice whose theoretical assumptions are now difficult to dislodge (for example, again, the Text Encoding Initiative).[28] McGann's closing argument about interface in the 'Rationale' (2001), however belated, was all the more valuable for pointing a way out of hypertext theory's closed circle of self-confirmation. In retrospect, hypertext theory now seems like a part of the conversation about digital textuality that mistook itself for the whole conversation, but the digital humanities' practical orientation should not mean a dismissal of theory. 'The implementation of the theoretical design', as McGann (2001: 74) calls it, has become no less a moment of *theoria* for the digital humanities, in the sense of Hans-Georg Gadamer's distinction of *theoria* as more than passive observation: 'It does not mean a mere "seeing" that establishes what is present or stores up information. [...] Theoria is not so much the individual momentary act as a way of comporting oneself, a position and condition. It is "being present" in the lovely double sense that means the person is not only present but completely present', as when one is present in an audience that is fully 'engrossed in their participation as such' and fully aware of each other (1998: 31). In this sense of *theoria* and *presence* as synonyms, the modelling of human presence in interface design becomes not just the implementation of a theory, but an act of *theoria* that enables one to think through these complex relationships. Textual scholarship has long exemplified this philosophy, as in Bernard Cerquiglini's pithy formulation, 'every edition is a theory' (1999: 79). Unfortunately, humanities computing practice has bypassed such moments of *theoria* in its tendency to think of interface design and text encoding as separate activities, each happening at opposite ends of the research plan. As Kirschenbaum points out, interface design too often comes as an afterthought, late in the project schedule as time and resources run out.[29] The deferral of interface thus represents not so much work left undone as a missed opportunity to articulate what's at stake in how the humanities understand texts.

---

subtly changes the meaning of this statement by altering its orthographical form to 'forms affect meaning'; see Finkelstein and McCleery 2006: 36.
28 For discussions of the structural impositions of the TEI tagset, with particular reference to the sometimes-vexing <fw> (forme-work) tag, see Lancashire 1996: 123-4, and Bjelland 2000: 24-6.
29 See Kirschenbaum 2004a: 524-5.

5. Serving the Particular

> [T]he universal in the humanities is in the service of the particular.
>
> K. Anthony Appiah, 'Humane, All Too Humane' (2005): 42

The search for human presence in digital artefacts is also the search for the humanities' place in digital scholarship. Both searches are underway even as the design of digital tools is moving in one direction while the theories of textual scholarship are moving in another. Digital humanists caught between the tensions described in this essay should be wary of two species of the same essentialist fallacy: one, perpetuated by theorists with only a screen-deep understanding of technical matters, asserts that digital texts are inherently unstable (productively or otherwise); the other, perpetuated by computing practitioners who neglect theory, asserts that that the only aspects of texts worth knowing are those which may be modelled digitally. Screen essentialism thus has its counterpart in computational essentialism, and digital textual scholars must somehow navigate between the two. The challenge is to design interface tools that do not force business or (social) science models upon humanists. This step involves developing traditions of programming native to the humanities, and recognizing that programming and computer science are not the same thing.[30] A further challenge is to determine how designing and prototyping, as keystones of the experimental tradition within the digital humanities, should relate to the archival and historical strengths of textual scholarship.

To put all this another way, what does the conjunction *and* signify in a term like *history and future of the book*? Is it merely a hasty splice between disciplines, or an expansion of an established field into new territory? In the most optimistic light, the *and* represents the imperative to find a synthesis between reading historical artefacts and designing for the future. Although interface is by no means the only important aspect of digital textuality, it is the area where such a synthesis is most needed. The response of textual studies should therefore be more strategic than simply pointing out when computing practitioners do not understand humanities materials. For a text encoder working under a computer science model to treat data as extricable from their presentation *is* consistent with best practice. For a literary scholar to treat texts as *in*extricable from their presentation

---

30 On the importance of decoupling programming from computer science in the digital humanities, see Crane et al. 2007: 54; for a pedagogical perspective on programming in the humanities, see Rockwell 2003.

is also consistent with best practice. This is the methodological crux facing digital textual scholars of the present and future.

The solution lies partly in rearticulating a simple but fundamental idea to all sides: even as we design new digital artefacts, we are still learning how books work, as well as manuscripts and other textual materials. By looking for something more than the authorial *genius loci* in texts, McKenzie introduced new ways to answer the question of what is at stake in textual scholarship's search for 'the human presence in any recorded text' (1999/1985: 29). The phrase *human presence* implies no less complexity than *any recorded text*, and digital artefacts, like any other kind, bear traces of the social worlds they occupy, not just of their creators. Just as Kirschenbaum rightly questions the easy binary that produces digital texts as unstable, so must we also be vigilant against the myth that, with the rise of digital technology, the human record is now moving from a period of fundamental stability to one of instability. As print- and manuscript-oriented textual scholars have long argued, past textual forms were never so immutable to begin with.[31] Textual scholarship may be the contrarian voice within the digital humanities, resisting those progress narratives which, in order to justify investments in tool-building, make texts computationally tractable by sacrificing their complexity on the altar of expediency. The serious study of digital artefacts does not replace that of pre-digital materials; rather, the two must progress together or not at all.

Readers of the May 27th, 1911 issue of *Scientific American* were shown a figure of the New York Public Library that revealed to them the textual depths beneath their feet. In the same gesture, the figure asserted a sense of mastery over the space of the archive, rationalizing it by means both of the retrieval mechanism and of the image's power to depict it. Digital humanists today are presented with similar representational systems promising a similar mastery. 'What do you do with a million books?' remains a worthwhile question, but only if we remember that the humanities' great advantage is the power to produce new knowledge using only a few books — sometimes even one text. That uniquely powerful economy of scale defines what Appiah calls the humanities' 'deeply idiographic character': discovery comes from 'a particular poem, a particular painting, a particular sonata' (2005: 42).[32] For digital tools and methods to share in that distinctly qualitative power, they must be able to serve the particulars of texts with-

---

31 For example, see the recent debate between Elizabeth Eisenstein and Adrian Johns in *American Historical Review*, mediated by Anthony Grafton (Grafton 2002).
32 On the term *idiographic* as opposed to *nomothetic*, see note 9 above.

out sacrificing them to the exigencies of the universal. The digital humanities now face a paradoxical challenge: being digital comes naturally; it's the humanities we have to earn.

5. Defining Electronic Editions: A Historical and Functional Perspective

Edward Vanhoutte

1. Introduction

Since Peter Robinson published the first electronic edition in a series designed to accommodate all of Chaucer's *Canterbury Tales*, he has been theorizing and writing about the nature and definition of electronic editions. Along with Jerome McGann and others, he has been at the centre of the debate on electronic textual editing since he began work on the collation and textual criticism of Icelandic manuscripts, for which he developed programs collectively called *Collate*. Because of his accessible papers on the subject of electronic textual editing, his software for automatic collation and his models realized in commercially available editions, Robinson has been the logical starting point for many a scholar wanting an introduction to the concept of electronic textual editing.[1] However, rather than looking for a general definition of an electronic edition, Robinson has consistently been specific about what kind of editions *he* wants to produce, first of the Old Norse *Svipdagsmál*, later of Chaucer's *Canterbury Tales* and Dante's *Commedia*, and more recently of the Greek New Testament. Since he admitted that he was mistaken to abandon the single (edited) text in the edition of *The Wife of Bath's Prologue* (Robinson 1996c) in favour of a set of different views of the text, he has moved from advocating the reader's freedom of choice among many texts, to recognizing the function of the one text, to looking for the ideal model of an electronic edition and its functions. Currently he

---

1   It would be informative to examine in how far this is true for non-Anglo-American digital scholarship, for instance in the work of French and German scholars.

advocates 'fluid, co-operative and distributed editions' that are strongly interactive and that are indebted to Peter Shillingsburg's concept of 'knowledge sites' (Robinson 2003a: 125, 2007c). At the same time, Robinson's ideas of 'electronic editions for everyone' (2007b, ch. 6 in this volume) correspond with Shillingsburg's concept of the convenient and the practical edition that must bridge both the theoretical and practical differences between textual and literary critics (2005). This concept recalls Fredson Bowers' idea of the 'practical edition' (1969).

Shillingsburg's and Robinson's ideas for distributed editions do not, however, provide a general model for electronic editions or a generally applicable and stable interface. These ideas may well be suited for classical, medieval, and Victorian Anglo-American textual traditions and may well respond to the needs of the broad communities interested in them. They seem unlikely to be successful for editors of texts from smaller traditions, such as the modern Dutch and Flemish. Editors of texts from such traditions work for an audience of only a few interested academics and a small reading public who for the most part want simply to read texts from printed books. The idea of the active involvement of a computer-literate and critical community with a knowledge site built around a modern Dutch or Flemish text is but an idle fantasy.

It is tempting to advocate a standardized interface to electronic editions for the convenience of the user. From a theoretical point of view, however, such an interface is as absurd as Stefan Graber's defence of the historical-critical edition as the only legitimized type for scholarly editing (1998). An interface should rather be conceived as an aggregate of means by which the user can interact with the text, commentary, and ancillary material. What the interface is called upon to provide is very much dependent on which underlying mechanisms have been provided to assist the manipulation of a particular text or set of texts according to the nature of that text and the editor's interpretation of it. Hence, imposing a general interface would render some perspectives difficult to impossible to realise. The electronic edition would then be reduced to a publication tool demonstrating a fixed set of options rather than a modelling tool for exploring the text and generating meaning with it.

Is it possible to define what an electronic edition is, given that it may be called upon to do so many different things? The range of requirements is large – from demonstrating 'the considered act of reproducing or altering texts' (Tanselle 1995a: 10) to providing tools to online communities for the

5. Defining Electronic Editions

enhancement of knowledge sites; from the digitization of a printed edition to the provision of user generated editions; from the publication of one text to the presentation of a textual archive. How should this question be answered? By a guide to good practice? By a survey of current theoretical positions and case studies, e.g. in the recent volume on *Electronic Textual Editing* (Burnard et al. 2006)? By normative guidelines like those of David Gants (1994), Susan Hockey (1996), Jerome McGann (1996a), and Peter Shillingsburg (1993, 1996b)? By several meditations on the technologies, functions, building stones, or characteristics of electronic editions (e.g. Karlsson & Malm 2004)?

My aim here is to propose a definition of an electronic textual edition and frame it in the historical context of earlier defining efforts.

2. Research Assistant

Robinson's edition of *The Wife of Bath's Prologue on CD-ROM* (1996c) is likely the first generally acknowledged example of a published electronic edition providing a real example of the rationales and principles articulated in the mid-1990s. At the time the new HTML-driven World Wide Web and the desktop computer seemed to support the widely proclaimed democratizing character of hypertext. The feasibility of electronic editions, for which these documents provided blueprints, was determined by the technological knowledge of textual scholars who had been looking into the advantages of computational techniques. The production model of encoding text-critical research in a platform independent markup language and publishing the scholarly edition in a hypertextual environment seemed to be a fair trade-off between the use of manageable text-based technology and the popular(izing) hype of hypertext publishing.

Although the idea of hypertext was devised by Theodor Nelson in the mid 1960s (2003/1965), it first became a useful technology with the release of the programmable hypermedia authoring tool and information organizer HyperCard in the mid-1980s. Before then the computer had been used extensively as a 'research assistant in scholarly editing' (Shillingsburg 1980: 31), relying on programs and tools developed for concordancing, collation, analysis of variants, stemma determination, reconstruction, building, and photo composition. In the 1980s sophisticated and integrated packages for textual editing, such as Shillingsburg's CASE, Robinson's COLLATE, Wilhelm Ott's TUSTEP (1988), Francisco Marcos Marín's UNITE and Robert

Cannon and Robert Oakman's URICA! were developed.[2] However, with HyperCard and the introduction of the personal computer came a new contingent of less technically sophisticated scholarly users. Consequently, computer applications in the field of textual editing consisted of 'sophisticated word processing' (Potter 1985: 95) whose most proclaimed advantage was the elimination of the need to retype documents whenever a correction was inserted.[3] Towards the end of the 1980s Hans Walter Gabler summarized the computer's function in textual editing nicely by saying that: 'l'ordinateur n'est donc pas instrument de recherche, mais un simple outil pratique qui peut, il est vrai, améliorer de manière notable l'efficacité et la qualité de nos travaux' (1989: 55).

This was corroborated by a survey of scholarly editors conducted in the fall of 1990 by Cathy Moran Hajo, mentioned by David Chesnutt (1991). This survey showed that computers were mainly used as word processors in the preparation of critical editions and their critical apparatus. '[E]ditors working in 1991', Chesnutt concluded, 'continue to use computers in many of the same ways they adopted in the late 70s and early 80s' (1991: 377). As a matter of fact, the 1970s and 1980s saw few new insights. When presenting TUSTEP as a suitable suite of software tools for critical editing in 1988, Wilhelm Ott confessed that the basic ideas and techniques presented were not new: 'Most of it could have been told (and has in part been told) ten years ago. [...] So you must be content with a more than ten-year-old concept, and with some results and experiences which we have achieved since then.' (Ott 1988: 82). Charles Faulhaber agreed: 'To date, most computerized textual criticism has conceived of the computer primarily as a tool to facilitate the production of printed texts both by automating the procedures of textual criticism, as well as by permitting a much greater consistency in the application of editorial criteria.' He further pointed out that the goal of the process was still the printed text itself, and he observed that 'as a byproduct, but only as a byproduct, the computer also produces an electronic version of the text' (1991: 123).[4]

---

2   The main difference between the integrated packages and other programs is that each program in such a package produces an output that can be used as input for follow-up programs so that a continuous editorial procedure from text comparison to typesetting the scholarly edition becames possible.

3   Even if the manuscript had been prepared on a word-processor, it was commonly retyped by the publisher in a second machine-readable version that included formatting codes.

4   Already in 1967, Martin Kay optimistically claimed that '[i]n a few years every printing house which wishes to remain competitive will produce a machine-read-

5. Defining Electronic Editions

With respect to the application of computational techniques to textual editing up to the beginning of the 1990s, Thomas Tanselle is probably right in commenting that '[w]hen people say that the computer makes possible certain kinds of textual research, such as locating all the appearances of particular words in a given text or group of texts, they are using the word *possible* inexactly to mean 'practically feasible"' (2006: 3). It is indeed true that when Miriam Shillingsburg claimed back in 1983 that her edition of Washington Irving's *The Conquest of Granada* 'could not have been produced without the aid of the computer' (1983: 654), she did not mean that it had been impossible to produce an edition of this complexity and size without the aid of the computer, but that it was unlikely a project to happen since it would have occupied a substantial part of one's academic career. 'The misuse of possible is not a trivial matter,' Tanselle argues, 'for it is symptomatic of the exaggerated claims one often hears about computers, and these claims do not provide a useful foundation for thinking productively about just what computers can in fact do for us' (2006: 3). In this respect also, Tanselle's conviction that '[p]rocedures and routines will be different; concepts and issues will not' (2006: 6) seems to be true. Fifteen years before Tanselle's claim, Jean-Louis Lebrave had already observed that the computer-assisted edition did not affect the concepts and issues of editing: 'les charactéristiques et la structure du produit imprimé ne sont pas modifiées par l'utilisation de l'ordinateur dans les phases de mise en page. De ce fait, la P.A.O [Publication Assistée par Ordinateur] n'affecte pas la problématique de l'édition' (Lebrave 1994/1991: 171).

3. Publication Medium

The exaggerated claims to which Tanselle reacted were also present in hypertext theory of the late 1990s. The introduction of the computer as a publication medium, however, and thus, in a way, as a modelling tool, started the transition from computer-aided or computer-assisted editions

---

able version of a text as a natural by-product of the printing process, and it is to be hoped that a systematic effort will be made to insure that this material is not destroyed as it usually is today'. The question is then: what can be done 'to make this data available to linguists and literary scholars and to enable them to profit as they should from the computer facilities that are so rapidly becoming cheaper and more powerful'? (Kay 1967: 171).

to true electronic editions that exploit the possible beyond the feasible.[5]

The idea of publishing scholarly editions electronically, then, began to gain ground, thanks to the wide availability of personal computer software and hardware, economically sound solutions to the 'input bottleneck' by the development of affordable scanning services and optical scanners with OCR software, the improvement of digital imaging equipment and techniques, the availability and exponential growing capacity of magnetic and optical storage devices and the overall falling cost of data processing and storage.

The ambiguity in the association of the concept of electronic edition with the photo-composition of printed editions, rather than with the production of editions for the screen, was criticized by Roger Laufer who proposed the concept of the *édition-diffusion éléctronique* (electronic distributed edition) as an alternative to *l'édition automatique* which was what computer-assisted editing was called in France (Laufer 1989: 115). Disappointed by the illegibility of his own edition of Alain René Le Sage's *Diable Boiteux* and inspired by translation software used on Apple Lisa and Macintosh machines, Laufer, at an international meeting in 1984,[6] promoted the implementation of the technique of *multi-fenêtrage* or multiple windows in a program which could turn the computer itself into a publication medium (Catach 1988). This technology would overcome the economic and static limitations of the elitist construct that is the printed scholarly edition, and introduce a social alternative for the dynamic and full realization of the promise of the critical synoptic edition that claims to offer the option of reading multiple versions simultaneously in the form of the apparatus of variants:

> Le recours à l'informatique permet d'obvier à ces inconvénients. Le lecteur choisit son texte de base et son ou ses textes de comparaison pour les lieux qui l'intéressent. Ainsi devient réalisable une édition critique entièrement variable selon demande. (Laufer 1989: 115)

---

5 As long as the printed paradigm remains the model by which the computer is used in assisting text-critical research, this transition will never take place fully. Statements about the computer as a mere tool to facilitate the text-critical process are mostly made by scholars who do not intend to explore the possibilities of the computer as a modelling tool, and who stick to the assistant role of the computer in existing areas of study. Reasons for this attitude can be manifold and include ignorance, resistance, peer pressure, and intentional compliance with certain schools and traditions.

6 Table ronde internationale portant sur 'Les problèmes techniques et éditoriaux des éditions critiques', 28-29 June 1984, Paris: CNRS. The proceedings of this meeting are published in Catach (1988).

5. Defining Electronic Editions 125

The use of the multiple frames on the screen as a manipulation tool for the dynamic reading or consultation of parallelized documents (versions, variants, facsimiles, annotations...) was the original idea Laufer added to existing technology.

Around the same time, George Logan, David Barnard, and Robert Crawford described the critical edition of Thomas More's *Utopia* that aimed to publish a machine-readable text not merely as a series of computer files which could be distributed and analysed in conjunction with (non-system) analytical software,[7] but as 'files linked to software that can display sections of text in desired configurations, maintain interconnections between the different files, and provide other appropriate services' (Logan et al. 1986: 319-20). The authors describe a variety of uses of the electronic edition, ranging from consulting the isolated component files of the edition, to dividing the screen into multiple windows for the simultaneous consultation of different component files, to simultaneously scrolling parallelized component files. Unlike Laufer, however, Logan et al. propose to publish the electronic edition alongside the printed edition. Because all the components of the printed edition are also present in the electronic version, the latter can be used as a replication of the printed edition, but as the authors point out, the greatest advantage lies in its 'power to facilitate coordinations which, though explicit, are virtually impossible to discover in printed books' (Logan et al. 1986: 322). They explain: 'the windows of the electronic edition can replace not one but several place-holding fingers [...] they allow appropriate temporary rearrangements of the pages of the edition' (Logan et al. 1986: 322).

Jean-Louis Lebrave commented that: '[l']innovation principale est peut-être que l'utilisateur devient partie prenante dans l'élaboration des matériaux qu'il consulte, et contrôle librement les cheminements qu'il effectuera à travers les documents' (1988: 127). He added that one of the implications of this technology was that the exclusive choice between a critical edition and a facsimile edition disappeared because 'on peut consulter simultanément un fac-similé du brouillon et telle ou telle forme d'édition ou interprétation de ce brouillon' (Lebrave 1988: 127). As an alternative to the conjunctive use of analytical software with the machine readable text in Logan et al. (1986), Roger Laufer predicted the integration of several analytical software tools such as collation and concordance software in this kind of electronic edi-

---

7 Towards the end of the 1980s machine-readable texts of literary titles became available as separately distributed products on CD-ROM or as part of electronic text centres. Often, the texts were encoded for use with specific analytical software packages such as WordCruncher or Micro-OCP.

tion (Laufer 1989: 124). However, as he pointed out, the specific software that would facilitate all this still had to be written.

Like Laufer, Lebrave saw recent computer technology as an alternative to the traditional codex. He described the electronic edition as 'a multi-media data base, giving access to facsimiles, to various transcriptions, to interpretation tools, like dictionaries or programs for automatic comparison of textual fragments' (Lebrave 1987: 142). The advantage of such a 'pluralistic system', according to Lebrave, is that it 'would allow any reader to construct his own reading according to the hypothesis he wants to build up' (1987: 142).

Although neither Logan et al. nor Laufer and Lebrave ever use the terms *hypertext* or *hypermedia* in their early presentations and writings, – Logan et al. speak of 'interconnections between the different files' (1986: 319) – their descriptions of the mechanics by which users of their editions could walk 'à travers les données génétiques sans être prisonnière d'aucune des formes de représentation utilisées' (Lebrave 1988: 136) undoubtedly describe the functionality of hypertext.

The explicit link between Gérard Genette's (1982) concept of hypertext as a form of intertextuality[8] – already in use in genetic studies (Marantz 1988) – and Nelson's concept of hypertext as *non-sequential writing* (2003/1965)[9] was made by Lebrave in a series of articles on hypertext and *avant-texte* in the early 1990s. Here, Lebrave highlighted the advantages of hypertext for the organisation and visualization of the *dossier génétique* and reported on some early experiments with the hypermedia authoring tool HyperCard.[10]

Although the concept of hypertext was considered to provide the ideal metaphor and technology to reconstitute the dynamics of the writing process (by the visualization of a number of documents and their regrouping according to several principles such as resemblance, difference, teleology, and chronology) the resulting edition was a closed hypertextual universe and remained as static as its printed counterpart. In other words, it only offered dynamism within its own pre-set boundaries and according to the enabled features of the hypertext application.

---

8   'J'appelle donc hypertexte tout texte dérivé d'un texte antérieur par transformation simple (nous dirons désormais transformation tout court) ou par transformation indirecte: nous dirons imitation.' (Genette 1982: 16).
9   Nelson describes: 'a body of written or pictorial material interconnected in such a complex way that it could not conveniently be presented or represented on paper' (Nelson 2003/1965: 144).
10   Namely genetic editions of the beginning of Flaubert's *Hérodias* by Lebrave and a genetic path through one of Joyce's *Finnegans Wake* notebooks by Daniel Ferrer (Ferrer 1995).

4. Analytical Tool

An interesting early suggestion of a dynamic system was provided by Todd Bender in 1976 and was echoed by Donald Ross Jr. in 1981. Both scholars conceived of formal textual editing as a computer project that 'should be set up and preserved in such a way that future scholars can return to it and use it in its electronic form' (Bender 1976b: 194). After analysing the Platonic orientation of modern textual criticism, as advocated at the time by the CEA (College English Association), and the incompatibility of this method in the case of modern literary texts where 'the printed page is inherently incapable of representing the work accurately or fully' (Bender 1976b: 194), Bender introduced computer technology as offering the possibility of retaining 'a version which more closely approximates the essence of a work without disregarding all the mutations which exist in the manuscript and printed representations' (1976b: 194). He proposed to recognize the electronic text as the primary form of the work and the '"real" repository of information' from which any printed expression and any form of textual analysis could be generated. With the publication of the concordance to Conrad's *Heart of Darkness* in 1973, Bender (1973) had demonstrated the generative power of this approach. Instead of basing the concordance on a printed text, which Bender argued is but 'one among many possible provisional, incomplete, and arbitrary formats of information' (1976b: 194-5), he based the concordance on the basic input data which included transcriptions of all significant printed and manuscript versions of the text and their collations. This genetic and transmissional information turns the repository into a three dimensional data pool that, although it cannot produce definitive editions, 'can easily search out for us and note every case in which a literal or punctuation variant occurs in this three dimensional matrix' (Bender 1976a: 333-4). As any printed edition is a two dimensional and 'simplified expression of a matrix of complex variables' (Bender 1976a: 336), Bender envisioned that the role of the textual editor might be the construction of the multidimensional model of variables which could be consulted from any 'scholar's desk console anywhere in the world' connected 'through radio or telephone circuitry' to 'one central data bank' (Bender 1976b: 195). The reader, Bender noted, will come to the electronic repository and ask for 'a provisional expression shaped to his needs' (1976a: 337). In order to facilitate a dynamic consultation and analysis of the data bank, Bender developed a system by which relationships among words or signs are represented not by positional notations, but by arithmetic notations that are semantic-neutral representations of the language. This system would allow the representation of interrelations in a set of complex variable information in which a word is seen as a constellation of significations (Bender 1976b: 196).

Some years later, Donald Ross Jr. proposed to turn Bender's model inside out. Instead of a textual database containing the transcriptions of the witnesses of the transmissional and genetic history of the text and their collations, Ross suggested storing the copy text as data together with collation information and expressing the traditional footnotes or apparatus of a printed edition as algorithms or a series of programs that manipulates the copy text into a representation of any selected stage of the textual history (1981: 159-61). This means that every single stage of the textual tradition or genesis, including the critical text established by the editor, would then be *assumed* data which could be called upon and produced by these algorithms. Editors would be responsible for the validity of the commands invoking the algorithms that produce a stage of the text and they would also have to document the procedures so that users of the edition could access any perspective on the textual history. The use of such a system would be threefold in Ross' view. First, this data organisation could produce traditional printed editions presenting any stage of the text. Second, the assumed data could easily be analysed, for instance to determine stylistic patterns by the generation and collation of concordances of various stages of the textual history. Just as in Bender's database proposal, statistical analyses of other stylistic features would also be options as well as an automatic analysis of genetic features. Third, the database could function as a 'front-end' for a document retrieval system that not only displayed the assumed data assembled by specific user-driven commands graphically, for instance to represent the author's working process, but that also provided access to all information stored in this database. 'Assuming this were possible,' Ross concluded, 'then the kind of information in the data base could be displayed to the scholar working at a terminal, where passages from all sources could be called up' (Ross 1981: 161).

5. Hyperedition/Database

Almost two decades after Bender's proposal, Marilyn Deegan and Peter Robinson (1994/1990) came to similar conclusions regarding the fact that traditional scholarly editions inevitably present a selection of the information used and produced in preparing such an edition, especially when the computer is used for the transcription, preparation, encoding, and collation of texts which produce much intermediate data that are not represented in the final result. The selection and presentation of data is traditionally left to the judgement and experience of scholarly editors who endorse scholarly editions with their authority. In Deegan and Robinson's proposal, however, all data on which editorial decisions are based could be presented in what they called 'an electronic hypertext edition' which would not substitute for but supplement the traditional edition. As Deegan and Robinson argued, 'viewed in the light of certain reasonable reading expectations, the legitimate exercise of editorial selectivity imposes arbitrary and subjective limits on the interpretation of texts, and what is a justifiable and intelligent limitation from one scholarly angle may appear, from another, an unnecessary restriction of possibilities' (Deegan and Robinson 1994/1990: 35-36). Less radical than Bender, who emphasized that the real information was located in the electronic memory, Deegan and Robinson preferred the on-screen representation of information with the aid of hypertext as a referential management and navigating system. By their proposal to not only present the results of critical research such as the edited text and several commentary sections and apparatuses, but also the research materials, such as encoded transcriptions and digital facsimiles of the documentary witnesses, they introduced the edition/archive issue which was commented on by Peter Shillingsburg (1996a: 161-71). However, they clearly expressed the need for the electronic hypertext edition to preserve the features of the traditional scholarly edition alongside the presentation of these data, as did Logan et al. (1986) and the 1997 CSE *Guidelines for Electronic Scholarly Editions* which claimed that the 'content of an electronic edition differs little from that of a print edition.'

In an instructive and elaborate essay on 'Textual Criticism in the 21st Century' Charles Faulhaber agrees with Deegan and Robinson on the content of a hyperedition. He describes the concept and function of what he calls 'the electronic critical edition' as follows:

> In an electronic critical edition the critical text will be the locus of a set of data connected to it by various kinds of links, some established specifically by the editor, others established automatically by software tools. The critical text will not exist as a self-sufficient isolate but rather as part of a rich environment which will enable users to study the text's internal structure – graphemic, phonological, morphological, lexical, semantic, syntactic, discursive – as well as its relationship to its genre, to its linguistic and literary tradition, to the interpretive tradition which surrounds it, to its historical moment, to its society, and, eventually, to significant aspects of its culture, understood in anthropological as well as artistic terms. (Faulhaber 1991: 128)

Deegan and Robinson (1994/1990) draw the attention to two issues that also feature in the later propositions and normative guidelines for electronic editions already mentioned in the introduction to this essay. The first was the requirement for a platform independent and non-proprietary markup language that could deal with the linguistic and the bibliographic text of a work and that could guarantee maximal accessibility, longevity, and intellectual integrity in the encoding of texts and textual variation. This was found in the work of the Text Encoding Initiative, which had issued their first *Guidelines for the Encoding for Machine-Readable Text* in 1990. The second issue was the need for a hypertextual navigation tool that could guide the user through an enormous amount of documentation and proof of textual variation, and that would overcome the shift from the singularity of the edited text to the multiplicity of the archive. Already in 1993 (although not published until 1996), John Lavagnino boasted that textual scholars were 'the avant-garde when it comes to the use of hypertext' (1996: 109).[11]

This vision is typical of the overall tendency in the 1980s and 1990s to ignore Donald Ross' generative database proposal, which took an algorithmic approach to produce assumed data in favour of Todd Bender's archive suggestion, which took a presentational approach towards articulated data. However, Manfred Thaller, in line with his perspective on humanities computing as a humanistic computer science, proposed to consider electronic editions as computer systems that are able 'to support historical *research*, as opposed to administering, in a convenient way, *results* of historical research' (1996: 254), which is what hypertext editions do. In Thaller's vision, the underlying structure of an electronic edition is best organised as a database system that browses texts as extended string data types. Using this data type as a replacement for the concept of a simple string in programming application systems enables the acceptance by the database sys-

---

11   The paper was written in 1993 but published in 1996.

tem of external information 'which is browsed into the internal extended string representation, processed in that form and re-converted into some kind of external representation before being displayed on an appropriate medium' (Thaller 1996: 252). Thaller is backed up by Dino Buzzetti (1996), who favours a database representation of the entire textual tradition that contains processable representations of text. But he also warned that 'the dynamic form of a database representation – a form of representation that affords a more faithful reproduction of the varied and diversified expressions of textual fluidity – should not be mistaken for the accomplished form of its edition' (Buzzetti 1996: 255). Like Ross, Buzzetti proposed to document the sequential textual tradition in a unique and consistent non-linear representation in database form, for which he used Thaller's extended string concept:

> A database representation can thus act as a consistent and unifying model of all different sequential representations of a text, a congruent structure onto which they can all be mapped simultaneously and consistently, and from which they can all be separately derived and individually displayed. (Buzzetti 1996: 255)

This entails a double economy of encoding a single sequential representation and processing a multiplicity of structurally different representations.

However, probably because of its embedding in computer science rather than in the humanities, this database model was not generally considered by humanities scholars who came to think about electronic editions. The hypertext edition, on the other hand, with its focus on the edition as an object and its realization of associativity and intertextuality, was championed by many a project. As Lou Burnard (1992: 17) explained: 'Where true database systems require a formalization of the information content of text, hypertext systems return us the view of information as an emergent property, resulting from a connection between one piece of discourse and another.'

6. Edition/Archive

The database concept, however, did turn up in Deegan and Robinson's description of hypertext as 'a document which is essentially a database with active cross-references allowing non-sequential reading and writing' (1994/1990: 36). This inspired Peter Shillingsburg (1993, 1996b: 31) to conceive of the electronic edition mainly as a database attached to a network. Next to the concern that the design of the electronic edition and the storage capacities of the archive must anticipate the desires of the targeted user community, Shillingsburg mainly addressed issues of usability, transportability, security and order, integrity, and expandability. The networked database model was shared by Susan Hockey (1996), who put more emphasis on the need for encoding strategies that could also handle documentation of meta-information about the text and the images. 'Ideally', Hockey argues, 'the master copy would consist of transcriptions of the text and digital images of the source material' (1996: 13-14). Deegan and Robinson likewise proposed that the electronic edition should contain encoded transcripts of all the manuscripts and 'possibly digital images of some or all manuscripts' (1994/1990: 36). Shillingsburg (1996b) turned this desirability of a full accurate transcription and a full digital image of each source edition into a condition of the electronic edition, echoing Tanselle who stated that '[d]igitized images of the original manuscripts and printed pages should always be provided along with the more manipulable electronic texts' (1995b: 591-2) – something which Lebrave (1987) had already requested before. Tanselle also required the inclusion of 'critically reconstructed texts [...] within the collection of texts available in a hypertext edition' (1995b: 592),[12] a suggestion picked up by Shillingsburg in his defence of 'both types of editing' (1996a: 95), that is historical and critical editing. In the context of his envisioned knowledge sites, Shillingsburg defends the logic behind the inclusion of a critical text in a documentary archive and asks: 'In what sense is it a gain to have in an archive a historical text that was poorly produced and represents the hasty and not-so-careful editorial work of a commercial publisher rather than the thoughtful, careful work of a scholarly editor – who just happens to pursue editorial goals with which you don't agree?' (2006b: 157). Interestingly, Shillingsburg designed his knowledge sites as documentary archives in which scholarly editions have

---

12 In 'Critical Editions, Hypertexts, and Genetic Criticism' Tanselle makes two explicit points about hypertext. First he defends the graphical possibilities of hypertext: 'Just as a scholarly edition in codex form is considered deficient if it does not provide a record of variant readings, a hypertext edition (or 'archive') should be regarded as inadequate if it does not offer images of the original documents, both manuscript and printed' (1995b: 591). Secondly he defends the inclusion of a critical text in a hypertext edition/archive: 'Indeed, the point can be made more positively: that critically reconstructed texts ought to be included within the collection of texts available in a hypertext edition' (Tanselle 1995b: 591-2).

5. Defining Electronic Editions 133

their place. Curiously, he seemed to have forgotten Tanselle's defence of the inclusion of a critical text in a hypertext edition 'or 'archive' (Tanselle 1995b: 591) when he reported 'I have yet to hear anyone suggest that the electronic scholarly archive should have a critical edition of each sort added to the collection of historical texts' (Shillingsburg 2006b: 157).

In his influential essay 'The Rationale of HyperText', Jerome McGann pointed out that the *Rossetti Hypermedia Archive* (McGann 2005b) is 'an archive rather than an edition', claiming that its indefinitely expandable 'webwork of relations' escapes the 'bibliographical limitation' of the edition which 'closes its covers on itself' (1996a: 27). McGann's concept of the archive is directly linked to the function of hyperediting, the result of which is 'theoretically open to alternations of its contents and its organizational elements at all points and at any time' (McGann 1996a: 29). Furthermore, '[u]nlike a traditional edition, a hypertext is not organized to focus attention on one particular text or set of texts. It is ordered to disperse attention as broadly as possible' (ibid.). In this discourse, McGann clearly used the word 'edition' when he referred to the traditional codex edition, and 'archive' to emphasize the hypertextual nature of the electronic edition. That this is not a useful distinction is proved by his own use, in the same essay, of the terms 'Hypereditions' and 'Hypermedia editions' when he refers to the results of 'hyperediting' (and not 'hyperarchiving'). The somewhat awkward distinction between edition and archive is not used consistently by McGann himself and it seems to reflect his aversion to the mechanics of the traditional critical edition shown in the following quotation:

> Editing in codex forms generates an archive of books and related materials. This archive then develops its own meta-structures – indexing and other study mechanisms – to facilitate navigation and analysis of the archive. Because the entire system develops through the codex form, however, duplicate, near-duplicate, or differential archives appear in different places. The crucial problem here is simple: the logical structures of the 'critical edition' function at the same level as the material being analyzed. As a result, the full power of the logical structures is checked and constrained by being compelled to operate in a bookish format. If the coming of the book vastly increased the spread of knowledge and information, history has slowly revealed the formal limits of all hard copy's informational and critical powers. The archives are sinking in a white sea of paper. (McGann 1996a: 14)

As McGann later reflected on this essay, '[t]he immediate focus of the argument was the debate among editorial theorists about the possibility of creating, in scholarly form, the 'social text' – that is, a critical edition that would not privilege the authority of one particular text or document' (2001: 25). In order to achieve this, McGann (1996b) sought to 'integrate for the first time the procedures of documentary and critical editing'. *The Rossetti Hypermedia Archive*, then, was created by McGann to demonstrate the practical feasibility of his social theory of the text that was at the heart of *A Critique of Modern Textual Criticism* (1983), and to promote the view that digital forms were open and interactive as opposed to the static and linear qualities of the traditional codex form (2001: 25).

Robinson (1996b) interestingly ranked McGann's *Rossetti Hypermedia Archive* together with Richard Finneran's *Hypermedia Yeats* project (Finneran & Bornstein 1994) in a 'more is better' kind of electronic edition which he opposed to the 'less is better' group in which he situated his own edition of the *Wife of Bath's Prologue* (1996c) and Anne McDermott's edition of Johnson's *Dictionary of the English Language* (1996). The distinction between these two kinds of editions is made on the basis of their respective intent to include all the relevant multimedia materials or only a selection. According to Robinson, editors of editions in the 'less is better' group aim 'to identify a particular textual domain and a particular audience, and to present that text for that audience as clearly, as richly, and as accurately, as is possible with the resources available' (1996b). In the case of *The Wife of Bath's Prologue* (1996c) the textual history under consideration is limited to the pre-1500 witnesses only, and the Johnson edition only presents the first and the fourth edition of the *Dictionary*. Further, Robinson pointed out that these editions are also 'rigorously exclusive: there is no discussion of the importance of Johnson's lexicographic work on the CD-ROM, and the Wife of Bath's Prologue CD-ROM contains no glossary and no study of the Wife of Bath herself' (1996b). Together with the explicit editorial presence in the text, this function is one of Robinson's arguments that an electronic edition should not be an archive, resource, or 'an accumulation of materials without any editorial "interpretation"' (1996a: 110). In a later reflection on the editions of the *Wife of Bath* and the *General Prologue*, however, he called them 'repositories of information, from which skilled scholars might quarry what they need' (Robinson 2003b). Robinson (2007a: 8) summarizes: 'for a digital edition to be all it can and should be, then it will let the editors include all that should be included, and say all that needs to be said.'

The distinction between editions and archives, however, is not made by Tanselle who observed that '[u]p to now, scholarly projects for publishing electronic texts have tended to take the form of archives' (2006: 5). Electronic editions and electronic archives, in Tanselle's view, are therefore synonymous.

At the same time, it is true that the meaning of the word 'archive' in connection with electronic textual editing has changed over the course of time. Originally denoting a mere repository of digital surrogates of material artefacts and processed data, the concept has come to include scholarly and critical material such as edited texts, annotations, scholarly essays and the like, alongside the digital resources. This transition has happened organically.

7. Critical Edition

The distinctions discussed so far such as print versus electronic, archive versus edition, database versus hypertext, or 'more is better' versus 'less is better' have been useful in the debates in which they feature, but they are problematic with regard to defining the electronic edition. Just as pointing to a tree does not define one, comparing a tree with something which is apparently not a tree does not work either. The discussion above illustrates that a definition as crude and basic as the one John Lavagnino suggested, writing in 1993, as the core of all hypertext editions, was even at the time of writing theoretically problematic: 'a system that would store both electronic texts and images of all the versions of the works in question, and offer the ability to display parallel texts of any two versions, as either images or electronic texts' (Lavagnino 1996).

Although it might have been true that this is '[w]hat a number of scholars have imagined a hypertext edition would be' (Lavagnino 1996), this definition clearly describes a very specific type of electronic edition and a very specific type of hypertext edition which requires a specific archival basis and a specific display. Toby Burrows (1997), in his proposal for building a typology of electronic editions, did not include any requirement with regards to the contents or the display of the edition, but instead looked at five more neutral characteristics of electronic texts, namely the markup scheme employed; the extent to which the edition is dependent on specific software; the method of distribution or publication; the overall structure or architecture of the edition; and the type of edition involved. Although this checklist could produce informative metadata on the edition as a bibliographical object which should evidently be documented as part of the edition, theorists of the electronic edition have focused on describing more functional requirements. John Lavagnino (1996) argued that the hypertext edition should facilitate four tasks: '*selecting* versions to look at; *comparing* versions; *constructing* new and possibly more representative versions of the text on the basis of the information available; and *integrating* all this study with other scholarship and criticism.'[13] A fifth possible task '*consulting* a critical text' is not listed here. By excluding the explicit requirement of the inclusion of a critical text, Lavagnino defended an electronic edition that is different from Faulhaber's 'electronic critical edition' (1991) which is centred on a critical text. The reason for this can be found in McGann's definition of critical editing: in an interesting discussion – at least from a historical and theoretical point of view – on the ESE (electronic scholarly editing) mailing list in 1994 (ESE 1994), about what critical editing is and what the nature of the electronic archive is, McGann made the following claim:

> critical editing is a mechanism whereby, through a programmatic study of textual variance in extant documents, one hypothetically reconstructs lost or absent documents (which may themselves be hypothetical). period. that IS what it is and that's all it is. [...] now although this editing tool is obviously designed for use in dealing with ancient texts, it was adapted by scholars to certain 'modern' circumstances where the documentary record was once again relatively broken and problematic. it was then re-adapted (by bowers) to situations where the documentary record was hardly damaged at all, i.e., in cases where one did not need the special tool of 'critical editing' to clear the texts of errors. simple collations would take care of the errors. the tool was used rather to construct 'eclectic editions' that represented hypothetical forms of some hypothesized 'authorial intention' (original or final, usually). (ESE 1994)

McGann continues: 'with the coming of electronic text, however, the use of 'critical editions' in the proper sense, for modern texts, changes.' Therefore, the real question in connection with electronic archives and critical editions, McGann argued, is: 'would a critical text be useful?' In other words, 'are there any cases where such an edition would be called for, where it has any point; what would make one want to produce such a text?' According to McGann, the documentary record of texts, as presented in digital archives,

---

13   When rereading his essay in 1997, Lavagnino pointed out that 'this essay looks to the future because most of its suggestions about things we need to be able to do with texts have not been implemented' http://hdl.handle.net/2027/spo.3336451.0003.112 [accessed 8/3/2010].

seldom demands such a text. Nevertheless he argues in favour of the inclusion of critical texts in digital archives such as his *Rossetti Archive*, but, he adds, 'I won't make such a reconstruction myself.'[14]

Robinson (2002) accepts McGann's reservation about the inclusion of a critical text in an electronic edition or archive, and mentions the presentation of an edited text as a mere possibility of a 'critical digital edition'. With the 'critical digital edition' Robinson proposes to extend the functions of a traditional printed critical edition in the traditional print library to the digital realm. Its main function is thus, according to Robinson, to 'think critically, and to help others think critically' (2002: 59) or, in other words, 'to help editors edit, [...] to help readers read' (Blake & Robinson 2000). Robinson's proposal reintroduces critical editing into the model of the hypertext edition as an archive whose main function is the creation of accessibility to certified materials. In an earlier meditation on the electronic edition, Robinson (2009; written 1997-2002) had defined the electronic edition in general terms as 'an edition conceived and executed exclusively for electronic publication, and impossible in any other form'. Here, he discussed six requirements which supplement this definition and which he sees as 'co-ordinates by which critical editions might be located' (Robinson 2002: 51). An electronic critical edition, then:

- is anchored in a historical analysis of the material
- presents hypotheses about creation and change
- must supply a record and classification of difference over time, in many dimensions and in appropriate detail
- may present an edited text
- must allow space and tools for readers to develop their own hypotheses and ways of reading
- must offer all this in a manner which enriches reading

Scholarly editions, as Ray Siemens (1996: 43) has reminded us, have a certain dynamic: 'The contents of a scholarly edition, to some degree, show the influence of previous scholarly work and, because scholars will rely on and refer to it, its contents also influence future study.' The quality and relevance of the scholarly edition depends on its capacity to document the no longer and to facilitate the not yet. Robinson's co-ordinates are all situated in this continuum with the first three leaning towards the documentation

---

14 In this ESE discussion, Morris Eaves asks McGann whether he thinks critical editing is dead? McGann answers that critical editing is certainly not dead and that a 'full bowersian critical editing process' is justified 'to clear a problematic documentary record'.

of the past and the last leaning towards the empowerment of the reader and user who are invited to conduct future study, part of which could be the creation of a critical edition. A critical digital edition is thus minimally a well-documented digital archive that overcomes the dangers of what Már Jonsson has called 'Utgeverisk impotens' or 'editorial impotence' (cited in Ore 2004: 35).

If McGann and Robinson are right in their assumption that the documentary records of texts in such archives or editions seldom ask for the inclusion of a critical text but are incubators for future scholarship, the digital archive should be an icon representative of the tangible and original documentary archive – Flanders (2009; written 1997-2002) called representation the textual condition of the edition/archive. The idea goes, then, that this representational archive of digital images, encoded transcriptions, records of difference over time, and contextual information provides the building stones from which different kinds of editions – which Robinson (1994: 93) calls 'nothing more than compilations of materials' and McGann (1994: 104) considers 'specialized organizations of materials' contained in the archive – are generated for different audiences. Mats Dahlström, however, has called this assumption 'overidealistic' (2001: 69). When taking into account Julia Flanders' observation that in an electronic edition 'the representation of documentary evidence is attached, conceptually, to the mode of knowing that the edition is offering' which substantiates in 'different theories about what counts as textual knowledge' and different internal economies of 'evidence, of substantiation, of utility' (1998: 306) we can begin to understand Dahlström's reservation. His reticence has nothing to do with a fundamental suspicion towards the reliability of reproductions[15] as voiced by Tanselle (1989), nor a distrust of the accuracy of the transcriptions – transcriptions of which text, one could ask, for no text is self-identical, as McGann has argued in *Radiant Textuality. Literature after the World Wide Web* (2001) – but with his analysis of the nature of editions, as he explained in his essay 'How Reproductive is a Scholarly Edition?' (Dahlström 2004). Dahlström's main argument is that the claim of reproductivity as a result of the scholarly edition's supposedly scientific nature ignores the limitations of the genre. The nature of a scholarly edition, Dahlström contends, is determined by its historical, medial, social, and rhetorical dimensions:

> To sum up, the SE [scholarly edition] is a subjective, rhetorical device. It

---

15   Issues of digital surrogacy, authentication of digital images, and questions of photographic truth, are passed over in this essay.

5. Defining Electronic Editions

is moreover both a result of and a comment on contemporary values, discussions and interests. It is situated in time, in space, in culture and in particular media ecologies (of both departure and target media). To all bibliographical genres, using derivative target documents as representations of departure documents, these are factors imposing constraints on their iconic force. The situatedness limits the representational and moreover the remediating force of bibliographic tools, including the SE. There are no absolutes here. The SE obviously has representational and reproductive force, the very abundance and undisputable value of SEs throughout history testify to that truism. The interesting question is what factors are at work to limit or to enhance this force. Another important matter is what force and purpose the remediated material itself might have, that is, to what degree the SE is valuable as laboratory, as working material for new scholarly editorial endeavours. I am not talking about the value of SEs for historians, for literary critics, for studies in the history of ideas, etc., but for the making of next SEs based on textual criticism. (Dahlström 2004: 27)

And he continues:

If such archives are to be used as laboratories for generating new scholarly presentational documents such as critical editions, i.e. turning the target documents into departure documents, one would have to stay alert to the derivative status of the archived material in the first place. An SE based primarily (if not solely) on the derivative documents of such a digital archive will always to some extent depend on the inevitable choices made by the persons building the archive, on the historical, socio-cultural, cognitive, and media particulars and on the pragmatic purposes and theoretic values defining and framing the final derivative documents in the archive. (Dahlström 2004: 28)

In the same essay, Dahlström mentions the 'mimetic fallacy' and the 'complete encoding fallacy'[16] as implicit and problematic assumptions of the electronic scholarly edition that aims to be reproductive. He also reminds us that the scholarly activities of transcribing and text encoding are subjective moments of selection. Since they are governed by one's theory of the text which, on the pragmatic level, is translated to 'thought, method, and decision' (Robinson, 2002: 55) and since they are straining after rhetorical and political effects, we could call them editorially intentionalistic.[17]

---

16 Willard McCarty defined 'mimetic fallacy' as 'the idea that a digitized version will be able to replace its non-digital original' and 'complete encoding fallacy' as 'the idea that it is possible completely to encode a verbal artefact' (McCarty 2003, cited in Dahlström 2004: 24).

17 See also Peter Shillingsburg's discussion of five formal orientations in editing, in particular the documentary, sociological, and bibliographic orientation (1996a: 15-27).

Tanselle (1995a: 14), however, has warned that the resulting texts 'may be inappropriate for certain purposes' and Dahlström argues that striving for a universal aim of the digital archive 'is doomed to failure because it is rooted in an assumption that both textual material and scholarly editing are context-free phenomena' (Dahlström 2004: 28).

Espen Ore advised that a basic archive – 'grunnarkivet' (1999: 143) – be a self sufficient digital archive whose creation 'is done as a goal in itself, not as a step in the creation of an edition' (2004: 42). Therefore, he requires that all documents have explicit source descriptions and that their creation as digital artefacts is documented.[18] Further, Ore stipulates that the documents are sufficiently described in terms of file types, resolution, character set information, and encoding schemes. This information must articulate the authority of the archive and must guarantee the preservation of the archive as a bibliographic artefact, as Marilyn Deegan has claimed as well: Deegan (2006: 366) suggests that a thorough documentation of data, metadata, links, programs, and interfaces may enhance the chances that the digital edition is preserved as a functional scholarly environment.

Interestingly, Ore (2004: 42) adds that digital archives *may* move on from being basic archives 'if they offer editing tools and make it possible for users to mark up texts', that is, allow users to apply their own theory of the text on the textual model. However, contrary to Shillingsburg (2006b), Ore does not consider this a formal requirement of the digital archive: 'The archive should be a possible data source for zero or more editions' (Ore, 2004: 42).

Elsewhere I have argued that an electronic (scholarly) edition should be processed from a platform-independent and non-proprietary basis or digital archive of encoded transcriptions, high–resolution image files, metadata etc. which can be stored for archival purposes and can be used as a reproductive basis for more editions. But I have also emphasized that this archive differs from and precedes the generation of the edition proper, which is the immediate result of textual scholarship; the edition proper is intended for a specific audience, is designed according to project-specific purposes, represents at least one version of the text or the work, and its creation and editorial status are explicitly articulated and documented (Vanhoutte 2006: 163).

---

18 'For digital facsimiles this would include the techniques used for photographing and/or scanning and information about post-scanning processing of the image files. For texts, transcription work and encoding (including proofreading) should be documented.' (Ore 2004: 42)

8. Ergodic Editions

In their fullest realizations, Robinson's model of co-operative and distributed editions and Shillingsburg's knowledge sites aim to incorporate both Ore's self-sufficient archive and Robinson's and McGann's models of the reproductive edition against the background of the history of electronic textual editing as recounted in this essay. The eventual product would no doubt have to qualify as an ergodic[19] text where the reader behaves as 'a user in a transcending, cocreative, author mode' (Aarseth 1997: 183) and from which electronic editions, as I have defined them, could be generated. Paraphrasing Aarseth (1997: 1), in an ergodic edition or text, nontrivial effort is required to allow the reader to traverse the text.[20]

Espen Aarseth developed his textonomy mainly for literature, but I argue here that his typological model is applicable to electronic editions and can help in typifying the different genres of editions as they exist today and as they are envisioned in the writings of McGann, Robinson, and Shillingsburg, and discussed by Ore and Dahlström. Aarseth's textonomy is especially helpful in describing these different genres because it uses a vocabulary that is not common to the humanities. By applying this textonomy to the province of electronic textual editing, he supplies the field with a better model for the defining debate than the dichotomous positions described so far between print and electronic editions, archives and editions, hypertext and dynamic editions, or critical and non-critical editions. It also explicitly incorporates the user in the descriptions which is relevant especially for those editions which, as target texts, present themselves explicitly as departure texts for future scholarship. The active interactivity and the fluidity of the edition as a co-operative and distributed model, then, is substantiated in the tension between the *textons* or 'strings as they exist in the text' (Aarseth 1997: 62) and *scriptons* or 'strings as they appear to readers' (ibid.). These two concepts are central to Aarseth's model.[21] Since textual editions are constructed with

---

19 Ergodic is derived from the Greek ἔργον - work and ὁδός - path.
20 Further paraphrasing Aarseth (1997: 1-2): if the ergodic edition is to make sense as a concept, there must also be non-ergodic editions, where the effort to traverse the text is trivial, with no extranoematic responsibilities placed on the reader except (for example) eye movement and the periodic or arbitrary turning of the pages or scrolling of the screen. Examples of such editions can be printed reading editions that are linear documents or simple text archives that only represent one version of the text.
21 This opens up the possibility not only of seeing the electronic edition as an electronic infrastructure for script acts, but also of applying Shillingsburg's *Script*

an implied or ideal reader or user in mind, often an avatar of the editor, the traversal mode of the edition as text should be of concern to its creators.[22] In his typology, Aarseth identifies seven variables 'which allow us to describe any text according to their mode of traversal' (Aarseth 1997: 62). Adapting the model of the traversal mode to the electronic textual edition results in the following schematic overview:

Variable	Possible value
Dynamics	Static, intratextonic dynamics, textonic dynamics
Determinability	Determinable, indeterminable
Transiency	Transient, intransient
Perspective	Permanent, impermanent
Access	Random, controlled
Linking	Explicit, conditional, none
User function	Explorative, configurative, interpretative, textonic

This expands as follows:[23]

1. *Dynamics:* In a static edition the scriptons are constant; in a dynamic edition the contents of scriptons may change while the number of textons remains fixed (intratextonic dynamics), or the number (and content) of textons may vary as well (textonic dynamics). In a knowledge site where users can add new markup, new variant texts, new explanatory notes and commentaries, and have their personal note space, the number of textons is not known. An edition produced on the basis of the archive provided can have a fixed or a variable number of textons, depending on the editorial model and technology implemented. The editorial model, introduced by Lancashire (1989) and discussed by Siemens (2001, 2005), with integrated advanced textual analysis software constitutes a dynamic edition.

2. *Determinability:* This variable concerns the stability of the traversal function. An edition is determinate if, for every scripton its adjacent scriptons are always the same. If not, the edition is indeterminate. As a scholarly

---

Act Theory to the edition proper (Shillingsburg 2006b: 40-79) – the electronic edition as a model of self-reference.

22   Aarseth defines the traversal function of a text as 'the mechanism by which scriptons are revealed or generated from textons and presented to the user of the text' (Aarseth 1997: 62).

23   This expansion applies Aarseth's original model to electronic editions and quotes, paraphrases, and adapts Aarseth's original text (1997: 62-64). Aarseth himself has suggested to readers to 'use these terms in any way you find pleasurable, please rewrite them, refute them, or erase them, if you want' (Aarseth 1997, 183).

5. Defining Electronic Editions 143

product, stability and hence determinacy appears to be a *conditio sine qua non*. However, one could envision an edition, probably based on game models, which is self reflective and generates simulated forms of meaning resulting in indeterminate text as Jerome McGann and Johanna Drucker's *Ivanhoe Game* attempts to do for literary criticism.[24]

3. *Transiency:* If the mere passing of the user's time causes scriptons to appear, the edition is transient; if not, it is intransient. Most, if not all, editions are intransient and do nothing unless activated by the user. However, one could conceive of a *play mode* which showcases the contents of the edition to the user as a recorded movie.

4. *Perspective:* If the edition requires the user to play a strategic role, then the edition's perspective is personal; if not, it is impersonal. Editions which present the user with no other possibility of action but reading are impersonal. In a reproductive edition, the user is (in part) responsible for what happens with/to the texts.

5. *Access:* In an edition or archive with random access the scriptons of the text are readily available to the user at all times. If this is not the case, then access is controlled. Random access is typically a quality of the printed edition. But electronic editions which have all data pre-processed qualify as random access as well. This is closely related to the perspective of the edition. Personal editions will generally offer controlled access.

6. *Linking:* An edition may be organized by explicit links for the user to follow, by conditional links that can only be followed if certain conditions are met, or by none of these (no links).

7. *User functions:* Besides the interpretative function of the user, present in all editions, some editions may be described in terms of additional user functions: explorative, in which the user must decide which path to take, and configurative, in which scriptons are in part chosen or created by the user. If textons or traversal functions can be (permanently) added to the edition, the user function is textonic. If all the decisions of a user about an edition concern its meaning, then there is only one user function involved, here called interpretation. When users must make choices about alternative paths and actions, the user function is explorative. Some editions allow the user to configure the scriptons by rearranging textons or changing variables. And finally, in some cases the user can extend or change the text by adding their own writing or programming.

---

24   McGann and Drucker's *Ivanhoe Game* can be found at http://www.ivanhoe-game.org/ [accessed 10/3/2010].

Aarseth has calculated that these seven variables create a multidimensional space of 576 unique genre positions for text, applied in this case to electronic editions (Aarseth 1997: 64-65). This space offers an alternative to the legacy typologies from conventional editorial theory with which current theory on electronic editions is wrestling. As Aarseth points out, 'the model works both on an abstract, synthesizing level and on a particularizing, predictive one' (1997: 74). He further explains that the 'open categories approach also allows for a prediction of hypothetical textual modes, by combining functions that are not found together in any existing texts' (Aarseth 1997: 74). On the synthesizing level, correspondence analyses of existing and envisioned electronic editions on the basis of this traversal model could shed new light on the defining debate and show that the recent participatory models of Robinson and Shillingsburg occupy just one of these genre positions each, next to many others. On a predictive level, the model offers a toolbox for the combination of functions into new genres of editions. But the main advantage of the adoption of this traversal model is probably that its reductionist perspective 'makes it easy to check, criticize, modify, or even reject if necessary' (Aarseth 1997: 74) conceptions of texts, readers, editions and their limits. As such, this textonomy of electronic editions does not offer a decisive end to the defining debate, but feeds it with another method of analysis, description, and definition.

6. Electronic Editions for Everyone
Peter Robinson

1. Books Defy the Digital Revolution

In January 2004, I gave a lecture on electronic scholarly editing at the University of Virginia.[1] At the beginning of the lecture I asked the audience, of around 60 people, three questions. The first question was: who among them had bought a movie on DVD in the last year; who had bought a piece of music on CD-ROM or by download in the last year; who had taken digital photographs? Almost everyone in the audience had done all three. The second question: who in the last year had bought an electronic book? Only three people — around 5% of those present — had done this. The third question was: how many people had bought a conventional, print book? Everyone had done this.

One could guess the answers to further questions. We may doubt that as many as three people in the group had bought a film on videotape, or music on vinyl record, or taken a photograph using film. In film, music and photograph, the digital triumph is near complete. Yet books — despite the frequent proclamation of the 'death of the book' — remain stubbornly locked into non-digital, old-style, analogue printed and bound paper format. Gutenberg would recognize a modern book; Monteverdi would be puzzled by a CD-ROM (let alone an iPod). Even among a highly-select

---

1   A version of this paper was given by myself with Barbara Bordalejo in the Digital Texts seminar organized by Willard McCarty at the University of London in March 2007. Although I am credited as the only author of this paper, much of Dr Bordalejo's contribution remains: particularly, the 'bird nesting in a rainbow' trope. As so often, acknowledgement is scant justice to the debt I owe (and owe to many others, some mentioned in the citations in this article, with whom I have discussed digital editions over the years).

audience at the heartland of digital texts, the University of Virginia, just five percent of the audience bought electronic books, while everyone bought print books, and everyone bought digital films and music.

Why have books defied the digital revolution? What implications does this have for those of us who are engaged in the making of scholarly editions in digital form?

2. No Problem with the Digital

One response is to deny the premise: one could argue that it is misleading to base this argument on the relative numbers of people buying films, music and books. It could be argued that the correct measure is readership, not ownership. By this measure, it is certainly true that we daily absorb massive quantities of textual information, of the sort that used to be exclusively printed, via computer screens: think of emails, news sites (many set up by traditional print organizations, such as newspapers), academic journals, online resources of all kinds (encyclopaedias, search engines), and the daily working deluge of memos, notices, circulars, papers, which arrive in our electronic inbox each day — not to mention SPAM mail. But this argument only points out, even more sharply, the contrast between the relative failure of electronic books and the success of every other digital medium. It appears we have no problem with digital text: we read digital texts all the time, just as we listen to digital music and watch digital films. So why is it so few of us buy digital books? Nor is it that digital books do not exist: publishers and computer companies have spent fortunes on trying to persuade us to invest in specialized machines to read electronic books, and on converting printed books into the forms required by these machines (see the Appendix). Yet, none of these machines have achieved anything like acceptance, few of us buy electronic books, and airport bookstalls continue their thriving trade. The determination of millions of people to go on buying print books is even more striking when one considers that the text of very many of these books (indeed, of almost every book of any popularity published before 1900) is available free on the internet. So why do we — hundreds of thousands of us a year — go on buying copies of *Pride and Prejudice* when we could get the same text, very likely in identical wording, from the Web (indeed, from the University of Virginia) — or even, just find the copy we bought a few years ago, which is probably lying somewhere around the house. Compare, again, the situation with films and music. Film and music publishers each year have to spend a fortune on stopping people illegally downloading digital films and music, in order to force us to buy what they sell. But print publishers (who, nowadays, are likely to be film and music publishers also) have to spend very little on stopping illegal book downloads, while the public continues to flock to bookstores.

3. Media of Distribution and Media of Performance

We can see, too, that there is a difference between books and both films and music. To enjoy films and music we need a player: the electronic file (or, in the pre-digital age, the film reel or the vinyl record) is firstly a distribution medium, requiring a separate performance medium. The performance medium might be a computer, an I-Pod, a Discman, or portable media player, or a home hi-fi or cinema system. The point is that distribution and performance media are separated in films and music, as they are not in print books. For digital films and music to succeed, they need only to provide a more efficient distribution medium — which, of course, the digital form does easily. One could phrase this in terms of 'compelling advantage.' Simply as distribution medium, digital media in film and music have compelling advantages in terms of cost, fidelity, portability and convenience. Add to these advantages in terms of content ('add-ons' such as deleted scenes, director's commentaries, interviews, alternate endings), and add too advantages in the ultimate performance, in terms of accuracy and detail of sound and image, speedy movement to any part of the work, replay, freeze-frame and magnification, and it is no wonder that in film and music digital media have, in just a few years, driven their vinyl and tape predecessors to the edge of extinction. We note too that, in essence, the film or music on DVD or CD is the same film or music as on the outdated analogue. There are a few additions, and a few improvements, but these are not decisive. Even without these, the digital distribution medium itself constitutes a compelling advantage. There is no need for the film or music itself to be fundamentally rethought. It is sufficient just to present the same film or music: just better, cheaper.

Let us now apply this distinction between distribution medium and performance medium to books. Firstly, let us consider distribution medium. For the great majority of books, digital methods carry little advantage in terms of distribution medium. Yes, digital methods might compress the book onto a computer chip, and might allow this to be sold for a few pennies, and might allow it to be instantly available, for download to your computer. But most books are already very small and convenient, and one could argue that a book on a computer chip is actually too small: how would you shelve it? (and, reader, consider too how many flashsticks — portable computer storage on a chip — you have lost). Further, books are already cheap: the difference between the few pounds most books cost and a few pence is not a compelling advantage.[2] Finally, books are already widely available: not just at bookstalls, or newsagents, but increasingly at supermarkets, pharmacists, anywhere selling anything — not to mention the immense success of online booksellers such as Amazon. There is an exception to this in the case of large, multi-volume publications: dictionaries, encyclopaedias, catalogues, scholarly journals etc. In these cases, the printed volumes are so large, and usually so expensive, that digital distribution constitutes a compelling advantage. There is a rule of thumb here: if the computer on which you want to read the book is smaller and more convenient than the printed book, then you will very likely read the book on the computer. Now, even quite small encyclopaedias are larger than laptops, and hence their disappearance from the bookstalls, while most scholars with appropriate access will routinely read scholarly journals online, not in print (or, will print from the online version and read that). However, these are exceptions: for most books, digital distribution is not a compelling advantage.

Secondly, as a performance medium, most printed books are far superior to any digital form of those books yet in existence. It is a cliché commonly repeated that one cannot read a computer in bed (or the bath, or on a beach). As with most clichés, this statement is much more than half-true, much more than half the time. Inescapably, we must conclude that for many kinds of book — literary and popular fiction, biographies, self-improvement or religious tracts, all kinds of specialist magazine — people prefer print books to electronic books for most forms of recreational reading. Indeed, we should not be surprised by this. The modern print book builds on five hundred years of refinement since Gutenberg, and indeed on

---

2   I here betray that I am writing as a reasonably comfortably-off citizen of the developed world. Where there is a desire for the book, but very little money, even a small difference in price might be critical: so that it is not surprising that a high proportion of downloads from the University of Virginia electronic text centre were, in 2001, to IP addresses in the less-developed world (personal communication, David Seaman).

more than a thousand years of the codex before that, and on many centuries of the roll before that. The major effect of the technological revolution on book publishing has been to bring this development to a new perfection, so that books are better printed, more attractive, and cheaper, than ever before (see the Appendix). Further, advances in paper, font, print and binding technology mean that publishers can tune the physical book to its content as never before. Reading a book is more pleasant (and cheaper) than ever before. Compared to such rich diversity, books on computer screens are bland and monotonous.

In summary: books are both distribution medium and performance medium. They both carry the text and allow it to be read. For electronic books to succeed they must have an overwhelming advantage in either or both of the distribution medium and the performance medium. Electronic books have a marginal (if any) advantage only as a distribution medium, and they are at a considerable disadvantage as a performance medium. Considered in this light, it is not at all surprising that print books are prospering in the digital age. Indeed, it is only surprising (and, a measure of the blindness of technological hyper-enthusiasm) that so many otherwise sensible and capable people should have thought that electronic books could completely replace print books (see the Appendix).

4. Scholarly Editions, Then and Now

So far I have been considering the general case of all kinds of text-based publication. Our primary concern, as textual scholars, is with scholarly editions. Given the context I describe above, how might scholarly editions fare? In the early days of the academic discovery of digital text (a whole decade ago, around 1995) the answer seemed clear. For scholarly editions, the future — then — was digital. Articles by myself, Jerome McGann, Susan Hockey, and others, laid out what seemed to us — then — to be the compelling advantages of digital editions (McGann 1995, Hockey 1996, Robinson and Deegan 1994). We could include all the material — all the images, all the transcripts, all the collations — which print editions have to leave out. By the magic of hypertext, we could do away with all the cumbersome mechanics of footnotes, appendices, front and back matter: everything the reader could possibly want could leap out at a mouse movement. In this analysis, digital scholarly editions would be superior both as distribution medium (all that information on a single disc!) and as performance medium (hypertext!). How could they not succeed?

Looking back, we failed to see some critical factors which might have undermined our confidence. Firstly: it appears that rather few readers (indeed, rather often, only the editors) actually want to see all the images, all the transcripts, all the collations. Traditional print editions acted as filters, straining out all this information so that readers did not have to see it: if readers do not want to see it, then including all this is no advantage at all. Secondly: as with other kinds of print book, scholarly editions in print form have developed highly sophisticated means of both compressing and expressing information. A superlative example of this is the Nestle-Aland edition of the Greek New Testament (Nestle et al. 1993). The 27th edition of this packs into a single volume, small enough to fit into a largish pocket, all the information anyone working to a high level of detail with the tradition of the Greek New Testament is likely to need: a full record of all significant variants in some thirty key manuscripts, including even marginal and other corrections found in these manuscripts, and a conspectus of key variants across the versions of the New Testament in other languages and in patristic and other citation (Nestle et al. 1993). Of course, one has to learn to understand the highly-abbreviated forms used by the Nestle-Aland, but each year thousands of students do just that. On this analysis, the advantages of digital editions as distribution media (people do not want what digital editions can distribute) and as performance media (print editions are really rather good) are less compelling than we supposed.

Further, we failed to reckon with some other points. There is the demon of copyright. Some of the most exciting digital edition projects focussed on modern authors. It can be difficult enough gaining permission for print editions for these; for digital editions, in some notorious cases, it has proved impossible. But even for older texts, where there should be no copyright issues, there have been problems. Arranging for digital photography and reproduction rights is, with very rare exceptions, arduous and too often forbiddingly expensive. Further, co-operative projects involving different scholars at different institutions can founder on copyright, as individual scholars or institutions (for whatever reason) attempt to enforce control over what they see as 'their' work. There is also the sheer expense and difficulty of making digital editions. For years, the audience for scholarly editions in any form has been shrinking. In this context, the commitment of resources necessary for making an electronic edition is difficult to justify

— and indeed, is likely to be justifiable only in a very few cases, usually of flagship texts by flagship authors. Finally, there is the conservatism of our community, which might long continue to use print forms even where the advantages of digital forms are decisive. There is a rather spectacular instance of this conservatism in the case of the Parliament Rolls of Medieval England, on which I advised. This is now available in two forms for institutional use. It is available in print, in sixteen rather large volumes, from Boydell and Brewer, at a little under £2000 a set (Given-Wilson 2005a). It is also available in electronic form, from Scholarly Digital Editions, by internet license to institutions for approximately half the price (Given-Wilson 2005b). By any reasonable standard, the internet version is superior to the print version: it is easier to use, it consumes no valuable shelf space, it can be used by any number of students and scholars, anywhere in the university, anytime. Yet up to August 2007 around three times as many institutions have opted for the print version as have subscribed to the electronic version.[3]

This appears to be leading us to a rather depressing conclusion: that the effort of making scholarly editions in digital form is not worth the candle. Is there a future for this work? Is there a place for digital methods, in the making of scholarly editions?

5. Imagination, Powerful Tools and Familiar Objects

Here, we offer two answers to these questions. The first, brief, answer is: there is certainly a place for digital methods in the making of scholarly editions, even though the final mode of publication is print, not electronic. Scholars may use computers to gather, order and explore data, while making an edition. In particular, they may gather information on variation between witnesses and submit this to different analytic programs to gain a rapid and clear sense of the development of the textual tradition. We have ourselves used computers very effectively in this way, and we can expect that computers may continue to be so used. In this respect, scholarly editors may be little different to many other scholars, who use a wide variety

---

3   Up to August 2007 Scholarly Digital Editions had sold 38 internet licenses of the *Parliament Rolls of Medieval England*. Boydell and Brewer printed 100 copies of the 16 volume edition, retailing at £1950, and had sold out by May 2007, and were printing additional copies to meet the demand (SDE company records; personal communication from Boydell and Brewer staff).

of computer tools (including standard email, word processing, internet and e-journal applications), but whose output goes through the normal channels of print. In this view, we would be using some new tools, and our scholarly editions will be better for them, but the editions themselves will not be very different from those scholars have made for centuries.

This falls far short of the kind of revolution we imagined ten years ago, and far short of what we thought scholarly editions in electronic form might do. However, I think that the potential of scholarly editions in electronic form remains as great as scholars first imagined it, though I and others were naïve about the difficulties of realizing this potential. The potential remains, and there may be ways this potential can be unlocked. But I think it cannot be in any form which looks and behaves substantially like any printed book, or any scholarly edition we have seen so far. I am reminded of the Chilean poet Vincente Huidobro. He initiated a literary movement called 'creationism' (completely unrelated to anti-Darwinian babble) about which he said 'when I say 'The bird nests in a rainbow' I present you with a new fact, something that you have never seen, that you will never see, and that however you would really like to see.'[4]

We could say that scholarly editions in digital form are rather like Huidobro's bird nesting in a rainbow: a wonderful idea that we would all like to see. Yet, anyone who has seen a Dreamworks film knows that in Hollywood — and so in every movie cinema in the world and in every home with a computer or a television — birds can nest in rainbows. All you need is imagination, and some powerful tools. So here is our second answer: we can make scholarly editions which do all that we have dreamed. All we need is imagination, and some powerful tools.

What can we imagine, then? Consider, further, Huidobro's bird nesting in a rainbow. The point of this is that we can imagine a bird nesting in a rainbow, because we know what birds are, what nests are, what rainbows are. These are familiar objects: it is the combination which is startling. One can extend this further, more generally, to the virtual world of the Web. Where the Web is at its best, transforming and enriching lives, it takes familiar objects and puts them in a new and liberating context. The world we call 'Web 2.0' is particularly rich in examples. For generations people have written diaries, people have sent messages to each others, people

---

4   'Cuando escribo: "El pájaro anida en el arco iris", os presento un hecho nuevo, algo que jamás habéis visto, que jamás veréis, y que sin embargo os gustaría mucho ver.' Huidebro 1925; I owe the idea and the reference to Barbara Bordalejo (who, however, is not responsible for the development of the trope in this paper).

have collected albums of photos and other personal memorabilia. These are familiar activities. But in the world of the internet, these familiar activities have been transformed into blogs, MySpace and FaceBook; all examples of 'social networks' on the Web. At the very least, the countless hours spent by millions now on these activities have the virtue John Shirley ascribed to reading Chaucer: they prevent people doing worse things.[5] But of course, they have far more virtue than this, as anyone who has spent more than a few minutes in these intoxicating environments can testify: they offer the sense of belonging, of being sustained by a myriad of contacts, built on near-instant communication in many forms. To take another example: for centuries, we have had all kinds of compendia of useful knowledge, usually in the form of encyclopaedias. In the Web, these have been turned into a new kind of compendium, the Wikipedia, written and endlessly rewritten by its readers. Here, the ordinary object has indeed been transmuted into something very new, an encyclopaedia with some of the characteristics of a social network, as its readers are also responsible for making and sustaining it. Recently, we have become familiar with scholarly web communities, such as the Digital Medievalist and Digital Classicist groups, which incorporate aspects of wikis, blogs, newsfeeds and other elements familiar from social networks into invaluable new environments for collaborative work.

If we can create digital editions on the internet which have even a fraction of the impact of these extraordinary objects, then indeed we may have made a new bird nesting in a new rainbow. How, then, can we imagine these? We have some clues. Firstly, we should identify the fundamental familiar objects which will constitute our bird in a rainbow. Secondly, we should imagine how these might be combined in a new way.

For we textual scholars, the first fundamental familiar object is this: knowledge about texts. We know where texts come from, how they were made and distributed; we know how their meaning is shaped by the circumstances of their creation and dissemination. Show us a book, or a

---

5   Shirley's remarks are in the 'The prologe of the knyghtes tale' prefaced to the copy of the *Tales* preserved in British Library Harley MS 7333. His words are: 'O . yee so noble and worthi pryncis and . princesse other estatis or degrees . what euer yee beo th[a]t haue disposicione , or plesaunce . to rede or here the stories of olde tymis Passed to kepe yow frome ydelnesse and slowthe . mescheuing other folies that might be cause of more harome filowyng' [O ye so noble and worthy princes and princesses or estates or degrees: whatever ye be that have disposicion or pleasure to read or hear the stories of old times past, to keep you from idleness and sloth, mischief or follies that might be cause of more harm following] (Published in Solopova 2000).

manuscript: we can tell you about how they were made and the texts they contain, and about other books and manuscripts containing those texts. Show us a text, and we can tell you about the books and manuscripts which contain it, and how they differ, and what these differences mean. The second fundamental familiar object is the methods we use to discover what we know; the painstaking work of finding and analyzing the forms of the text. So we can offer anyone interested in texts two things. We can offer what we already know; and we can offer means to find what we do not know.

6. Mediating Textual Scholarship

Most of the time, this knowledge, this method, comes to us in a second hand way through books, articles, notes, catalogue entries etc. Indeed, we have become so used to receiving knowledge of texts in this way that it seems to us that textual scholarship is, actually, printed textual editions. But of course it is not: the print editions are simply the way in which most of us receive textual scholarship, most of the time. Textual scholarship precedes print editions, as what textual scholars know and do. Usually, we know textual scholarship only in severe print. But it does not have to be this way. In 2001 I had the extraordinary experience of being in the National Library of Ireland with Hans Gabler and Danis Rose as they examined a page of the Joyce's draft of the Circe episode of *Ulysses*, then on display there.[6] This is a very difficult page to interpret, and the two scholars fell into an intense discussion on exactly what Joyce wrote, in what order, how he changed it, why, and how these writings connected to the rest of the novel. Not only was I fascinated: in a few moments everyone in the gallery had gathered around Gabler and Rose, to hear what they had to say. One can suppose that few of these onlookers would think of reading (say) any of the Joyce editions made by Gabler or Rose, but that day they were rapt (Gabler 1984; Rose 1997).

This incident suggested that not only are there other ways of communicating textual scholarship beside print, but that print may not even be

---

6   This was on 15 June 2001. The following day (Bloomsday), Gabler and Rose together examined the Eumaeus notebook of *Ulysses*, on display in the Sotheby's showroom in Dublin prior to its auction, again before a large and impromptu audience. The notebook has since gone into private hands, giving extra significance to this public examination (Private communications, Hans Gabler 7-10 September 2007).

6. Electronic Editions for Everyone 155

the best way to communicate textual scholarship. Consider how one might read (say) the first page of Joyce's *Ulysses*. You might have your reading text; then you might (if you are fortunate) have a copy of Gabler's and Rose's editions close by; you might also have the relevant volumes of the Joyce Archive, with copies of the key Rosenbach (1975) manuscript, and of various typescripts and galleys.[7] These could be spread out on a large desk, open at various pages, with an apparatus of bookmarks pointing at other pages. It has been a commonplace of commentary on hypertext editions that the advantages of the digital medium could allow any reader to have access to all this material, with a rapidity and convenience never before possible. But I think our early attempts to do this have foundered, on exactly the lack of imagination which cannot see a bird nesting in a rainbow. What we have done in the digital form is mimic the way all the materials on this first page might be accumulated in print form. For example — to change the example from Joyce to my speciality, the *Canterbury Tales* — we have made digital copies of single manuscripts, with transcriptions, collations, descriptions and analyses (Canterbury Tales Project, Robinson 2003b). This is a rather comprehensive collection, but it is still only one collection, of only one aspect of the *Tales*, presented from only one point of view. There are many other materials one might want to consult which we have not included. Particularly, one might look for a tale-by-tale, line-by-line commentary, such as is found in the *Variorum* volumes. One might also wish to examine other editions, beside our own, and hunt down discussions of particular lines by various scholars.

So far, digitization (where it has happened, and there are many areas where it has not) has presented all these disparate resources as distinct from each other. Just as the scholar in the library must find the various volumes he or she wants and lay them out on the desk, ready to consult, so the digital scholar has to locate the various resources he or she wants, work out how each one works, and spread them across the digital desktop. There are advantages, in speed and convenience, but there are also significant disad-

---

7   The James Joyce Archive has, in 63 volumes, facsimiles of almost all Joyce's notes and drafts for the novels and other creative works, and was published by Garland in 1977 and 1979 (Groden, 1977-79). Only 250 copies of this were published and these are now rare. There is an excellent account of the making of the archive (and other matters) in Michael Groden's 'Perplex in the Pen – and the Pixels: Reflections on the James Joyce Archive, Hans Walter Gabler's *Ulysses*, and 'James Joyce in Hypermedia' (Groden 1998). The major exclusion from the James Joyce Archive is the Rosenbach manuscript of *Ulysses*, published in three volumes of facsmile in 1975 (Rosenbach 1975).

vantages. The greatest is that while all books work in much the same way, this is emphatically not true of digital resources. We have all experienced the sinking feeling, when opening up the latest grand digital resource, that there are wonders here which cannot be found: or, even more frustrating, having found them once, being unable a few weeks later to find them again. Further, the cataloguing of digital resources is uneven, at best: a search engine is not a catalogue, but that is what we have to use most of the time. So, we are looking at the first line of the Canterbury Tales, in the Hengwrt manuscript. We have the splendid Estelle Stubbs edition of this, which includes a collation of every line of Hengwrt with the Ellesmere manuscript (Stubbs 2001). We ask ourselves: is there somewhere, out there on the net, an alternative transcription to this line, as given by Stubbs? There is: in the University of Michigan Corpus of Middle English Prose and Verse. We ask ourselves: is there somewhere an image of the first page of the Ellesmere manuscript? There is: at the Huntingdon Library website, in San Marino, California. We know that Norman Blake edited the *Tales* from the Hengwrt manuscript. Is there an electronic version of this first line, in that edition, somewhere? There is: at the Oxford Text Archive (though, unfortunately, with restricted access). We could ask: are there electronic versions of other editions, including this first line? There are: for instance, at the University of Virginia, and in the Michigan Corpus of Middle English Prose and Verse. It is up to the reader to find all these.

From this sketch, one can see how far digital scholarship remains bound by the model of print: each scholar (or group of scholars) makes a separate digital object. It is up to the individual reader to locate all these separate objects, and make sense of them. In the worst cases, this is like one of those wonderfully circular games: you can only find what you want if you know what it is you want and where it is. As most readers know only the text in front of them, they are unlikely to find the riches lying about them, and are unlikely to be able to make sensible use of them, if they do find them.

7. Imagining Otherwise

It is time to imagine a bird nesting in a rainbow. The way we have it now, all these transcripts, descriptions, facsimiles, commentaries, translations wait passively on the Web for someone to find them, just as print books wait in a library for someone to read them. Suppose instead that they did not

6. Electronic Editions for Everyone 157

wait, but they went out over the Web to find someone who was reading something closely related to them. Imagine you are reading the first line of the *Canterbury Tales*. In Michigan, a computer server thinks: that person is reading the first line of the *Tales*. I have a transcription of the first line, and it sends a message to the computer on which you are reading to that effect. Simultaneously, in Oxford, in Virginia, in San Marino, other computer servers realize they have something relevant to what you are reading, right now, and they too send messages to your browser: we have something for you. Instantly, on your browser, a message appears, indicating that there are relevant materials waiting for you, at all these sites. With a little intelligence, the materials could be sorted, into transcripts, images, commentaries, etc, and the message on your browser tuned (or removed altogether) to reflect just what information you are interested in. This is the equivalent, if you like, of books in the library shelves realizing that you are reading Chaucer, and unobtrusively shuffling off the shelves onto your desk.

Does this sound like science fiction? It should not. Something like this already works every time you do a Google search: the links in the margins of your screen are generated by Google itself, calculating from your search just what you are interested in and creating links accordingly. Every time you log into Amazon, you will see a list of books which Amazon has chosen for you, based on your past purchases. There are many other instances. All these are examples of a key aspect of 'Web 2.0': expressions of the principle that web applications should not simply wait for the user to do something, but should try to anticipate what the user might desire and should set to drawing together resources to satisfy that desire.[8]

This vision has many implications for readers. In our study, or our library, we take books from the shelves and spread them on the desk. In the digital world, the reader may choose from the resources supplied by servers around the world, and spread them out, as he or she chooses, on the digital desktop. Again, we can see something like this in personalized pages such as that offered by Gmail, where you can populate your live desktop with newsfeeds, reports on the weather, stock market updates, clocks, and more. In the examples I have given so far, I have spoken of access via the text: through the first page of *Ulysses*, or the first line of the *Canterbury Tales*. Equally, access could be by the source object. I am looking

---

8   See the Wikipedia definition of 'Web 2.0', http://en.wikipedia.org/wiki/Web_2.0 [accessed 15/8/2007]. The term was coined and given currency by O'Reilly Media: see http://www.oreillynet.com/pub/a/oreilly/tim/news/2005/09/30/what-is-web-20.html [accessed 15/8/2007].

at a digital image of the first page of the Hengwrt manuscript. Around the world servers gather material relating to that manuscript (descriptions, discussions, commentaries), to that page (digital images, observations), and to the text on that page, line by line and word by word (including, other versions of that text on that page). All this is then available for the reader, to explore as he or she wishes.

There are implications for scholars, too. Up to now, if scholars wished to make a digital edition, they had to do everything, from initial encoding to final publication. In particular, they had to create a publication interface, so readers around the world could read what the scholars had made on their computer. This required access to considerable resources, usually only available to a few well-funded projects, and in turn meant that each of the editions so made were digital islands, entire in themselves and separate from others. In the vision here offered, scholars have only to make the individual components of the edition: the transcription of this line in this manuscript; the collation of the various versions of these words in this line; the commentary on this line etc. These are then placed on servers, from where they are harvested into each reader's browser. This removes entirely the need for the scholar to provide any kind of interface (though they still might, if they wish). The effect is to open up scholarship: no longer will scholars need to be part of an elaborate and expensive project to contribute to digital scholarship. This raises further questions: if anyone can make a transcript of the Hengwrt manuscript and put it on the Web, how will the reader choose which of these to read? The restriction of scholarship to the academy provided forms of control and quality assurance; do we need these; how could they be provided if we do, and if we do not need them, how will we fare? And where will publishers be in this world?

We said above that to make the bird nesting in the rainbow, we would need imagination and powerful tools. Here is what we have imagined. What tools will we need to make what we have imagined? In fact, most of the tools already exist. There are many protocols, in the form of 'web services', which allow computers to talk to computers, and then send information back and forth between them, exactly as described here. It is now straightforward to embed commands into browser interfaces to access these web services. Thus: you start reading a text, any text, of the *Canterbury Tales*. As each line of the text is loaded into the browser, a command is triggered: find materials related to this line. The browser broadcasts a message: what do you have for me? Around the world, servers are waiting for such a message. They send replies; the browser gathers the responses, and adjusts the display accordingly. The technical infrastructure for this is widespread. However, we do lack a key component. We need agreed referencing schemes, so that the browser knows exactly what it has, and servers recognize that they have relevant materials. Again, the fundamental encoding infrastructure for such agreed referencing schemes has been laid down by the Text Encoding Initiative in general, and more particularly by the Canonical Text Services project.[9] These are not yet worked out in sufficient detail to support applications of the sophistication here described, and this is work to be done.[10]

8. Realizations

In a previous article, I characterized this model of editions as 'fluid, co-operative and distributed' (Robinson 2004). Some key elements of this model can be seen in the ongoing work on the digital edition of the 28th Nestle-Aland Greek New Testament, on which I am advising the Deutsche Bibelgesellschaft and the Münster Institute for New Testament Research.[11] This is described in more detail in an article I have written for *Ecdotica* (Robinson 2007b). In summary, this is arranged so that for any verse of the Greek New Testament, the reader may choose what elements should appear on the screen: the Nestle-Aland text; the conventional apparatus, as printed; a new digital apparatus, providing more detail for key manuscripts; full transcripts of the key manuscripts; a German-Greek dictionary; and an 'explanation' window that gives a brief summary of the symbols and conventions used by the edition. In the Nestle-Aland work, all the elements are being provided by a single editorial group. However, the design of this work is such that it could be opened out by allowing other elements to be added to the desktop which are not provided by the editors (for example, different dictionaries for different languages, different commentaries). In the reverse of this, elements from the Nestle-Aland could be exported to other

---

9   See http://www.tei-c.org/index.xml and http://chs75.chs.harvard.edu/projects/diginc/techpub/cts-overview respectively [accessed 12/3/2010].
10 A draft paper prepared by the author on the encoding and technical infrastructure needed to realize what is discussed in this article was placed at http://www.interedition.eu/index.php/WG2:Architecture [accessed 12/3/2010].
11 The ongoing work, and the final edition, may be seen at http://nestlealand.uni-muenster.de/ [accessed 12/3/2010].

interfaces. This deconstruction of an edition into separable parts, possibly held on different servers, each capable of being made by separate scholars, and each capable of being linked with others in an infinity of ways, takes us a considerable way towards our vision.

I believe that this model of editions provides the compelling advantage which will (at last) lead to readers routinely consulting digital editions on-line, and to large-scale creation of digital editions for readers. For readers this will provide immediate and convenient access to information about the text they are reading, with the ability to order, filter and arrange this information onscreen as they wish. For scholars this will remove the need to build complex publication interfaces for the editions they make. Rather, they can concentrate on the intellectual work of making transcripts, collations, analyses, commentaries (indeed, just as they would have done for print publication), leaving it to the well-organized magic of the Web to bring these to the readers. Such editions will be our bird nesting in the rainbow: familiar things, in a remarkable combination. They will be electronic editions for everyone.

Appendix

The first part of this article advances the premise that books that we read (such as novels, biographies, recreational literature), as opposed to books that we reference (encyclopaedias, dictionaries), have failed to cross the digital divide. Publishers produce books in print; we buy them and read them in print, much as we have for six hundred years.

There have been determined, and very expensive, efforts to break this pattern, so that printed books would go the way of the vinyl record. There was a particular flurry of activity around the turn of the millennium. In a 1999 article written for *The Economist*, with the somewhat menacing title 'Beyond Gutenberg', Bill Gates promoted the advantages of eBooks, without going quite so far as to suggest that they would drive print books out of existence (article available on http://www.microsoft.com/presspass/ofnote/11-19billg.mspx, accessed 14 August 2007). (Gates is rather fond of declaring obsolescence: besides books, a Google search for 'Bill Gates obsolete' shows that he has declared television, DVDs and US High Schools obsolete.) On 6 January 2000 Barnes and Noble and Microsoft released a press release proclaiming that 'the sale of electronic books will reach US

6. Electronic Editions for Everyone   161

$1 billion in 3-4 years, and could overtake the sale of print books in ten years.' (Reported in *Wired*, 6 January 2000; http://www.wired.com/techbiz/media/news/2000/01/33488, accessed 14 August 2007). A 2001 review article on eBooks and eBook readers by Sarah Ormes in the online journal *Ariadne*, 10 January 2001 (http://www.ariadne.ac.uk/issue26/e-book/, accessed 14 August 2007) lists a range of e-book providers and technologies.

In retrospect, Ormes' article marks a high-point of what now appears as misplaced confidence (though even in this, she strikes a note of caution: 'But finally these electronic dreams seem to be about to come true': note the 'seem'). What did happen to the Barnes and Noble/Microsoft prediction? Industry sources (http://www.mbendi.co.za/notices/ebooks.htm, accessed 14 August 2007) suggested that in 2002 500,000 eBooks were sold in the US. While this number is not negligible, it should be compared to the 1.6 billion print books estimated as sold in that year. The same site estimates eBook sales in February 2004 as $900,000, and cites a figure of $2,591,469 for eBook sales for the third quarter of 2003. This would give an annual figure of around $10 million for 2004. According to the Barnes and Noble/Microsoft prediction, electronic book sales in 2003-4 should have been $1 billion, not $10 million. Barnes and Noble ceased electronic book sales in September 2003 (http://handheldlib.blogspot.com/2003/10/electronic-book-web-weekly.html, accessed 14 August 2007).

Electronic book readers have fared no better. The Rocket reader, in 2001 the market leader according to the Ormes article, was taken over by Gemstar, to become the Planet eBook reader, which appears to be no longer available: the Planet eBook site now does not mention the reader at all, and the company appears to have adopted Adobe pdf technology (http://www.planetebook.com/, accessed 14 August 2007). Franklin Electronic Publishing (http://www.franklin.com, accessed 14 August 2007), who created the eBookman, still exists, though the device does not.

One cannot say that the failure of electronic books is due to a lack of supply. There are a very large number of books available in electronic form, to be read using software on general computer devices (some of the software is tuned for particular platforms, such as Franklin's Mobireader, intended for mobile devices). Franklin lists over 25000 fiction titles and nearly 12000 nonfiction titles on its website, available for individual download at prices generally somewhat lower than the equivalent print book (e.g.: the Oxford Advanced Learner's Dictionary is $29.95 on Franklin, $34 on Amazon, against an Oxford list price of $46; *The Best American Erotica 2006* is $9.99 on

Franklin, against $11.20 on Amazon and a list price of $14. It is revealing, however, that from the Franklin web homepage it appears that this company concentrates on 'niche markets' (particularly of language students, for whom they offer a range of handheld dictionary readers) rather than on their general eBook offerings. Many more titles are available in Netlibrary (over 100,000 titles, according to http://www.netlibrary.com, accessed 14 August 2007), but Netlibrary appears to concentrate on supplying the library market rather than retailing direct to consumers.

The experience of Microsoft appears particularly relevant. Microsoft continue to offer their eReader software, able to run on any handheld using the Microsoft Pocket PC standard. The Microsoft Reader website (http://www.microsoft.com/reader, accessed 14 August 2007) offers outlines of popular titles and an extensive catalogue of eBooks (over 29000 fiction titles – *The Da Vinci Code* is third on their list, at $5.94). Again, prices for books listed on the Microsoft site are only slightly lower for eBooks than for print books: Nancy Gibbs' *The Preacher and the Presidents: Billy Graham in the White House* is listed as an eBook for $16.14, against a new price listed of $26; Amazon had the title at $17.81. For both Franklin and Microsoft, however, one has to dig rather deep on their websites to find the electronic book catalogues. It appears that electronic books are ancillary to the main business of both companies. One could draw a similar conclusion from the way in which Amazon treats electronic books (at least, for www.amazon.com on 10 September 2007): where electronic books are available, their presence is signalled as a note against the listing for the print book, rather than as saleable items in their own right. There is a section 'Digital downloads' on www.amazon.com but this leads only to downloads of films and music, not books (10 September 2007).

One could summarize this state of affairs as follows: there are a very large number of eBooks available, able to be read on the most-widely used computer platforms. However, there appears no imminent likelihood that these eBooks will completely supersede print books. They appear to coexist with print, targeting a niche market of particular users, rather than the general reader. (Since first drafting this Appendix in August 2007, the launch of the Amazon Kindle reader has dramatically increased the profile of eBook readers. However, the determinedly print-like presentation of the books on the reader, and the marketing of print and eBook versions together, suggest co-existence rather than replacement.)

On the other side of the ledger, there is plentiful evidence to document

6. Electronic Editions for Everyone 163

the thriving state of printed books. Statistics gathered by the International Publishers Association (IPA) suggest that in the period from 1990 to 2000, the number of individual titles published across the world increased by around 50%. The figures offered by the IPA are incomplete, with some countries not providing data for all years. However, there are comparable statistics for a few typical countries: in the UK, individual titles published grew from 63756 to 110155; in Spain, from 42207 to 60426; in the USA from 46743 to 64711 (see http://www.ipa-uie.org/statistics/annual_book_prod.html, accessed 13/8/07). For the period after 2000, Bowker reported that book production in 2004 showed a 14.1% annual increase in titles published, with a 43% increase in fiction titles. Even university press output – often cited as a problem area for academic publication – was higher, at a 12.3% increase (Press release May 24, 2005; see http://www.bowker.com/press/bowker/2005_0524_bowker.htm); the Bowker figures, available on their website, for 2006 and 2007 suggest a slight decline from this all-time high; see also the cautionary notes concerning the difficulty of counting titles at http://www.pushthekey.com/2007/08/09/british-book-production/, accessed 14 August 2007. There is an extremely useful summary of statistics relating to world-wide publishing, with links to websites and comments, at http://www.parapublishing.com/sites/para/resources/statistics.cfm (accessed 14 August 2007). Overall statistics on the number of publishing houses (for example, on the 'parapublishing' site) give a similar picture to those on individual titles published. Statistics on print runs and on actual books sold (let alone read) are harder to come by, and do not appear to be available in any systemized form. It is possible the overall increase in titles published in the last decades has been accompanied by smaller print-runs, with the rise of 'print-on-demand', so that fewer books overall are sold but a larger number of titles. The 'parapublishing' site gives somewhat anecdotal information on actual numbers sold (e.g. 1.6 billion books sold in the US in 2001, around 7 for every person in the US). Overall, these figures hardly suggest an industry in decline.

Useful articles on this subject are Robert Darnton's *New York Review of Books* article 'The New Age of the Book' (46.5, March 18, 1999; http://www.nybooks.com/articles/546, accessed 14 August 2007) and Mark Moss' The Future of the Book', *College Quarterly*, 7.3 (2004), at http://www.senecac.on.ca/quarterly/2004-vol07-num03-summer/moss.html, accessed 14 August 2007.

7. How Literary Works Exist: Implied, Represented, and Interpreted

Peter Shillingsburg

This essay is a companion to another titled, 'How Literary Works Exist: Convenient Scholarly Editions' (Shillingsburg 2009), which together examine the nature of the 'things' that textual scholarship tries to identify and analyse, in order to see how best to represent them in electronic scholarly editions and archives. The other essay focuses primarily on electronic problems and solutions for edition and archive representation. This essay prepares the ground for the other by examining the nature of textual existence and representation.

1. Physical Texts and Electronic Representations

The description of the seminar series in which this essay began states that the presentations were 'meant to engage all those who are interested in a *digital future* [my italics] for the book.' I hope it is engaging in that way, but I wish also to engage those who are interested in a *future for the book* in a digital world. If we ever come to believe that a digital representation of a physical book is an adequate or complete representation then textual studies, bibliography, and history of the book will have lost the battle to persuade us to understand how books exist, how communication happens, and how understandings of texts are achieved. If, on the other hand, textual studies, bibliography, and history of the book fail to embrace the challenge of electronic representations of books, they will have lost a valuable opportunity to broaden and enhance the understandings they have developed of books as physical objects, media of communication, and loci of understanding.

When one looks at the development of public policy as represented in the expectations of funding agencies for electronic dissemination of research results in the fields of scholarly editing and archive accessibility, one can see the enormous importance of getting the relationship between physical texts and electronic representations right. If we get it wrong by missing out on the proper preservation of physical books, and, no less so, if we get it wrong by missing the opportunities for electronic potential, we will be remembered by future textual scholars for these failures. Our ability to get it wrong is not limited to some simple opposition between physical and electronic books. We can make disastrously wrong choices in the practical ways we embrace electronic books, even if we continue, as we must, to collect and protect physical books.

Funding agencies tend to base their judgments, about what editions and archives to fund, upon the soundness of the scholarly investigations and upon the importance of the works selected. A completion date is set, and a request, almost as an afterthought, is made for electronic access and dissemination. Scholars comply because they primarily care about the texts and textual scholarship. Electronic dissemination all too often seems a relatively simple job of porting to the screen what traditionally was printed. For this, technical assistance in the form of a 'techie' seems sufficient. But agencies and scholars alike are missing out the third wheel of the tricycle by supposing that there are thoughtfully constructed long-term electronic vehicles for presenting the fruits of editorial scholarship; despite XML, TEI and SSLT, there are not. No one with funding for an editorial project has asked for very long the question, 'What is the best way to construct an electronic scholarly edition?' That question is swept away almost immediately by the far more practical question, 'What is the best way, given our deadlines, to mount a presentable version of this research project?' Furthermore, funding agencies famously hive off research questions from dissemination questions, thus failing to see that, in the electronic world, catering to differing audiences such as fellow researchers on one side and students on the other is no longer a matter affecting the treatment or construction of foundational texts and analytical results but is, instead, an aspect of interface design, offering options for tailored access to common research materials. The results of existing funding policies have been projects that invariably provide only local solutions to local problems.

It is the aim of this essay, and of its companion on 'Convenient Scholarly Editions', to survey the issues at stake in the crossover period when momentous and expensive decisions are being made about libraries, about electronic access to books, and about the construction of electronic scholarly editions and scholarly archives.

2. Goals of Critical Editing

It is now generally believed among textual critics that in former times, under the influence of Lachmann in the nineteenth to Bowers in the twentieth centuries, editors believed their job was either to restore the text of a work to the form it once had in a now lost archetype or to emend an existing text so that lexically it would resemble what its author aspired to but was prevented from achieving by various agents or circumstances. Put simply, editors strove either to *re*construct the text of a lost archetype or construct a text that achieved its author's intentions for the first time. Whether anyone ever actually saw the work of editing in these ways, the two concepts at least provided clear goals, though neither could be achieved definitively because both frankly and explicitly required the exercise of critical judgment and what Fredson Bowers once declared was, 'the boldness to edit'. (Parenthetically, and provocatively, let me insert a little worm in the argument to come: To these two types of critical editing there are being proposed, by those seeking to minimize or eliminate critical judgment in editing, alternatives that might be more adequately achieved by photocopy machines and scanners than by scholarly editors.)

At least two important shifts in thinking about literary works and criticism of them have intervened to alter the goals of critical editing or at least to alter how editors talk about them. The first shift replaced a quest for lost archetypes and unachieved ideals with practical materiality and a search for order in extant documents. The second replaced the ideal of original authenticity and of aesthetic sensitivity with social awareness. These two shifts have focused the attention of both literary critics and textual critics onto extant documentary texts as intrinsically interesting because of their historical status and their ability to index through time the social conditions of authorship, publishing, and reading. Gone are the romantic genius of the author, the noble hand-maidenly efforts of the editor to restore, construct, or reconstruct ideal texts, and with them the hopes for urtexts or well-wrought urns. Presumably, also gone is the subjectivity that bolstered genius, construction, and ideal texts.

The new editorial order appears to be on much safer ground, for it has minimized its reliance on the editor's critical acumen, a quality unfortunately distributed unevenly by fate amongst historians and textual critics. The new goals of textual scholarship are grounded in the materials, economics, and social actualities of book production, not in the airy mists of aspirations, intentions, or séance-like efforts to commune with dead authors. Thus, fevered agitation about irrecoverable intentions has been replaced by calm analyses of material documents. This double move was self-reinforcing because the extant material documents appeared to form corroborating, if not sufficient, evidence for new interests in cultural and social forces affecting authorship, publishing and reading. Aesthetic concerns for the integrity of art achieved through ideal, intended texts (so rarely achieved in extant texts) have taken a back seat or been forced off the bus entirely.

Two related shifts have taken place in the last forty years that bear strongly on current notions of the work. The first shifted attention from the author to the reader, from intention to reception. The second shifted attention from questions about how to edit in print to those about how to edit for electronic publication and distribution.[1]

The present paper does not trace the history of these shifts but rather takes them for granted as having taken place. It does not, however, take for granted that the shifts have been beneficial, successful, or without loss. Obviously, they have been sufficiently beneficial to be successful enough to have affected the profession of letters. But enthusiasms often come at a price and can blind one, at least at first, to the losses involved.

So, in looking at how literary works exist, I am eager to see if these shifts have entailed losses and, in particular, if a re-examination of how literary works exist might help us to see how they should be or could be edited for electronic representation.[2]

---

1 Key texts in the shift of attention from author to reader include Barthes (1986/1968), Foucault (1989/1969), Fish (1980), Tanselle (1990), and Greetham (1991). My own discussion of the shift from print to digital forms, in *From Gutenberg to Google* (2006), is just part of ancient and continuing discussion. The arguments in the present essay did not occur to me, unfortunately, until after I had published the book.

2 Arguments about the nature of 'work' in relation to 'texts' and 'documents' and about whether editors should concern themselves with a notion of a work as a concept rather than as a physical object, such as a manuscripts or printed text, form

3. How do Literary Works Exist?

At first glance it would seem that, if the goal of editing and of critical analysis is to examine material documents as socio-cultural and historical evidence, then the original documents themselves or high-resolution digital images of them are basic beginnings. That is so because any transcript or new edition would be a witness to the social conditions of its own production, rather than of the production of the original it was trying to (re)-present. Likewise, it would seem, in that case, that we need not be overly concerned with what forms the text might have taken in documents that no longer exist or with what forms the text might have taken had the vicissitudes of history not interfered. Those lost or unachieved forms do not exist and any attempt to 'see' them would be mediated by speculative emendation and new representation. But that seeming logic may be superficial, and the shift in editorial goals outlined above may fail to address the full range of critical needs for texts of works.

My purpose, then, is to ask 'how do literary works exist?' and to explore that question by applying to textual works the words 'implied,' 'represented,' and 'interpreted.' The essay will end with some suggestions about how literary works might be edited and represented electronically if researchers were but given the time, money and expertise to pursue such issues before undertaking the daunting task of producing a literary research project by a particular date. Perhaps what is wanting is a call for project proposals where the outcome is to be an analysis of current best electronic practice, recommendations and prototypes for a new electronic environment (where fundamental questions are addressed about interface design, coding practices, file structures, analytical and presentation tools) and the economics of development, dissemination, access and maintenance. Though I have recently published a book, *From Gutenberg to Google: Electronic Representations of Literary Texts* (2006), which is about the nature of literary texts and about electronic editing, I have tried to take a different tack here toward issues explored in that book.

I speak not primarily or only as a textual critic, but as a student of literary works. I believe I speak for many students of literature who are interested in the materials that contain or convey literary works; who are interested in the authors, publishers, and production personnel that constructed the chief dividing lines separating editorial methods. Key texts are Greg (1950-51), Tanselle (1989), McGann (1991), Martens (1995b), Plachta (1999), and Greetham (1999). An introductory analysis of competing theories is in Shillingsburg (1996a).

those materials; who are interested in the discourse communities in which the words were written; who are also interested in the people who bought and read the works, not only at the time of first publication but through the years and into our own time; who are interested in literary works as currently re-imagined and marketed material objects; and who are concerned about how our modern identities and 'presentness' affect our reception of literary texts. In short, one way to put the problem of electronic editing is that we wish to serve the needs of people who want to understand the work of art in a variety of artistic, critical, historical, material, social, and intellectual ways. Funding for literary projects (the works of Thackeray, the *Canterbury Tales*, the poems of Jonathan Swift), each with a deadline looming, normally omits funding with which to re-examine and revamp the computer infrastructure within which to mount archives and editions of Thackeray, Chaucer, Swift or what have you. But here I want to consider the question of electronic editions in that latter light. The aim is definitely NOT to establish how our understandings of literary works can be contained in humanities computing. The question is, rather, how can humanities computing support and enable our understandings of literary works -- though perhaps it would be even better to think of it as a two-way street.

To extend and attempt to explain this problem, I hit upon the title of my presentation: 'The Work Implied, the Work Represented, and the Work Interpreted.' The work, the literary work, to be understood has these three characteristics, and the interesting thing about this division of the problem is that in every case the two excluded characteristics invade the chosen focus at every point. Nevertheless, any computer solution would need to address these characteristics.

4. The Work Implied

When I was revising the first edition of *Scholarly Editing in the Computer Age* in 1986, my fellow scholar, Price Caldwell,[3] in an attempt to understand what I was getting at by talking about notes, drafts, manuscripts, magazine publications, and book publications, asked if I meant that the work consisted of the sum of all these things. I imagined he was suggesting an

---

3 Caldwell's interest in ordinary language led him to develop a system he calls 'molecular sememics' as a way of understanding the functional dynamics of natural languages (1989, 2000, 2006). I applied this theory to editorial concerns in *From Gutenberg to Google* (2006).

7. How Literary Works Exist

edition that somehow added all the bits from all the versions to produce a work that was a sum of its parts and of course rejected the notion out of hand. 'Oh,' he said, 'Perhaps what you mean, then, is that the work is implied by these material documents but is not equivalent to any one of them?' That is, no one copy was the full and definitive container of or representative of the work, but that each contained or represented it in some way. I thought perhaps that way of putting it might get me into trouble, but I liked it. The work is not equivalent to any material representation of it, but is (partially and particularly) represented by each version of it.

If the work is *implied* by the documentary text, it cannot itself *be* the documentary text. But if it is (partially and particularly) represented by each documentary copy of it, do we not mean that a version of the work is the text found in some document? Well, yes, at some rudimentary level each document represents a version (though it must be said that some documents are incomplete and do not represent a whole version) and further, that some documents (manuscripts for example) often contain more than one version: original, intermediate and last. And sometimes a version becomes recognized as a version only when it has been extracted and constructed from texts found in more than one document.

But to speak of the Work Implied in this simplistic way as if it consisted of a series of snapshots of a THING, a static object, or as if it consisted of a developing series of attempts to construct a final static object, is to understand the processes of composition, of production and of reading in only one of their potentially interesting ways. If we are talking – in an everyday sense – about a work of art, whether as short as a sonnet or as long as *War and Peace* itself, then we are generally talking not about a thing as a whole, for which some document can stand as a snapshot, but rather we are talking about what Willard McCarty has called a machine: a tool for making our way bit by bit sequentially (mostly) through the work that is only implied by any one form of the machines that represent it (2006). It is worth pausing to meditate on the notion that a literary work is never looked at as 'a thing' that can be taken as 'a whole'. Literary works are travelled through more or less linearly with a focus of attention on smaller sense units in a sequence that achieves a sense of wholeness only in our memory of the experience of reading. That process is similar to the processes of writing and of manufacturing literary works as well. So, the idea of a snapshot version of the work as a whole is at best a metaphor on the verge of collapse.

I leave the question of representation for a moment to focus first on the processes of composition, production and reading. When one reads one version alongside another, rather than reading a single text in isolation, one frequently gets a bigger bang for the buck. My colleague, Professor Julia Briggs, recently brought two good examples to my attention. The 18th chapter of *To the Lighthouse* (the last in the first section titled 'The Window') in the American edition ends with Mr. Ramsey's aloof detachment registered as his ability to know; the same chapter in the British edition ends instead with *Mrs.* Ramsey's triumph. Both versions contain approximately the same statements but in different climactic orders. Alone, each of these versions has whatever effect the reader derives from that particular arrangement of the details. In opposition to each other, a reader encounters tensions of dissent and difference that raise a range of questions: who did this; why; what difference is being made; was it an accident; do the versions target different audiences as conceived by the author; do they just represent different potentials; or, is one actually the 'right one'? I suppose that if one version *is* the right one, rendering the other one wrong, it could be an act of kindness to readers to suppress the erroneous reading. But in fact the surviving evidence does not indicate that one is wrong. We know that Americans read one version and the British read another. Notice, then, that for persons reading only one version this range of questions will not be raised or addressed. And note further that if such a single rightness were desirable in a scholarly edition, it would have had to be created in its single rightness by an editor who, first as a reader, had to enjoy the richness of the tension offered by the two versions in opposition and then spoil it for all other readers by making a decision on their behalf. Each version implies the work in a different way; in juxtaposition, the versions imply the work in a more complex way.

The other example Professor Briggs brought to my attention was from Thomas Middleton's *The Second Maiden's Tragedy*. The husband spends his life in passionate suspicion of his wife, who in fact is unfaithful to him. But just as he dies at the end of the play, in the first version, he is convinced by his wife and her lover that they are innocent, and the husband dies in the blissful belief that his wife is truly his, but he simultaneously dies in the sad truth that his whole married life has been wasted and embittered by groundless suspicion – never mind the fact that the audience knows that is false. In the alternative ending, the wife and lover come clean at the deathbed, admitting all, and so the husband dies in the full satisfaction that he was right in his suspicions all along and in the sad certain knowledge that

7. How Literary Works Exist   173

his wife had indeed cuckolded him. Now, we might think that one or the other ending is better, more authentic, or more final; but in fact the ironic twists of both endings in tension against each other might be better than either of them alone.

So, to sum up so far, the work is not a document. It is not a single text. And it is not the sum of all of its texts. It is implied in part by each document and the texts of versions that can be extracted and constructed from documents. And it might, in some instances, be implied differently by the tensions between two or more versions at once than by a single version.

Thus, even though we may not believe in ideal archetypal or intended texts, the proposition remains that literary works do not exist as fixed material objects; they are only implied variously by surviving materials. That proposition entails problems such as, who shall be in charge of constructing the edition that acknowledges these conditions of textuality? And who decides how readers wishing to understand the work of art in historical, documentary, social, and intellectual ways are to access and interact with the edition? And we must not forget that one reason we wish to develop some sophisticated sensitivity to the condition of literary works in their multiple selves, their implied forms, and their chronologies of dynamic existence is that we wish to create an electronic equivalence which enables and does not ignore or deny these sensitivities.

And so, an electronic archive with digital images of documents and accurate, searchable transcriptions is a good start; but it isn't good enough.

5. The Work Represented

Imagine you have gone to one of the world's great libraries to see the manuscript, or the first edition, or the even rarer third revised cheap edition of a work. You fill out a call slip, pass it to the librarian's assistant and in due time you are handed a typed transcript of the work. After a moment of speechless surprise, you say, 'No, no. Please, may I see the original'. 'But', says the librarian, 'look, this is not just any transcription. See. There is a full header recording who prepared the transcript and how it was proofread. Not only that', says the librarian, 'it is from a TEI conformant XML encoded original file'. 'No, no', you say. 'I don't care who transcribed it or how many times it was proofread. I don't care if it is TEI conformant. I want to see the *real* original'. Thank goodness librarians do not act that way. So, why, when we come to the electronic archive / edition / work site as a place to study a work of literary art on-line and we click on the icon or hotlink to 'The Blessed Damozel' or *The Songs of Innocence* or *The Origin of Species* or *Vanity Fair*, why oh why do we get a transcript? We do not want a transcript; we want an image. And we don't want just any image. We want a choice of the manuscript, the 1821 newspaper, the 1848 first edition, or the 2002 critical edition, and what we get when we make the choice should be an image of what we asked for, not a transcript.

This is not an idea that goes without saying. Ninety-nine percent of electronic sites offering literary works offer only transcripts. Ninety-nine percent of websites do not identify the source text for the transcript or say who transcribed it, how it was transcribed, how it was proofread, or when it was transcribed. Ninety-nine percent of electronic literary works were mounted by people who think that a text is a text is a text and any text will do. Even most of those who identify a particular source text offer only a transcript as if the transcript and the source were interchangeable equivalents. They are not. They do not imply the work in the same way, as has been argued too many times to count by the followers of D. F. McKenzie (1986) and J. J. McGann (1991).

Nevertheless, I begin with the electronic archive because, of all things that have been done electronically with texts, digital image archives seem to me to be what we have, so far, done best. I'm not sure we have ever done it perfectly; we have frequently done it imperfectly. But there is a sense of satisfaction about the potential for electronic archives that makes us think that if we are not there yet, we are almost there.

An archive of transcripts, by the way, is not a book archive. It is a collection of reprints, and possibly a valuable thing. But electronic transcripts do not constitute an archive in any sense of that word that I understand.

So, we begin with images of texts. These too are not an archive. They are images of an archive. To be accurate we should call them virtual archives to distinguish them from real archives. And when the virtual archive is done right, it contains the images not just of the text but of the medium on which the text was written or printed, so that we can know something about the paper, the margins, the condition of the material, the quality of the printing, and the sense of age. The virtual archive, furthermore, can be better than a real one because of the capacity to produce images of high enough resolution that the virtual reproduction can reveal more than the original reveals to the naked eye. Certainly virtual archives can be better than microfilm which has served our profession so well for so many years, but which has also taught us reams about the inadequacies of photo-reproductions.

In electronic image archives we have much more than photo-reproductions because we have mechanisms for searching, with the help of optical character recognition (OCR), text files which can be hidden behind the image files or as 'a facing page'. There is, of course, the slight disadvantage of OCR not getting everything right and therefore if one performs a machine search of a raw OCR file one will miss all the instances of the search words that have been mis-transcribed. But, what am I saying? Of course scholars do not expect machines to do what they are supposed to do before releasing their work to the public i.e. proofreading, double checking, vetting, verifying and approving the transcripts first. So, with electronic archives we have licked the problem of images and searchable texts. And this is to say nothing about the semantic web and data mining, which in our case we have not got.

Virtual archives can be better than real ones in other ways. First, because the internet and storage devices are capacious, we can add images and files to our archive until it is comprehensive. If we have not always been comprehensive, we sense that it is just a matter of time and money. And, second, and perhaps even better than that, we have licked the distribution problems too: unlike a library archive, the electronic library can be made available in Timbuktu via the Internet. Timbuktu scholars do not have to go to great academic institutions such as Cambridge, Oxford, UCLA or TAMU[4] — or if they still have to, we feel that in time they will not have to.

So, if we think of the electronic representation of texts and documents in these terms, we might with justice feel that the electronic age has reached a milestone: that the technology and the methodology for representing texts and documents awaits the will and direction of scholars to fulfil the promise of a new but present age.

But if *texts and documents* have now the potential (and in some cases have already realised the potential) to be represented electronically in scholarly, reliable and useful ways, what can we say about the representation of *works*?

The easiest thing to say is that works are represented in texts and documents and that without documents there are no works. I would of course agree with this but suggest that, good as it is, it is not good enough. It does

---

[4] University of California, Los Angeles; Texas A&M University

not go far enough. If we revisit the notion of the 'Work Implied', and if we restate the notion that the work is not equivalent to any representation of it, is not fully represented in any one version of it, then the *work* cannot be essentially *documentary*. While it is true both, that at some level each document represents a version of the work and that the work cannot exist except through material forms, it is also true that an incomplete document does not represent a whole version, that manuscript documents frequently contain more than one version, and that sometimes an implied version of a work becomes recognizable as a version only when it has been extracted and constructed from more than one document. Thus, the complexity of works exceeds the complexity of texts and requires more than imitation on a computer's screen of hand written and machine printed texts. If we hope to create a system for representing works electronically, it must cater to a range of views about how works can and should be represented and not just to a view that is satisfied by the archive of images of historical documents, not even when those digital images are backed by accurate searchable transcripts.

It might help us to see this range if we imagine briefly just three different kinds of edited texts to produce:

First, edited texts of documents in which only demonstrable errors are corrected and to which editorial notes are attached.

Second, edited texts of manuscripts or other documents from which early, intermediate and final versions can be extracted or distinguished, or which can be provided with some navigation aids to help readers see the processes of composition and revision contained within the one document.

And third, edited texts that draw from two or more extant historical documents to provide an edited version that fulfils one or another view of what the text should or could be.

This third type, eclectic editing, as I began by indicating, has been widely criticized in recent years, and yet it is still, at least for English language texts, one of the most practiced forms. At its least defensible it is practiced by editors who want to produce the most artistic, or most politically correct, or most aesthetically pleasing form of the work. The resulting forms may not only be eclectic, drawing emendations from historical documents, but also 'enhanced' by speculative emendation. It is worth remembering in this context, however, that all historical variants, excepting those produced by the author, were originally speculative emendations. In its most defensible form, eclectic editing seeks to incorporate in one text the guiding influence of that person or persons to whom the greatest authority for the text is attributed. It is an approach used in attempts to reconstruct archetypes when all the historically extant documents are centuries removed from their originals and where many documents have a claim to some share of authority. And it is also used when manuscripts, proofs, and authoritative printed documents bear the evidence of carelessness, censorship, or heavy-handed interventionist editing.

Whatever one might think of these ways to edit texts — to alter what is found in the raw documents — it is the case that editors practice all these forms of editing. Despite objections, there are responsible scholars who advocate each of these editorial approaches. The fact that one can find examples of abominably edited texts representing each of these approaches does not demonstrate that the approach itself is abominable.

And the point of this exercise is to demonstrate that in developing the tools for electronic editions and archives, the needs of scholars who use any or all these approaches must be acknowledged. But before proceeding with that thought, let us pause to think about the work interpreted.

6. The Work Interpreted

My argument in brief is this. That if each material instantiation of a literary work implies it in some way — in some admittedly partial way and not in a definitive way — then it follows that each electronic representation of the work implies it in yet a different way from that in which the material form does. But that is not the most important part of the argument. If the work is implied by, rather than fully inherent in, the documents that represent it, then the only way to know what is implied by each form is to try one's best to interpret that form and to say what one thinks is implied by it. And, when one does that, one is confined to saying what is implied by the particular copy of the work one is reading; it does not necessarily apply to other copies nor is it necessarily generic to the work as a whole. In short, if it is the nature of a work of literary art to be partially implied by each copy of it, any interpretive engagement with a copy of the work apprehends the implications only of that particular copy. That which is implied by a Yeats poem published in the *Irish Times* at a time of incidental public turmoil of 1913 is not what is implied by that same poem safely ensconced in the Norton Anthology of English Literature, volume II in 1997 or 2007.

It is clear from the traditions and habits of readers, however, that there are frequent and important congruities amongst readers of different copies of a work, such that in spite of reading different copies, each implying the work somewhat differently, there is a strong sense that they have indeed read the same work. This overlap is usually enough to make readers overlook, or consider as trivial, the differences arising from the fact that they are not referencing the same lexical or bibliographical form of the work. Nevertheless, it is worth remembering the potential for interpretive difference deriving, on the one hand, from the bibliographical and lexical particularities of the copy being read and, on the other hand, from the contexts of origination that exercised an operant force on the construction of the copies of the work at important events in the work's life, and on, if one but had one, the third hand, from the critical and interpretive communities influencing the present reader.

For the first of these, the bibliographical and lexical particularities of the copy being read, one probably needs only to say 'coiled fish' vs 'soiled fish' or perhaps 'too sullied flesh' vs 'too sallied' or 'too solid flesh' or 'early editions of Henry James' vs 'the New York edition of Henry James' or to refer to the examples from Middleton's *Second Maiden's Tragedy* or Virginia Woolf's *To the Lighthouse*, mentioned earlier to get us thinking that textual differences often lead directly to conflicting interpretations. The already complex task of interpretation is rendered both more complex and more precise by attention to the particularities of the copy being read and to its differences from other copies.

The second potential for interpretive difference arises from knowledge or ignorance of the contexts of origination surrounding the significant events in the production of copies of the work. If in the act of interpreting a work we are inclined to use locutions like 'What Shakespeare did so well here' or 'Only Melville could have thought to use such a word' we had best be sure not only that the author is responsible for the locution being quoted but that we know enough about the circumstances of its utterance to know that our insight is supported by evidence that 'went without saying' for the author, production crew, and first readers of that copy of the work. If, however, we avoid sounding as if we knew what the *author* had meant by claiming instead that 'the *text* says so and so' or 'the *text* means so and so' we speak the nonsense that paper and ink molecules have independent volition. Texts do not mean things; people mean things by texts. But if I say that the text means such and such because I read and interpret the text in relation to what can be known about the contexts of origination, then the interpretation is plausible in reference to textual and historical evidence supporting it. In order to produce informed reader response, readers need texts that are particular, that look like what they are, and that are surrounded or supported by the materials that at one time may have gone without saying but now do not.

Asking readers to express their opinions about texts concerning which they have no information about the contexts of origination is like asking anyone you might meet on the street to express an opinion about when we will pull out of Iraq or if it will rain tomorrow or who will be the next president. People usually have no difficulty in expressing opinions but one had just as well ask a crystal ball or a cat because the opinion will be an act of the imagination unimpeded by knowledge, not the result of analysis of the full panoply of relevant evidence. Offering readers a historical text without also offering the fruits of scholarship into the contexts of origination is not good enough. It wasn't good enough in print anthologies and it isn't good enough in electronic forms.

Recapping: first, the work is implied by its material instantiations, not coeval with them; second, each representation of the work, material or electronic, is particular and partial; and third, the only access we have to the work is through acts of interpretation of representations that imply the work. It follows that the work itself exists only in deferred forms – not in immediate, transparent, unambiguous forms. A text is never a mere text or a simple text or a correct text, not even if it is well edited. We should be suspicious of locutions like 'the work itself,' for the work exists only in our constructs of it. While the text and the document are clearly material, the work is a mental construct. The German Historical/Critical editors make this same point by distinguishing, in the words of Gunter Martens, between textual evidence (the textual document) and the aesthetic object (the work extracted from it) (Martens 1995a, 1995b). Historical/Critical editors err, I believe, in assuming that editors can focus all their attention on the textual evidence and leave the aesthetic object for critics to worry about. For, even editors are prevented from unmediated, transparent interaction with the work because textual evidence is evidence *for* the work, not the work itself.

The work is implied and represented by material texts and interpreted from material texts and thus will never be nailed down and made fixed for ever — not in print and not electronically. The textual condition leads inevitably to arguments about how to interpret and how to represent works.

There are many legitimate ways to approach works of literature. And, so, while our job as editors is most immediately with the material representations of the work, we must acknowledge the elusiveness of works when we make decisions about how to represent them electronically. No edition of a work fully represents it. An archive of representations of a work only begins scholarship relative to the work by providing the foundation for full engagement with the work. Adequate electronic designs for archives and editions will make it feasible and easier to produce new literary criticism that is more broadly based in relevant texts and contexts. New electronic text projects should not only provide the evidence that will support a greater number and a wider range of interpretive possibilities, it should do so in an electronic environment that enables augmentation. My personal bias inclines toward the belief that such archives of texts and contexts will make historical readings both richer and more precise, but they will certainly not prevent readings that ignore history. I think that is okay.

There is no group of people on earth, and especially not textual critics, who can make readers read in historically rich and precise ways. Readers have legitimate or at least compelling reasons to read in other ways and we must, I believe, accept that as a fact of life. It is not self-flagellation to say textual critics have, in the print world, not done the best possible job of making text and context readily and invitingly available to critics. Important textual differences and revealing contextual facts are routinely buried in forbidding apparatuses and historical introductions. Better presentation and better interface designs can help readers achieve historical readings. With electronic scholarly editions we have a greater opportunity than ever to provide readers with particularized and contextualized editions. But I believe we still have formidable infrastructure and design problems to solve.

Those infrastructure and design problems are the natural results of a new medium with no traditions seeking local ways to solve local problems. In the book world every project had to be finished before it could be published. And we find big electronic projects following that model – finished and presented to users not as a dynamic growing site for scholarship but as a finished product to be seen and not touched. In the book world every project was cut down to size by compromise. And we find big electronic projects compromising in similar ways – by the size of hard discs, the speed of downloads, and the size of budgets. The state of modern electronic archives and editions represents a failure of imagination — a failure to see the problem whole or to recognize the shortfalls of local solutions for local problems. We have thought too small. The goals of electronic archives / editions for any work of literature are too great for any one editor or one small team of editors to fulfil. But we have yet to see electronic editorial projects as partial contributions to work sites where our best collaborators may have only just now been born. Can we do our work in such a way that textual critics, instead of ignoring existing electronic editions and looking for ways to rebuild from the ground up, can build on what is already done, or could attach their own scholarly work to the existing site as developing contributions to knowledge? If that is to happen how must we undertake our work?

7. Conclusion

My argument has reached this point:

First: That we acknowledge editing as an attempt to deal with a complex set of materials for which there are a variety of viable and necessary approaches.

Second: That editing, especially in the electronic world, is a task that cannot and should not end with one project's vision of the product but instead serves as a foundation, requiring maintenance, repair, replacement of parts and extension beyond the capacity of any one person.

Third: That there is a large and future community of scholars that can contribute to basic editorial work, to the construction of contextual matter and to the structure of critical understanding of the works represented in our electronic archive editions.

These three conclusions have much to say about how we do our work and how we lodge our scholarly endeavours in electronic form. In order for scholarly editors in the electronic medium to make a difference in the way students and critics read and interpret texts they must do the following four things:

1. Make access to texts in scholarly editions as convenient and inexpensive as paperbacks, but not oversimplified.

2. Construct editions so that readers can not only see but touch, manipulate, personalize, and alter their copies in whatever way they wish.

3. Construct editions so that other scholars can participate in the further construction of the work site by adding new materials, new links, new comments, new information, new texts, new tagging, new views.

4. Protect the integrity of the original textual foundation and the discreteness of each contributor's offering whilst accomplishing points 2 and 3. This will require a completely new environment and storage and retrieval system for electronic projects – one that separates texts from commentary by stand-off markup, protects integrity by check-sums and engagement histories, ensures longevity by multiple distributed online storage, and provides for spontaneous aggregation and integration to incorporate all new contributions to a given project for new users.

The final word in this first part of a pair of essays on the subject[1] is: until funding agencies supporting editions and archives add the third wheel to their funding scheme — development of a *Collaborative Literary Research Electronic Environment* — new electronic editions and archives will continue to imitate print by continuing to create closed, finished or abandoned, look-but-don't-touch products.

---

[1] See Shillingsburg (2009) for the second of the pair of essays.

8. Text as Algorithm and as Process[1]

Paul Eggert

1. Electronic Text and 'Text'

Elsewhere in this volume Peter Robinson relates an anecdote from a lecture he gave in 2004 in which he surveyed his audience to discover how many of them had in the previous 12 months acquired an electronic book as opposed to other common digital products. Nearly everyone had done the latter, but only five percent the former. Everyone had bought a printed book. The expectations of the early 1990s about electronic texts and how they would change our reading habits had not materialised by 2004. E-books will succeed, Robinson concludes, only when they have a compelling advantage over their printed counterparts.

What could this be in the case of scholarly editions? Despite considerable efforts on the part of many scholars around the world since the widespread adoption of the internet in the early 1990s results have been at best modest. We cannot claim that electronic editions are an unqualified success. They have not swept the field. As Robinson notes, while music, film

---

[1] The thinking in this paper has been stimulated by many conversations with my collaborators in the successive Just In Time Markup (JITM) projects at the Australian Scholarly Editions Centre (see www.unsw.edu.au/ASEC and www.unsw.adfa.edu.au/JITM). For reports, see Berrie et al. 2003; and Berrie et al. 2006. For a commentary on the wider meanings of the JITM projects, see Eggert 2005. I thank Peter Robinson for giving me access to three papers of his prior to their publication: 'Electronic Editions for Everyone' (in the present volume), 'Current Directions in the Making of Digital Editions: Towards Interactive Editions' (Robinson 2007b) and 'Documenting Texts and Text Sources for Exposure and Retrieval' (Robinson 2008). I also thank De Montfort University, especially its Centre for Textual Scholarship, whose support made possible my lecture to the London Seminar in Digital Text and Scholarship in 2007, on which this essay is closely based.

and photographs have not had to be fundamentally re-thought for the new medium in order to succeed, the book will have to be. Nowhere is this truer than in the case of the scholarly edition. That is why, I conclude, fundamental rather than purely technical questions have to be asked when we are considering the fate or future of the electronic scholarly edition.

Some basic questions about the nature of written and printed texts have been asked by members of the encoding community as they have struggled to define what it is that they are encoding. This ought not to be surprising. The act of encoding texts for computer processing involves a blatant intervention in text-files of a kind that scholarly editors in the print domain are normally shielded from, however heroic their emendation of corrupted wording of a literary or biblical work may be. Traditionally they have treated many aspects of the physical presentation of text as irrelevant to their pursuit.[2] However, this self-preserving instinct finds itself in a tighter corner in the electronic domain, where complete specification is crucial for computer processing.

The different requirements of the electronic medium can help to throw new light on some of the enduring questions of what texts are and how they function. Recent commentary has been tending in this direction, bringing bibliography and some aspects of editorial theory to bear on electronic texts.[3] My aim here is, accordingly, to inspect some of the recent text-encoding debate, and then the far-reaching proposals put forward by Jerome J. McGann in his provocative book *Radiant Textuality* (2001). I have some tough things to say. To get to that point I first offer a meditation on textuality, from which certain conclusions flow. At the fundamental level, textuality and electronic textuality, I believe, fold back into one. If *this* level of clarification can be achieved, then clarification of the continuing dilemmas in the computer representation of text should follow.[4]

My aim in the second part of this paper will be to express what can now be described as a convergence in thinking by some pragmatic commentators on the future of electronic editions — people who have *not* been won over to McGann's vision but who do see a way forward for an area of scholarly editorial endeavour that has not yet been unambiguously successful. I

---

2   Editorial self-preservation usually means that physical evidence is ignored or suppressed: cf. Eggert 2004, 162-4.
3   See for instance: Aarseth 1997, Dahlström 2000, Kirschenbaum 2001 and 2002, and Hayles 2001 and 2003. For a commentary, see Eggert 2005.
4   For the importance of modelling as a route to knowledge in humanities computing, see McCarty 2004.

refer to Peter Shillingsburg, especially in *From Gutenberg to Google* (2006b); Peter Robinson and his soon-to-be-announced plans, already circulated in draft form, for a new direction for his endeavours in Chaucer and Greek New Testament editing; and some aspects of the DISCOVERY project funded by the European Union's *eContentplus* scheme.[5]

The argument here has been anticipated in Eggert 2005, where I develop the wider implications of the methodology and aims of an Australian editing experiment called *Just In Time Markup* (JITM). By 2002 the JITM project had implemented stand-off markup as part of a system to guarantee the authenticity of a text file. We then realised that stand-off markup provided something we had not been looking to achieve: a basis for ongoing collaborative interpretation.

2. Defining 'Text'

In 1995 Alois Pichler declared that the aim of encoding must be 'to prepare from the original text another text so as to serve as accurately as possible certain interests in the text', and he added: 'what we are going to represent, and how, is determined by our research interests ... and not by a text which exists independently and which we are going to depict' (1995: 691, 690). Allen Renear, who has been deeply involved in the TEI (Text Encoding Initiative) movement, rejected this claim as 'antirealist' (1997). But his objection to Pichler's argument is based on an under-problematised notion that text is or must be abidingly and objectively real, and that this condition demands encoding that is aimed at elucidating the object's actual features.[6]

The new light thrown upon textuality by developments in editorial theory is relevant to this text-encoding debate. Gone are the days when scholarly editors could safely invoke the authority of Sir Walter Greg's 'Rationale of Copy-Text' to justify a reading text established on the basis of final authorial intention (1950-51). The form of presentation — a single text, together with the rejected and variant forms recorded in the back of the book — was itself, in every edition, an enactment of an under-specified and narrow theory of textuality. It was both narrow (in that its quarry was a verbal text abstracted from the material forms that had carried it) and

---

5 For DISCOVERY, see Pichler and Lanestedt 2007 and, more generally, Hayward 2006.
6 Renear 1997, 117-24. My counter-argument is in Eggert 2005.

Neoplatonic (the approximation of an ideal) at the same time. By the late 1980s a newly self-conscious understanding of texts was being cultivated. Texts now emerged as always in process, as meaningful both in their verbal forms and their physical presentations, as anchored not only in authorship but also in the publishing process and in their successive readerships. Text now was recognised as having social, performative and artefactual dimensions that editors' prior concentration upon its abstracted verbal form had not so much ignored (since they at least partially recorded it) as occluded.

This realisation bears out Pichler's comment negatively — that is, that we can only represent certain interests in a text — although he was thinking about text-encoding, not critical editions. The realisation also exposes the inadequacy of the realist position espoused by Renear. Texts are anything but self-identical: whatever their ongoing existence consists of, our view of them is perspectival. A phenomenology of text has replaced a simpler ontology. And yet, a phenomenology of multiple perspectives is not necessarily inconsistent with the belief that there is *something* abiding about texts. We know from experience that we wish, selectively, to absorb texts into our imaginative lives, just as, in the act of reading, we pour part of ourselves into them. We are dealing with something, a persisting something, but what is it? How do we define it?

We know for one thing that we all live in bodies. Our reality is conditioned by this corporeal existence. These bodies of ours live in an analogue world, but one whose communications and many other functions are increasingly enabled, and extended in their reach and speed, by digital technologies. Books in their analogue format have a comforting familiarity. They sit nicely in the hand. Like cats, they're up on our laps and we've started to handle them — tenderly, almost unawares, indeed we are still savouring the pleasure in store — even as our thinking minds are getting to work on the book's contents. The stream of words and punctuation — the text — is what we have now begun to read: isn't it?

Certainly, traditional page designs cater to this assumption by aiming for layouts that are transparent. The best design is said to be the one we can't see, that we look straight through to the content and never notice. It took some hundreds of years to achieve such designs. But of course the recent developments in editorial theory show that every reading is affected, consciously or not, by the page design, including the characteristics of the chosen font, the amount of leading and white space, the binding and paperstock, and more obviously the accompanying illustrations; or the competing matter beside a magazine serialisation being read week by week. All this needs to be considered before we get to the wider contexts of the reading: when it happens, to whom, for what purpose, under what conditions, with what history of prior reading.

So now it becomes harder to define what a text is. But we can't duck the question. We *have* to think about text, its material condition and its reception if we are to understand what it is that we are encoding when we say that we are encoding texts.

3. Text and Codes

I go for regular walks up Mt Ainslie near my house in Canberra. It's actually less heroic than it sounds, and so if friends are visiting I take them too. About halfway up there is a striking gum tree to the left of the path, which I have frequently looked at (see cover image). It has various markings on it. An American friend, with a bent for editorial theory, saw that I was serious when I stopped in front of the tree and asked him whether he was now looking at a text, or not. There in front of him was potentially a document, a textual carrier — the nearly white, virtually smooth bark of the tree — and there were, without doubt, brown squiggles on it, more or less in a vertical line, and conveniently at eye-height. He looked. Could they be in a Tai script, of which he was only vaguely aware? He had been to Thailand. Or was it conceivably in a sinuous Bengali script of which he had seen examples but could not read? He knew that Canberra is a multi-cultural city containing people from all parts of Asia and the Middle East. He took a while to declare that he had tried but he could not make any sense of it, and that in fact he doubted that it was a text, even though he could not explain how the markings came to be there. The fact, once explained, that these markings are the trail gouged by an insect burrowing under the bark that the Scribbly Gum later sheds, thus revealing the markings, clinched the matter. This was not a text. There was no human communicative intent.

In contrast, consider the period up until 1799 when the Rosetta Stone was discovered. Egyptian hieroglyphic inscriptions were unreadable, yet there was agreement that they would probably have a meaning, if only the code could be broken. There was little doubt that the stone inscriptions in the tombs were texts of some kind due to their regularity and repetitiveness. This of course proved to be the case when (by the 1820s) the code was articulated. There was, after all, proven human communicative intent demonstrated by the use of an alphabetic, syllabic and pictographic code that the original inscribers had held in common. The markings had proved to be not just mindless repetitions but real inscriptions, and the inscribed stone had therefore proved to be a document. What we had, now, were texts.[7]

The decisive change in status from natural or physical artefact to document, and vice versa in the case of the Scribbly Gum, occurs at the same time that it is decided that markings are or are not textual inscriptions. In other words, the documentary and the textual dimensions are interdependent. They are separable for purposes of discussion, but they are not separate. In a private communication, Mats Dahlström disagrees. He instances the case of the prisoner on death row who is given paper and ink on which at last to record his confession of the crime, but stolidly refuses to do so. The prisoner has created no text. But yet there is a document: the paper, Dahlström says.

I would disagree. The assumption that there is one seems justified only because the context has set up the expectation of normal documentary-textual interdependence. The physical paper is about to achieve a documentary status, but it fails to happen. If the same unused sheet of paper were then turned into a paper aeroplane by the perversely silent criminal it would no longer be thought of as a document. So the objection only confirms what I contend: that the documentary and the textual dimensions are fundamentally interdependent.

This fact is something we would have noticed long since as important did we not spend most of our reading lives assuming that we could essentially ignore the document. The basis of the document may be physical, it may be computational, or it may be the sound waves of orally declaimed verse: but in all cases there is a material condition for its newly declared status. Materiality is not a sufficient condition, for the documentary dimension is always in relation to the textual. Neither is self-identical, and both have their histories: the histories of writing and production, and the histories of reading. The two histories are intertwined.[8]

---

7 Cf. the 3rd-century BC Greek shorthand systems known as tachygraphy. They are yet to be deciphered despite the existence of a prayer in both normal handwriting and three different types of shorthand.

8 The first reader is the writer. At every stage of composition and revision, writers are reading what they just wrote, or wrote before. Typesetters, before they do anything else, are readers too, and obviously editors are; but so too are encoders of e-texts. All these people intervene between an earlier document to create the new document (printed or computer-processed) used by the readers. See further, Eggert

The space that we nevertheless open up by distinguishing conceptually between the documentary and the textual allows a number of otherwise puzzling things to fall into place. The first is that the *material* document can be seen now as the basis of the persisting something that we know reading reveals to us — whether the text is screen-evanescent, a temporary visualisation, or whether it arises as we read from a document that has hardly altered in hundreds of years. What related conclusions may we draw? First, we note the space between, yet the intertwined nature of, the documentary and textual dimensions; and second (although I do not enlarge on it here), the central relevance, when considering texts, of agency and time.[9]

4. The Humpty Dumpty Approach to Text

How can computer-encoding respond to these fundamentals? One way forward was proposed in 2001 by Jerome McGann in *Radiant Textuality*. Before I get to his ambitious proposal, which most commentators seem to have passed over, I have to deal with the aspect of his book that has dominated discussion so far: the Humpty Dumpty argument that words, and therefore texts, can mean whatever we want them to mean. A discussion of this ludic argument, which is conducted as a conversation between different voices animated by McGann, will finally point a way forward.

David Hoover has given McGann's Humpty Dumpty argument a mauling in 'Hot-Air Textuality: Literature after Jerome McGann' (2005). McGann's repeated rescanning of the same double-column document, a process which he describes in his book, resulted in textual variation: 'therefore,' he concludes, 'the text is not self-identical since the machine produced somewhat different texts from the same document' (cf. 2001: 144-6). Hoover shows, by repeatedly scanning a simpler document, that variation can be trivial. Thus for most practical purposes, he claims, texts *are* self-identical at least within a tightly defined readership (2005: 76).

Hoover next turns to McGann's account of a class on Keats's 'Ode on a Grecian Urn'. McGann writes it, teasingly, in the form of a discussion between various characters with names such as Instruction, Printer's Devil and Footnote. The student who claims that the phrase 'O Attic shape!' refers to a ghostly shape in an attic, such as his grandmother's attic, rather

---

2009, chap. 10.
9 See further, Eggert 2009, chaps. 8-9.

than to a Greek or Attic urn, is robustly defended. Although the student has deformed the poem's meaning by reference to her own experience, isn't this (McGann implies through one of the voices, but without fully committing himself) what *always* happens? The critic who brings historical information to bear on the reading to defend the poem against such subjective deformation deforms it also but in a different way. This argument has upset traditional scholars.

Hoover's counter-argument is that literature does not need to be opened up (quoting one of McGann's characters) 'in lots of new and interesting ways'. Radical forms of deformation are not worth pursuing. Rather, Hoover argues, 'interpretation requires new, interesting, and *reasonable* ways of constraining the wide array of possible meanings that literary texts typically make at least marginally possible' (2005: 90). In a more recent article, 'The End of the Irrelevant Text: Electronic Texts, Linguistics and Literary Theory' (2007), Hoover gets further onto the front foot. His argument reflects the remarkable growth in empirical resources now available to us that can aid, guide and check literary interpretation: bibliographic databases, text corpora, computational stylistics, reliable scholarly editions, and biographies of writers and detailed chronologies of their writings.

It is easy to get hot under the collar about McGann's proposals, except they are not quite his. He is only dramatising the dispute, giving voice — impiously, even wickedly, yet also sweetly and reasonably — to a normally repressed desire for a plenitude of meanings that anarchic students (such as, Dear Reader, we once were too?) must at least sometimes have felt whenever a teacher was determined to assert his or her interpretative authority on this or that line of a poem. 'It's mine too, isn't it?' we muttered darkly to ourselves as our suggested interpretations were cast ignominiously aside.

The alarmed response to McGann's book is understandable. Hoover's articles are more importantly indexing a general shift in the critical scene after the winding-down in energy of the Theory (the capital T Theory) movement since the late 1990s. But I think the actual importance of McGann's book lies elsewhere. He is setting up a principle of reading as inevitably and unavoidably one of deformation, a principle that he needs to invoke later in the book as a counter-weight when he finally gets down to his serious proposals. They are what I wish to discuss now. It will become clear that my objection to McGann's proposals takes a different form to the empirical ones of David Hoover.

5. Text as Algorithm

McGann's agenda was canvassed in a working paper published electronically (probably in 2000), 'Rethinking Textuality', where he talks of the need 'to rethink the work's textuality by consciously simulating its social reconstruction'. The computer game called *IVANHOE*, which he and Johanna Drucker developed to simulate textuality, is something I discuss later. The basic problem for encoding, McGann points out, is that literary texts are not like informational texts. They are inherently incommensurable. Poems are not just *about* a subject; they are also about their vehicle of transmission. They exploit capacities of sound, image, metaphor and movement; they get in behind the ratiocinating mind. Put another way: noise is part of their communication. It does not separate readily from signal. This is the conundrum faced by anyone who is sensitised to poetry but wants to specify the aspects of poems' functioning susceptible to knowledge representation that the computer can deal with, and that would allow it, in a specific sense, to 'read' the poem. This is the ultimate goal that McGann foresees, while recognising that there will always be limits (2001: 185).

The term that McGann invented in 1991 to cover the meanings emerging from the physical instantiation of the linguistic text — what he calls the 'bibliographic code' — seems custom-made for the computing environment, and certainly he takes on the challenge in *Radiant Textuality*. He hopes to set off a general effort to encode physical aspects of documents: he is eloquent on the subject of page-space (say, versus scroll-space or cave-space). He affords some hope that basic aspects of the *mise-en-page* that are below the level of our notice may after all be precisely specifiable and therefore rendered intelligible to the computer. Could we one day, then, have a machine called an OBR — an Optical Bibliographic Reader — exploiting new forms of digital pattern recognition?

I am sceptical. It is not that I question whether advances in digital pattern recognition will be made. Advances are very likely. Rather, I question McGann's notion of bibliographic code itself. The term has been taken up by a raft of editorial commentators and theorists but the attraction of it is, I believe, mainly rhetorical. If one is to be strict about the term, then there clearly is no such thing as bibliographic code. Dictionary definitions stress the systematic nature of codes: rigorously collected and arranged, as in legal codes; and the strictly defined substitution of words for other words, as in secret military codes. But the unpredictabilities of the gap between the physical features of a book and their meaning are poor conditions for the specification of a code. We can talk about the *art* of page design and book binding. Such work can be highly conscious and aimed at achieving particular aesthetic effects or even meanings: so that we could perhaps go so far as to claim the existence of a documentary or bibliographic semantics. But *code* is going further than the evidence permits. It would require a full-blown semiotics.[10] It seems to me that there can be no specifiable and invariable meaning for any particular *mise-en-page*.

Compare the criticism of paintings. Art critics sometimes refer to the visual 'vocabulary' of a particular artist or movement, and sometimes profess to be 'reading' paintings. In truth, these claims work only at a loose, metaphoric level. While paint or page designs involve the production of physical markings, neither invokes, in their physical appearance, a specifiable code that would allow the site to be duplicated without loss or change of meaning. With written or printed pages, then, to profess to be specifying the full material range of their possible significances — to our senses of sight, touch and smell — in order to turn them into a *code* would involve having to close the gap between the documentary and the textual, the gap between the material stimulus and the meaning for the reader. Given that there is no pre-existing code that can be drawn down for analysis, how is a 'code' to be specified? Clearly, it is impossible.

With what McGann calls the 'linguistic code' the chances are far higher, since a socialised agreement about the use of alphabetic or other scripts and about the functioning of syntactic arrangements, pre-exists both the writing and the reading of a text. The 'code' is, in effect, drawn down by both writer and reader. It is the document's *supplément*. It can be described, with varying degrees of success, structurally. It has commensurability. But meanings based on it notoriously vary so, although the conditions for the specification of this code are propitious, even here they are far from perfect.

There is also a larger, philosophical idea that the claim of a specifiable bibliographic code is presupposing. McGann envisages that it should be possible to articulate the rules for the reading of a document — as he puts it, 'a set of protocols for negotiating the textual scene' — so that a computer could read it (2001: 143). He claims that texts, because they are '*coded* bibliographically and semantically' should be seen as 'sets of rules (algorithms) for generating themselves' (2001: 138). These rules are the linguistic and

---

10   If it ever *were* to be defined, C.S. Peirce's semiotics might be the key to the advance: his account of the sign incorporates the interpretant of the sign into the semiotic transaction: see further, Eggert 2009, chap. 10.

8. Text as Algorithm and as Process

bibliographic codes. This is a breathtaking idea, but what does it imply? McGann realises that he is sailing close, here, to the holy grail of structural linguistics (2001: 151), only he wants to expand its purview to include the graphic (pre-semantic) markings in which the codings are embodied. McGann knows well that texts are not self-identical, and he says so several times in the book. But his new position on encoding is drawing him into the orbit of a transcendental idealism that would underwrite the continuing identity of any text. Indeed, he stresses it, relying on argument from 1960 of the Italian aesthetic philosopher Galvano della Volpe: 'As della Volpe shows, it [a 'true critical representation'] stands in a dialectical relationship to its object, which must always be a transcendental object so far as any act of critical perception is concerned.'[11]

When McGann writes that 'A text is a display and a record of itself, a fulfilment of its own instructions' (2001: 151), he is postulating the existence of bibliographic and linguistic systems that he hopes to see fully specified in ways that the computer can rapidly analyse when, say, presented with printed matter for scanning. A computer-algorithmic explanation of text is proto-structuralist; it requires no human participation. Yet such participation is crucial for the principle of deformation, which, as we have seen, McGann also maintains. By this principle he means that we can have a textual idealism while at the same time all our perspectives on that text can be different: 'they cannot be measured on a scale of equivalence' to the object of encoding, he says. All representations of it are, therefore, a deformation.

He hangs onto his earlier rhetoric of historical explanation of actual (what he calls 'determinate') productions and readings. Yet he also, in *Radiant Textuality*, refers to 'fields of perception and systems of conception' (2001: 178). Why 'systems'? The proto-structuralist explanation is working against the historical case. The effort starts to sound positivistic. Diachronic explanation collapses into the synchronic, and the idealism is not far away — as was also the case for Husserl, as Derrida famously pointed out (1973: 50). Reinvoking the transcendental ideal is too profound a philosophical step, or reversion, to be based on so little. In a sense the idea of system has been slipped in quietly to replace the human subject as the thing that underwrites and engages the transcendental ideal. There is, I believe, a more defensible model for textuality needed here.

---

11   McGann 2001: 173. Della Volpe (1895-1968): his principal work in aesthetic philosophy was *Critica del gusto* (1960), transl. Michael Caesar as *Critique of Taste*, London: NLB, 1978.

6. A Model for Textuality

When in 1994 I first criticised McGann's idea of bibliographic and linguistic codes it was because I felt the idea vaporized the writerly and readerly witness of the document. It converted the documentary dimension instantly into the encoded meaning and thus made the role of individuals in relation to it more or less irrelevant (Eggert 1994, 22-4). I find that this objection remains, but with a significant caveat. Since McGann's *The Textual Condition* of 1991, on which I was then commenting, he has found ways, both conceptually (via his principle of deformation) and in computer-assisted practice (in his IVANHOE game[12]), of incorporating readers' dealings with texts. But, as I see it, the advance is essentially only additive — i.e. what we end up with is system plus dealings — which explains how his position can be both like Renear's *and* Pichler's, realist and anti-realist, at the same time. There is a dilemma here that McGann's additive approach is trying to bridge: how can the text have a stable identity that can be encoded, and yet be always different?

Once we remove the transcendental assumption that McGann invokes, once we recognise what editorial theory has been pointing to in richly different ways now for years — i.e. the diachronic lives of texts in our lives — then it becomes clear that text will always be a messy affair, that our knowledge of it will always be partial, and all the more intriguing for that. But, if so, what can we point to that sufficiently stabilises a text's identity so that when we indulge in one of our culture's primary and most productive games, discussing texts, we can be sure that we are not only or merely discussing ourselves?

In 1998 I first adapted an idea of Adorno's that a negative dialectic between the textual and documentary dimensions can be thought of as underwriting the continuing identity of works and as therefore eliminating the need for McGann's or anyone else's idealism.[13] A negative dialectic has no synthesis. It describes an ongoing, antithetical but interdependent relationship. Document, taken as the material basis of text, has, by virtue of its physical or computational nature, a continuing history in relation to its productions and its readings; any new manifestation of the negative dialectic necessarily generates new sets of meanings. The work emerges only

---

12 For literature on IVANHOE, see the articles cited at www.ivanhoegame.org/wordpress/?page_id=2 [accessed 26/02/2010].
13 Eggert 1998, further adapted in Eggert 2009, chap. 10.

8. Text as Algorithm and as Process 195

as a regulative idea, the container, as it were, of the continuing dialectic. The ongoing existence of document is enough to link all the textual processes that are carried out under the name of the work. And bibliography is a technology for describing and relating allied documents. What McGann calls a 'deformation' is, from this point of view, simply another manifestation of text-in-process. And editions and text-encodings are only more excavatory and reconstructive forms of the same basic cultural dynamic.

Historical-materialist approaches to text are typically diachronic whereas semiotic (or algorithmic) modes are typically synchronic. As modes of explanation they have little respect for one another, and while in process are typically intolerant of one another's truth-telling claims. They tend to consume one another, to explain away one another's capacities to explain. My objection to McGann's argument is that he wants to be able to invoke both at the same time. But they never come together like that. They are constantly in real or potential conflict. As the philosophers say, they *sublate* one another over time; hence my invoking of the idea of a negative dialectic as a way of modelling explanations of textuality.

In *Radiant Textuality* McGann (2001) seemed to be seeing the principle of deformation as the next step for literary criticism. He subsequently employed games theory to incorporate the reader into the textual field and to record the resulting interactions. A paper he gave at the conference of the Society for Textual Scholarship in New York in 2003 substantiated this development. It offered a form of modelling of what texts are and do, and in this sense it was a prospect of things yet to come.

The computer game IVANHOE, which he developed earlier with Johanna Drucker at the University of Virginia, allows participants to role-play within what he calls the discourse field of Scott's novel. This is defined as including its production history and subsequent receptions; what editorial theorists, following the aesthetic philosopher Roman Ingarden in the 1930s, would call its life, including its textual evolution. None of the players of IVANHOE stands outside this life; all are role-players in it. Players must respond to new information claimed to be factual but which may, for the sake of the game, be duplicitous. Each move they make is played in the knowledge of the public (i.e. recorded) moves of all the other players; and the players keep a private log explaining each of their moves to which the computer itself has access and can make arbitrary moves to unsettle things.

In *Radiant Textuality*, McGann stresses what he calls the quantum effects of being always self-conscious of one's position within the game as a participant rather than an outside observer (2001).[14] As I see it, the game models the cultural field in which all works participate. Reviewers normally write their reviews, and critics their later articles, in at least partial knowledge of the views already expressed about the work in question, and about, say, what the author said in interviews on radio or television. If parodies of the work spring up, they themselves assume an existing knowledge of the work, or at least its mediation by commentators. All are operating in the same discourse field, for the real world of texts is always in a state of dynamic process.[15]

So this line of experimental modelling of text is potentially a fruitful one.[16] But if my account of the negative dialect between the documentary and textual dimensions of works is persuasive; if works are indeed in a process of continuous unfolding; if synchronic explanations of text are inevitably partial, then totalising or exhaustive schemes for text-encoding cannot be brought to fruition — although less ambitious schemes may, particularly if they accord with the model of textuality that I have described.

7. Stand-off Markup and Other Modest Advances

Theodor (Ted) Nelson, the original theorist of the internet, has long advocated the idea of external or stand-off markup rather than loading the text-file, as is typically done at present, with increasing amounts of interpretative markup subject to the same document-type definition (DTD) and therefore to the same hierarchy of content objects. Take XML[17] files for instance. They mix data with data referring to the data and with data referring to itself, all in the same file. This is very disadvantageous for some applications. Stand-off markup on the other hand offers a way of data-modelling and enhancing a text from multiple points of view. There is the opportunity to proceed with encoding what we already know about texts and to accumulate new knowledge about them without the worry of overlapping hierarchies, since

---

14 Cf. Schreibman 2003.
15 For a case-study, see Eggert 2009, chapter 9.
16 The IVANHOE game, and also the virtual-reality environments called MOOs*, such as the one developed for the Romantic Circle, MOOzymandias, may ultimately yield useful information about the ways in which readers process the physical qualities of books. See Fraistat and Jones 2003. *MOO stands for Multi-user dimension Object Oriented. See also Schreibman 2003.
17 Extensible Markup Language (a set of rules for encoding documents electronically).

8. Text as Algorithm and as Process

conflicting models need not be applied to the text simultaneously. This method leaves open the capacity to add layers and new kinds of interpretation that may emerge in the future. It also allows the signing of interpretative stand-off files by their creators, simplifying copyright concerns that the mixing of contributions within the one expanded file otherwise creates.

While better solutions will probably emerge, we know already that the use of stand-off markup using a checksum algorithm can resolve the problem of guaranteeing the ongoing authenticity of any text-file that is undergoing interpretation and enhancement. In the standard paradigm — i.e. using in-line markup — every addition of markup to a text-file necessarily creates a new state of the text. Text-files can quickly become so heavily encoded as to be beyond human capacity to proof-read them.

This is a problem for scholarly editions. Those who prepare them get jittery if asked to depend upon, without checking, the authenticity of newly processed text-files. Repeated human proof-reading is, strictly speaking, necessary because how can the editor *know* whether something has not accidentally been changed? Scholarly editors get jittery because they know from ample experience of manuscript and print production the normal fate of texts over time that are themselves undergoing repeated acts of copying. In the electronic environment, intervention, correction and enhancement bring with them new forms of this ancient fallibility.

The use of stand-off markup external to the text-file, applied to the text upon the user's call and incorporating an authenticating checksum algorithm in the act of incorporation, has emerged as one answer. Since the experimental JITM projects, mentioned above and reported in Berrie et al. 2003, Eggert 2005 and Berrie et al. 2006, there has been new interest in the potential of stand-off markup. In *From Gutenberg to Google* (2006b), Peter Shillingsburg assumes it as a given, and it helps him to strike out in new directions. Peter Robinson has informed me that he intends to give stand-off markup a significant role in foreshadowed technical developments for his e-editorial projects at his editorial institute in Birmingham. And as of late 2007 the programmers in DISCOVERY were giving the technique consideration as part of the likely development of a tagging tool aimed at collaborative interpretation of text-files within an RDF (Resource Description Framework) environment.

I mention these developments only to point to what I see as the emergence of a less totalising alternative to the structural one that underlies one side of Jerome McGann's thinking in *Radiant Textuality*. These developments lean, without toppling, towards the opposite, deformative side of his thinking. While one has to admit that all interpretation is an appropriation, a collaborative working environment for interpretation is surely preferable if it lets scholars hang on to what has been hard won: reliable transcriptions of the versions of literary works, and thoughtful rounds of emendation and interpretation. The interpretative files (or 'tagsets') created by scholars need to be accessible as a gradually evolving tradition of commentary and scholarship. This methodological requirement, familiar from the print environment, will not go away because of a change in medium. Scholarly agreement and disagreement need to be explicitly enabled in an environment where the commentaries are themselves authenticated i.e. electronically signed and dated and thus essentially anchored in their own tradition and history, rather than being free-floating and changeable, able to be deformed by others at will.

Of course, McGann's deformation is in spirit a ludic methodology designed to open up critical and interpretative possibilities, so David Hoover's censoriousness seems to me at moments to mistake its target. But his implicit question: 'Is life long enough to entertain open-ended possibilities?' answers itself with a confident *no*. This is partly because scholarship is basically collaborative. It needs to be in relation to something shared. It is a conversation over time about an abiding something. Interpretation of that something calls out counter-interpretation. Error calls out correction. But unless all of the participants can continually refer to the documents that carry the texts under investigation, their remarks will pass one another by without ever meeting. To play the fool with the documentary-textual continuum definitely creates more instantiations of it, just as treating it seriously does. But some instantiations are going to be more productive, more enlightening than others. Finally, the criterion has to be pragmatic, and I mean this in C. S. Peirce's sense of the word.

If this is the modest direction that electronic-edition development is going to go, will the medium *ever* supersede the printed book? Even in its scholarly forms the book is reasonably compact, sometimes cheap, often expensive but not ruinously so. And it has developed ingenious ways of condensing multitudes of evidence in tables, footnotes and cross-referenced textual apparatus. The fact of looming publication brings out heroic efforts on the part of the scholarly editor to finalise and complete the complex task — to get it *done* — thus answering to an all-too-human desire and capacity. And, as Peter Robinson points out, the printed scholarly edition

8. Text as Algorithm and as Process

filters out the surplus of information typical of electronic editions to date, an overload that readers cannot deal with profitably anyway.

Robinson and Shillingsburg have given the best answers to date as to the conditions under which the electronic edition will be able to supersede the printed book. Both concur with an argument of mine (Eggert 2005): that we will get to the new phase only when editors stop treating the electronic edition as something that they must keep jealously under their control, letting users consult but not re-build. Robinson's projects have so far been in this mould. His recent system ANASTASIA gives impressive functionality in its engine room, and impressive displays on its interface. But editions based on it are hard to reissue in a revised form when errors are detected in so complex an array of cross-referencing files. Worse, the whole wonderful thing depends to a dangerous extent on the welfare of its creator. Everyone worries how long the editions that depend on ANASTASIA would remain fully functional should Robinson happen to go under the proverbial bus.

Perhaps he worries too. His new emphasis is on distributed servers, each giving access to whatever materials relevant to an edition have been lodged on those servers prepared by various scholars or other individuals. Editions must henceforth be interactive, he says and in this he joins hands with Shillingsburg. He imagines Web 2.0 (and presumably semantic-web) capabilities gradually learning to predict the reader's needs, automatically finding, on other servers around the world, equivalent passages to, or relevant commentaries on, the lines of text that the reader is currently viewing. The hope is that, when relevant images, transcriptions, collations and commentaries automatically appear to gather themselves into our working or reading environment, editors will find the advantage compelling and will forsake the book. Readers will forsake it too, as soon as the web gives them a better experience. But we are not there yet, despite all the extravagant predictions about the imminent supersession of the book that were made in the early 1990s.

Is there an archival problem from this scattering of textual resources that Robinson predicts? My sense is: not as long as computers exist. Bits are tenacious creatures, probably more so than books, and they are very easily transferred. The digital resources of which I speak will achieve a permanent, effectively archival foothold purely through their wide distribution and use. Regathering them at the moment of reading in a relevant and authenticated form, and allowing interested parties to make further enhancements, is the challenge.

Common encoding standards and, as Robinson argues, agreed addressing protocols that ensure that exactly the same text fragment is being referenced, are required to make this happen (2007b).[18] Of course we still lack many of the basic tools. But this vision of a common, interactive type of scholarship and readership that democratically puts the reader in a box-seat while also empowering the scholar to make and sign more expert editions, doing much of the discovery work for us, is a very attractive prospect.

We should not fear the barbarians entering the gates of the scholarly city. They have usually got less arduous things to do anyway, and even when they do decide to interfere (as in contentious passages from books of the Bible whose wordings they object to) or even if they are empowered to make their own editions, my response is: Let them! Existing scholarly protocols of assessment and refereeing will doubtless be adapted to sort the electronic sheep from the goats. Authentication routines will keep the scholarly transcriptions safe, and when emendations are proposed by other scholars we should be able to provide keys that securely link the emending file to the target edited text-file, with permissions or refusals to emend built in. Stand-off interpretative files written for the original edited text should be able to be applied to the emended one once authentication routines or signed files with appropriate keys become easily available.[19]

Peter Shillingsburg's emphasis on modularity is important here (2006b: 80-125). He usefully lists everything that a well-constructed and adequately populated electronic edition should contain: all of the textual, contextual and facsimile materials, the receptions and adaptations. It is perhaps best to think of this as a wish-list. To achieve it, the editorial team will in practice

---

18   In his unpublished paper, 'A Specification towards Distributed Editions' (2007c), Robinson proposes some new TEI attributes and authoritative addressing protocols for different versions of the same work. The Functional Requirements for Bibliographic Records standard should assist with the addressing. FRBR defines a descending hierarchy of Work, Manifestation, Expression, Item, with adaptations treated as separate works but linked at the level of subject matter. FRBR's first large-scale implementation was the AustLit database (www.austlit.edu.au): RDF and Topic Maps enmesh all instances of the fundamental concepts of *agent* (author, publisher etc.) and *work* into a spider's web of relationships that themselves effectively define the agent or work rather than treating each one as a self-identical entity, robustly separate from all other agents and works.

19   JITM (the development of which ceased in 2005) was a step in that direction. Its system degrades gracefully. Markup written for text elements that are subsequently emended cease to authenticate those text elements when applied to them, but the remainder continue to be functional: see citations in n. 1, above.

inhabit what I have called the 'work-site' or what Shillingsburg calls the 'knowledge site'. Whatever we call it, the activities on that site will be the same: those of preparing, gathering, encoding, comparing, presenting and interpreting materials relevant to the work being edited. All this will be happening on a site on the internet. Equally, elsewhere, any number of other people not engaged in building the specific work-site, could be seriously or playfully or merely curiously handling copies of the same files at the same time. The work-site will be merely a more focussed and serious arena using the same — or mostly the same — materials. I say *mostly* the same, because the dragon of copyright is always at the gates, limiting the textual work we might do, limiting the free play that readers might otherwise have.

Since its editor-constructors will have inheritors or adapters or popular re-users, the work-site will, or ought to, consist of modules — materials and tools — that are individually reusable and repurposable, rather than forever locked together refusing entry to users. This imperative, about which Shillingsburg is persuasive, has to find a balance with the scholarly needs for textual authenticity, for precise citation of an ongoing tradition of interpretative commentary and, as Robinson points out, for precise addressing of the text fragments under discussion.

As I see it, the work-site will grow gradually by accretion, not by means of a grand scheme to enunciate the complete range of linguistic and bibliographic codes. It is virtually certain that the capacities of the computer to learn from our inquiries will bring to our attention information and materials for which we would never have thought to look. The computer's use of inferential logic, especially when assisted by formalised models and ontologies, and its capacity to compare files and to enable their collaborative enhancement, will multiply our knowledge. In these ways it will help us to build work-sites. It will allow us to understand works differently and anew. Its slow growth will reflect our gradual accumulation of knowledge about texts.

8. Conclusion

How, finally, does this vision of the future sit with the theoretical relationship between the documentary and textual dimensions sketched above? The material basis of electronic texts is obviously their computing environment, just as that of printed texts is the printshop. The routines of both environments affect the storage, processing and generation of texts. We become aware of this only when we refuse to naturalise the format and environment, when we stop to think about them.

I have referred easily and casually to texts being generated or visualised on screen. But in truth what we call a text on a computer screen is not a text: it is a computer artefact, an encoding and visualising of a binary flow of data, just as ink on a page is not a text till the material medium can be understood to be a document; or *not*, as in the case of the Scribbly Gum. For working purposes, because it simplifies matters, we normally agree to call a particular computer file visualised on screen a text. But as I hope I have shown, computers cannot strictly actualise texts — that is a human accomplishment — but they can process, manipulate and visualise *bits* with astonishing speed, often illuminating results and can allow cheap worldwide distribution. For this, all book readers will eventually be grateful, even if they are not now.

9. 'I Read the News Today, Oh Boy!'[1]: Newspaper Publishing in the Online World

Marilyn Deegan and Kathryn Sutherland

1. News Media Inherited and in Flux

The desire to receive and impart news is part of our social fabric: we all want to know 'what's new?' or 'what's up?' with our friends, families, or neighbours; as well as what is happening on a local, national, or international scale. As Mitchell Stephens (1990) observes, 'the frenzied, obsessive exchange of news is one of the oldest human activities'. News is also information with a time stamp: if it is not new, it is not news but something else. The oldest form of news is oral: word of mouth, which, before the advent of electronic media, could be conveyed only as fast as the fastest form of transport. Even before mechanization, this could be fast, and the stuff of legends: Pheidippides' two-day run in 490 BC from Marathon to Sparta (150 miles) to bring news of the Persian attack; the ride of Paul Revere, in the American War of Independence, to alert his compatriots that the British Redcoats were on the march. Jungle drums, smoke signals, yodelling have all been used over time and in different societies to communicate news faster than the human body; in recent ages, better roads, trains, and boats have accelerated word-of-mouth communication. The complexities of production and delivery processes mean that newspapers cannot, and never

---

1 The first line of the Beatles's song 'A Day in the Life', written by John Lennon and Paul McCartney; released in 1967 as the final track of the album *Sgt. Pepper's Lonely Hearts Club Band*.

could, compete with the speed with which individual items of news can be delivered by direct means. Where newspapers excel is in the comprehensiveness, variety, and range of their content, in the expansiveness of their comment on events and current affairs, and in their low cost, convenience, and portability. It is many decades since anyone relied upon newspapers for the football results, but sports pages remain hugely popular in all general daily and weekly newspapers, with football the most popular sport, and readers almost as eager for opinion, comment, nuance, gossip and even bias, as they are for the bare news. Though the advent of the telegraph in the nineteenth century (the first technology to convey news and information across vast distances instantaneously) and of radio and television in the twentieth century changed news reporting, they have not yet obviated the need for newspapers.

Periodical newsbooks, the ancestor of the modern newspaper, appeared in England in the 1620s, while London newspapers became widely available throughout the country during the course of the eighteenth century. For the last 200 years newspapers, magazines, and journals have been among the most widely and regularly consumed and the most influential print objects. Over this time, newspapers have been the threshold for our adult relationship to print, the basic tool of our literacy that we all aspire to: people who never read anything else will read newspapers. It is estimated that some 500 million newspapers are sold every day worldwide, though their circulation is likely to be much higher than this, with papers passed around within the home, the workplace, and other public spaces. In regions where literacy levels are low, the literate will read newspapers aloud to the illiterate. At the same time, printed news has always shared porous boundaries with other, higher literary forms: poetry, fiction, and criticism have regularly found a place, and often a first articulation, in the columns of a daily or weekly paper. In the newspaper, and its allied forms the journal and periodical, distinctions between high and low culture that might operate elsewhere have conventionally broken down under the pressure of variety in voice and subject, but also in authority: a common editorial practice dating back to the eighteenth century was the collapse of the writer-reader distinction in letters and opinions pages. Newspapers can thus claim to represent the demotic reach of the printed word: we all read or, perhaps, we must now say we all used to read news.

Over the same 200 year period, the newspaper industry has been at the frontier of technological innovation. It is important to register the interconnectedness of the two phenomena — the mass appeal of newspapers and technical development — because the one fuelled the other. It was the offices of the London *Times*, not of some book-industry entrepreneur (though such existed) that installed in 1814 the first steam-driven press for commercial use. The book trade, generally untroubled by the need to produce long high-speed print runs, lagged comfortably behind by several decades. By 1816 press production on *The Times* accelerated from 250 to 900 perfected sheets an hour. It is difficult to overestimate the consequences of such growth: the high-circulation newspaper and a mass-reading public together represented an explosive information alliance. A repository of current events and organ of opinions, the newspaper's regular punctuation of the working week and its centralizing overview formatted its readership, for good or ill, as a collective consciousness; both were the direct consequence of steam-power. The last twenty years have seen similar momentous technological and distributive change, and equally momentous shifts in how we relate to news. Change began in the 1980s with the move to an almost totally electronic workflow, in which production processes — from submission of copy, editing and typesetting, to page composition — were streamlined. Though constituting a major high-cost investment, this switch was practically invisible to the readership because the final product was still a printed paper. But electronic production meant that the industry was poised to move relatively rapidly into electronic delivery of various kinds; for example, e-papers are derived from the same files as those for the printed paper. The whole point of a paper, especially a daily, is that it reacts fast to news and new developments; it stays ahead of the competition or its sales wither. The pursuit of the scoop, the exclusive interview, the fastest breaking news are all aimed at outwitting rival papers, stimulating the readership and keeping circulation up, generating advertising revenue, and making money. If one paper implements a new feature, others soon follow. But currently the fear is that the Internet is changing reading and communication habits, and with them newspaper production and consumption, beyond all recognition, to the point where some fear newspapers as printed products may soon be a thing of the past.

The developed world has seen a slow but steady decline in printed newspaper production in the last ten years, though over the same time span some countries in the developing world have experienced an equivalent upsurge. Declining circulation is not the consequence of a diminished hunger for news but of a rapid increase in different sources of news, in particular online sources, and in the availability of portable devices, such as mobile phones, to which news can be delivered directly. The driving factor for these recent developments is the Internet: the pervasiveness of broadband connections, the increased capacity of processors, and improving quality of screens on desktop and mobile devices mean that the Internet is fast becoming the medium of choice for news and information. Some of this news and information is supplied by the traditional public and commercial broadcasting and publishing organizations, which have diversified their operations and established an online presence, but the new technologies have also ushered in a huge increase in alternative providers. There is a predictable demographic division in this narrative of changing news access, with younger age groups turning to the Internet more regularly for news than older.

The key to the health or otherwise of newspapers is of course economics; they are hugely profitable and many fortunes have been built in newspaper publishing over the last 200 years. They are also hugely expensive enterprises. Indeed, the cost of newsprint is so high that the cover price does not even pay for the paper the news is printed on. Content, journalism, analysis, comment, etc, are all funded from advertising revenues; if these revenues decline, corners must be cut. Since the mid-1990s and the early days of the Web, most major national newspapers throughout the world have established a serious online presence, delivering a version of the daily paper together with other enhancements such as audio versions, blogs, and premium content for subscribers. Initially, such web sites acted as little more than trailers for print. For example, the WayBackMachine, the Internet Archive's access point for archived web sites,[2] has a version of *The Guardian* newspaper's web site from 5 November 1996, referred to as 'a jumping off point for Guardian web projects'. The interface is plain, and the content a greatly curtailed version of the paper. *The Guardian* launched its full news site, *Guardian Unlimited*, three years later in 1999, by which time it had developed from a print 'taster' into a digital repurposing of the print object; far more extensive than its 1996 e-presence, it incorporated, for instance, a 'Breaking news' facility updated throughout the day. By 2003/2004, *Guardian Unlimited* was Britain's second most visited news site, after the BBC. Its print newspaper, a serious, left-of-centre broadsheet, then had a circulation under 400,000, but *Guardian Unlimited* had 7.5 million unique visitors per month, 2 million of those from overseas; it now reaches 12 million readers each month.

---

2   The Internet Archive http://www.archive.org [accessed 8/10/2007].

Online sites are highly successful, clearly achieving the market penetration (for advertisers) and user satisfaction (for readers) they seek. They are largely free to readers and these days most do not even require registration. Revenue comes, as it long has with printed news, from advertising (with such massive hit rates they are hugely attractive display cases) and from charging for premium services like the daily crossword. In the case of *Guardian Unlimited,* readers can also opt for an ad-free site for only £20 per year. The impetus for creating a strong online presence for newspapers is partly visibility and partly falling print sales, especially during the working week. In common with other newspapers, *The Guardian* and its Sunday sibling, *The Observer,* see an upturn in paper sales for weekend editions, when readers have more leisure to peruse comment, analysis, reviews, and all the other supplementary materials.

How do we classify online versions of newspapers? They share visual features with the printed product — banner and layout — though contrary to print, they all use sanserif typefaces. But they also share visual and structural characteristics with news sites that do not have a print counterpart: BBC, CNN, Fox News, Yahoo News, for example. They are hybrids, clearly related to their parent printed publications but because material is not bounded by the confines of the physical page, whether broadsheet or tabloid, stories can be longer; in some cases items are published online when space constraints dictate they do not make it into the print paper. Conversely, if the information supplied by online news sources may be 'unlimited', only a fraction of it is visible; by contrast, a five-minute scan of the whole edition of the print version can give a good overview of what is available. Once the workflow was electronic and text for newspapers was marked up in some form of SGML[3] (originally for print purposes) it could be directed down two different channels with little extra cost in terms of finance or time. The next step is a decoupling of print and online versions: they are clearly related products, share the same copy and similar design, but they are not two manifestations of the same thing. Unlike print, online news can be updated throughout the day, so it begins to be a news site, not a newspaper. Another way to think about the relationship might be to invoke the 'Stop Press' column, that small section once a regular feature of twentieth-century newspapers, by convention reserved on the front page of a paper issue for very late or breaking news items.

---

3   SGML, or Standard Generalized Markup Language, is a standard for how to specify a document markup language (which indicates a document's structure and other attributes).

Though now discarded from print, what online papers permit is the burgeoning of 'Stop Press' into a leading characteristic of news delivery and a further refinement of the underlying principle that news is information with a time stamp.

Besides offering an online edition of a newspaper, a large number of titles now also offer 'e-papers', also called 'digital papers' or 'smart editions'. These are surrogate newspapers with all the presentational features of print, but available online for viewing or printing. Full pages are displayed in single- or double-page view, and individual features can be magnified (zoomed) for reading. All the various supplements and magazines are available as with the printed version, and a number of e-tools are provided — searching, bookmarking, and 'smart' navigation. But this digital paper is (largely) identical to its paper form, costs more for access to the same information, and is not updated as regularly as online news. It is difficult to know what to make of e-papers. Do they represent a failure of confidence, a temporary blip in digital progress? They purposefully recouple what online delivery decouples – digital and paper characteristics – and from the technological point of view they make little sense. But they do make limited economic sense in terms of an overseas market anxious to replicate some of the comforts of paper while avoiding the freightage costs of the real thing. British daily newspapers cost around three euros throughout Europe, and weekend newspapers up to five euros, but a one-off payment of £1.50 (at the time of writing, around 2.20 euros) will give 24-hours of electronic access to the last thirteen issues of *The Guardian* and the last four issues of *The Observer*. Thus British e-papers are currently targeted at an expatriate rather than a home audience. *The Guardian* group, for example, states:

> Now you can read the Guardian and the Observer anywhere in the world, just as we do in the UK. Page by page. Picture by picture. Exactly as it appears in print.[4]

What the e-paper claims to offer is a newspaper reading experience as close as possible to that of a print edition from a traditional source; what it does not offer is up-to-the minute electronic currency, as generally only one edition is available per day.

The difference between an online newspaper and an e-paper seems to be the degree to which the one publication is customized to the latitude of the online environment and the other simulates the print object. The two

---

4 http://www.guardian.co.uk/digitaledition/subscribe [accessed 8/10/2007].

e-forms represent an uneasy accommodation — to the old technology, to the new, and to each other. E-papers are a back-formation, *after* the development of online news sites, and represent, however bizarrely given their electronic delivery, a nostalgia for paper and print. David Crow, writing in *The Business*, suggests that:

> while newspaper websites are constantly improving, some customers dislike viewing content online and miss the feel and design of the printed product (Crow 2007).

With this particular print object, the familiar formula may be as valuable as the content it carries; or as Harold Evans, a former editor of *The Sunday Times* and *The Times*, pointed out in his 1973 book *Newspaper Design*, 'the design cannot be separated from the product. The format, the typography and the printing are as integral a part of a newspaper as the words' (McKitterick 2002: 7). This is a point worth dwelling on: much of any newspaper's significance or message has long been acknowledged to lie in its form; form has always played a constitutive role in structuring content and guiding the reader's interpretation. We need only think of paper size (tabloid or broadsheet), the ordering and layout of an article on the page, the mix of font sizes, width of columns, and the interposition of photographs in the text block, to realize how rich in connotation such visual signals are — far richer and far louder than the visual signals incorporated in other common print objects, like novels, for instance.[5] To confuse things further, some online newspapers now offer a print version as a kind of crossover between the two digital formats, giving readers the chance to print off a PDF of a section with stories updated all day. *The Guardian*, for example, announces the G24 service with the invitation 'Print your own PDF'.[6] There are five PDFs to choose from: Top stories, World, Media, Business, and Sport. *The Daily Telegraph*, whose stated aim is the creation of a 'digital universe, without distinction between print, podcast or pdf' produced *TelegraphPM* (described as 'your multimedia afternoon newspaper') in September 2006. It was made available at 4.00pm and updated at 5.30pm, and offered a 10-page digest to be downloaded as a PDF; the reader was encouraged to, 'Read it on screen or print it out to read on the way home.' This was discontinued as a daily service in January 2008.

These examples would seem to indicate that, just as early printed books simulated features of manuscript copies, in moving from a print to an

---

5 For a recent example, see the comments accompanying *The Guardian*'s redesign in 2005 in Berliner format, http://www.guardian.co.uk/theguardian/0,16390,1552451,00.html [accessed 8/10/2007].

6 http://www.guardian.co.uk/g24 [accessed 8/3/2010].

online world we too are reluctant to lose functions familiar to us from the older technology, even though in this case the shift is larger, and the fit between the old and new technologies less evident. News publishers, traditionally in the vanguard of print developments, may be taking advantage of new possibilities, but they are also hedging their bets. This is particularly true when it comes to evaluating the look of a site in relation to its functionality: should online news sites look like web sites or like print papers? Which will ultimately have the greater appeal to the customer? How do we assess the intermediate forms, which mimic closely the printed object onscreen, in some cases even trying to reproduce the experience of analogue interaction by offering a 3-D-like appearance of the 'original' with facilities such as page-turning. Anyone using digital page-turning devices will soon find that they do not perform well in moving from one part of a digital text to another; false imports, intended to make us feel comfortable in the new environment, they actually impede our naturalization within it. By contrast, in the digitization of historic newspapers, a close simulacrum of the printed paper is a huge advantage to a sense of the real value of the object in its social and cultural time.

If in newspaper publishing we are currently witnessing a gradual decoupling of news from paper and print, with hybrid signs of both experiment and formal nostalgia along the way, there is an undeniable significant collateral benefit of electronic technology — aggregation. To achieve economies of scale in the digitization of news, the same underlying software is used to present, in aggregation, all the titles licensed by a single supplier. NewsPaperDirect, a key supplier, has created an integrated solution to the availability of newspapers for worldwide access. The company offers (as of April 2008) 650 newspapers from 77 countries in 37 languages, including many of the world's most-read dailies and weeklies, in the form of e-papers or printed papers through a print-on-demand service and using a browser called PressDisplay which claims to be 'redefining the reading experience'. This has increased from 470 titles in just a year. The front page of PressDisplay can be customized in a variety of ways to operate across a number of titles or chosen subsets of titles simultaneously, allowing the user to personalize the view of any particular paper and make comparisons across a range of publications, by title, country, language, or author. This means that several news titles can be cross-searched from one screen and search hits from different titles can be merged and listed together in order of relevance rather than by individual title. The benefit to the reader is in comparative searching of different versions of the same news item. Since searching and the list of hits is usually free, the benefit to the papers themselves or to the aggregators is collateral in as much as it leads people to more content that they will then spend money on. The sites make their money through recoupling, that is, print on demand of individual issues. By contrast, one of the disadvantages of many individual online news offerings is the disaggregated or 'silo' approach to information, in which it is possible to burrow deep into one resource, but difficult to move across to another and look at the same topic from a different perspective. (But see below the discussion on RSS feeds and personalization of news for further exploration of these issues).

Over five hundred years, the textual desires of literate societies have taken shape as print. We are now transferring what seems to us best about print into the digital realm and the online environment, at the same time as we are learning to accommodate the new things we believe the new technologies do best. There is a view that technology is something that does not work yet; or, put another way, nobody recognizes as technology those devices we take for granted, like books, alphabets, wheels. Current computer and communication technologies offer storage and retrieval, searchability and interconnectedness; but the price we pay is an expensive, cumbersome, and unreliable machine interposed between reader/writer and text. Print offers portability and cheapness, as well as a seemingly 'direct' experience. There are still, and there may always be, some things that paper does best: the access mechanism of the codex book in the hands of an experienced reader, for instance, can offer faster retrieval of known information than a computer. In the case of newspapers, the page is a highly sophisticated and evolved piece of design, offering fitness of purpose as well as ease of use. The screen-page assembled for paper printing does not yet work as well; on the other hand, a great deal of ingenuity and expensive software development have gone some way towards producing digital solutions which are surprisingly successful for both current and historic newspapers. Where e-papers score over online papers is in their translation into something just like the day's newspaper; where online papers excel is in their currency. Online news can be updated as the day goes on and as a story breaks, and it is interactive: through blogs and comment forms, readers can have their say and engage in a dialogue with journalists and other readers. The difference in e-papers and online papers actually comes down to how each handles the logical units that make up a complex textual object like a newspaper. These logical units are articles, ads, pictures, etc., which are mapped onto physical structures such as pages or pixels. When the page is the physical structure, this has a fixity that the pixel lacks, being an electrical phenomenon. In the case of e-papers, the fixed page composition is a delivery decision, not a physical necessity. With online papers, the logical units are delivered in ways that suit the electronic medium, though they may continue to share some design features with their paper or paper-like siblings: type design, banner, etc. The advantage of the logical unit unbound from a page is that it can be delivered in different ways to different devices (including paper). The reader can opt to personalize the news and have it delivered to computer screen, mobile phone, MP3 player, and other handheld devices. Currently, the disadvantage of the unbound pixellated news unit is the doubtful status of the long-term reliability and preservation of its information, given the frequency with which that information is updated. What, in this new world is the paper of record? Probably the printed paper still.

2. New Forms, Ideas and Functions of News

While strategies for decoupling and recoupling content from and to a paper vehicle still shape many of the ways in which we interact with news, there are other areas where the formal properties and the idea of paper have disappeared completely, and where news is genuinely paperless. Google News, for example, currently aggregates 4,500 news sources in English (of many different kinds) for searching or browsing, with a front page which can be customized according to interest. Google News is also available in other languages, including all the major European languages, Arabic, Hebrew, Chinese, Japanese, and Korean, where several thousand more news sources are aggregated. The news in all languages is updated continuously, and is computer-generated from these thousands of sources. Google News groups similar stories together displaying them according to each reader's personalized interests; links are offered to several versions of every story, permitting the reader to choose by topic and version of topic. Articles are selected and ranked by computers which evaluate, among other things, how often and on what sites a story appears online. As a result, Google claims that news stories are sorted without regard to political viewpoint or ideology. If the claim appears disingenuous — there can, after all, be no such thing as a neutral perspective on news; the choice of sources to search itself determines a viewpoint — Google's declared neutrality is particularly ironic in light of the agreement they reached to help the communist government in China block access to websites containing politically sensitive content (i.e. references to the Tiananmen Square massacre and criticism of the politburo) (Watts 2006) — a move which Google later admitted had caused the company's reputation damage in the United States and Europe (Martinson 2007).

Where Google makes a parade of its aggregated non-bias, there are highly influential paperless sites which are openly and vehemently partisan and politically-driven. The Drudge Report began as an email newsletter and has, since its inception in 1994, become one of the most powerful media influences in American politics. The plain and functional website, drudgereport.com, has received an estimated four billion hits in the last twelve months and is regarded by many as the first port of call for breaking news. Matt Drudge and his army of informants trawl television and the Internet for rumours and stories which are posted as headlines on the site. Mostly, these are direct links to traditional news sites, though Drudge sometimes writes the stories himself: in 1998 he was the first to break news about Monica Lewinsky, and in 2008 broke the news that the UK's Prince Harry was on the front line with troops in Afghanistan. According to Naughton (2006), many of his critics, especially those on the left, 'view his reportage as biased towards conservatives, careless, malicious and frequently prone to error'; but also, he has been hailed (by Camille Paglia) as 'the kind of bold, entrepreneurial, free-wheeling, information-oriented outsider we need more of in this country [USA]' (quoted in Naughton 2006). Whatever one's view, Drudge's importance in the American news arena is undisputed.

Salon.com is an influential and successful online-only news magazine, describing itself as a 'smart tabloid'. It prides itself on its provision of original, professional-standard media content over the Internet. Started by journalists in San Francisco in 1995, it had its origins in a newspaper strike:

> When the San Francisco Examiner was shut for a couple of weeks in 1994 a few of its journalists taught themselves HTML and had a go at doing a newspaper with new technology. They found the experience liberating, and David Talbot, the Examiner's arts editor, subsequently gave up his job and launched the kind of online paper he had always wanted to work for (Naughton 2006).

Salon attracts contributions from a wide range of well-known American writers and journalists, including Camille Paglia and Arianna Huffington.

Its name, borrowing associations from the regulated intellectual and conversational space of French Enlightenment salon society, reflects its policy of linking professional contributors with readers; and Salon has established two extensive discussion board communities, available only to subscribers: Salon Table Talk and The WELL. Since 2005, comments on editorial stories are open to all readers. The publication is strong on news and opinion, and claims to feature:

> some of the most in-depth and hard-hitting political coverage found anywhere, as well as breaking news, investigative journalism and commentary, and interviews with newsmakers, politicians and pundits. The War Room is updated throughout the day with breaking news.[7]

Salon is popular and successful, but without major commercial sponsors has always had a precarious financial basis.

Salon is a good halfway point between different modes of publication and aggregation in the mainline news industry, and less conventional publications available only online. There are other sites with the specific brief of reporting news outside the mainstream. One such is OhmyNews International, which has the tagline: All The News That's Fit to Share With You.[8] Founded in South Korea in 2000 'after decades of authoritarian rule had left the South Korean media deeply co-opted' (Grossman 2006), and initially available only in Korean, OhmyNews is 'Part blog, part professional news agency' and 'gets up to 70% of its copy from some 38,000 'citizen reporters' [...] basically anyone with a story and a laptop to write it on' (McIntyre 2005). An English language version was launched in 2004, and OhmyNews now claims to have, besides its army of Korean reporters, 1,300 citizen reporters in over 100 countries outside Korea. It also has around twenty 'featured writers', information professionals and free-lancers, contributing quality content on a regular basis. OhmyNews publishes about 150 stories and gets one to one-and-a-half million page hits a day. Contributions are edited and fact-checked by professional editors to filter out inaccuracies and potentially libellous claims. If a contribution is deemed extra-newsworthy, the editors give it a higher billing and a token $20 fee. OhmyNews is now one of Korea's most powerful media outlets, credited with influencing the outcome of the last Korean presidential election (McIntyre 2005).

As a concept, citizen journalism (sometimes also known as participatory journalism, grassroots journalism or public journalism) is difficult to define.

---

7   http://www.salon.com/press/fact/ [accessed 8/10/2007, 08.50 GMT].
8   *OhMyNews International* http://english.ohmynews.com [accessed 8/10/2007].

The boundary with professional journalism can be fuzzy, but it seems to marry the role of reader and writer in the news arena. In Korea, citizen journalism is a response to a deeply compromised professional media sector; it works less well where the mainstream product is trusted. Audience participation in mainline news media has, in the analogue world, hitherto been limited by the technology to readers', listeners' or viewers' letters, and radio and television phone-ins. On the Internet, the technical barriers and costs of making available material contributed by the public are slight, and people's desire to participate is considerable, so blogs and reader comment facilities attached to news sites are well used. This is not journalism, but once the boundaries between news and opinion producer, and consumer become less fixed, the parameters of what is and is not journalism change. A general feature of paperless news is the erosion of the paper-based notion of an expert editorial team selecting and directing news and opinion to readerships whose identities are, in some senses, group-constituted by the paper they read. This model now comes under pressure from informed users who interact with sophisticated tools and services provided by news suppliers (which may be online papers or paperless aggregated systems) to generate, and on occasion to respond to and initiate, news as a more personally or locally tailored service. This is potentially a momentous shift in the newspaper's function — from mass collective identification to mass individuation.

The Fort Myers News-Press in Florida, owned by Gannett, the world's largest newspaper chain and owners of *USA Today*, is experimenting in the redefinition of newspapers in direct response to lost readership and revenue to the Internet and other new media. Their solution is radical: 'the chain's papers are redirecting their newsrooms to focus on the Web first, paper second. Papers are slashing national and foreign coverage and beefing up 'hyper-local,' street-by-street news.' (Ahrens 2006). This news is provided by mobile journalists, or mojos, out on the streets every day looking for local stories, backed up by dozens of 'reader experts' who review documents and data on local issues and produce reports. Gannett has coined the term 'crowdsourcing' to describe this kind of outsourced journalism. This initiative is actually a return to an earlier mode of journalism, dying out because it was too labour-intensive and costly: by enlisting amateur, and therefore cheaper, assistance news publishers are effectively reinstating the local roving reporter.

The greatest costs in running a news source are editorial. Serious, in-depth, investigative journalism and professional editing do not come cheap, and many publications have been cutting their editorial costs as revenues decline. As Andrew Marr pointed out, in an article in which a number of media professionals gave their views on the future of news, there is a huge increase in the sources of news, but most of the actual information is recycled; there is not much more new reporting:

> Although there's an enormous amount of online news-related material, if you analyse it, very, very little is actually new fact, new information - it's almost all parasitic journalism carried out either by broadcasters or newspapers [...] what you have not got, obviously, is a new source of original proper journalism, because that costs money and someone has to pay for it (quoted in Burrell 2006).

According to *The Economist,* the decline in 'proper' journalism is a consequence of dwindling newspaper revenues in the face of stiff competition from the new media. Its current policy is to take a middle view on citizen journalism: it welcomes the opening up of 'the closed world of professional editors and reporters to anyone with a keyboard and an internet connection' and cites a number of cases where bloggers and citizen journalists have called attention to critical issues; but it argues that for 'hard news' reporting, as opposed to comment, their contribution is limited (Leader, *The Economist,* 2006[9]). Citizen journalists are outside the mainstream and often untrained, but sites like OhmyNews have shown that if you use professional editors and writers as well, their contributions can be valuable. Where problems arise is when the use of non-professionals is seen by the paymasters of the mainstream media as a way to save money or, by new entrepreneurs as the way to set up a lucrative business without investing in skill. Robert Niles, editor *of Online Journalism Review,* comments scathingly:

> Perhaps this frenzy to create a 'reporterless' news publication is simply the logical extension of the disdain that many in news management have had for employing actual journalists over past decades. It's the ultimate Wall Street fantasy — a newspaper without reporters (Niles 2007a).

Niles is not averse to the use of grassroots contribution to news publications, just to the lack of any professional journalistic or editorial leadership in such enterprises (Niles 2007a). Professional journalists themselves are concerned about the incursion of the amateur into their realm, and one can understand why: surgeons would be worried if members of the public with the skill to apply a band-aid or administer an aspirin decided they would like to carry out operations. Just because people can use a keyboard and

---

[9] Leader comment, 'Who Killed the Newspaper', *The Economist,* 24 August 2006.

have an opinion does not give them journalism skills, though when they carry a camera phone and are in the right place at the right time, it can make them news photographers: the terrorist attacks on the London transport system on 7 July 2005 were captured visually by hordes of bystanders on camera phones and used extensively by the media. In a July 2005 posting on his 'Complete Tosh' blog, Neil McFarlane, head of editorial development at *Guardian Unlimited*, has suggested that we stop using the term 'citizen journalist' and instead refer to such contributions as 'citizen *storytelling*'. For Macfarlane, the desired aim is not a society with "citizen journalists' overthrowing the professionals', but an integrated ecology of news reporting in which 'countless individual stories [are] told, and then highlighted when they happen to touch on a matter of mainstream interest.' For Robert Niles, this integrated ecology is actually a benefit for the mainstream, with readers and writers, professional and amateur, joined together in a news enterprise:

> 'Citizen journalism' provides professional reporters the chance to collect many more data points than they can on their own. And 'mainstream media' provide readers an established, popular distribution channel for the information we have and can collect. Not to mention a century of wisdom on sourcing, avoiding libel and narrative storytelling technique. And our readers don't care. They just want the most complete, accurate and engaging coverage possible. They don't know how we make the sausage, or even who makes it. They just want to eat (Niles 2007b).

3. Scale and Fine-tuning

The paperless, unbounded availability of vast and diverse news sources seems like a benefit to a world constantly hungry for news; but how do we cope with the volume? If we have seen everything we can find on a topic, are we well-informed? And how much is everything? One answer to dealing with the flood is personalization: choosing only the sources or parts of sources that seem to match our interests. Either we can choose for ourselves what news we want to receive from whom, or regularly visited sites might learn our preferences from our behaviour and cater for us up front, much in the way that book sites like Amazon give us recommendations based on our past purchases. If we want to personalize our online news sources, we might set up RSS feeds permitting the user to collate and access a constantly updating stream of material from a web browser; or we might create a Google personalized page integrating various news feeds with useful tools, including calendars and calculators. RSS is the acronym for 'Really Simple Syndication', and establishing an RSS feed involves downloading a small program to a browser and then choosing the feeds. As described by *The Times*, 'It's like having a very efficient butler who cuts out the headlines of your favourite newspaper and serves them to you on a tray'.[10] This could be the answer to controlling the volume, but what do we gain and what do we lose from this kind of targeted approach? We can receive information that matches our interests closely, but where we gain in precision, we lose in range: the degree of serendipity which may save each of us from tunnel vision. The beauty of a traditional paper newspaper is the opportunity to find out about things we did not know we were interested in. The seemingly random page layout is in fact well composed, with a balance of large and small items, images, and advertisements, and the opportunity for radial reading described by Jerome McGann as 'the most advanced, the most difficult, and the most important form of reading because radial reading alone puts one in a position to respond actively to the text's own (often secret) discursive acts' (McGann 1991: 116, 122). Lateral reading across, or constantly updated reading within, a space tailored to our individual tastes does not equate to this. And yet, the interesting thing is that such reader refinement or second-guessing has long characterized the kind of highly commodified text that newspapers represent in the alliances they forge between disparate items. Throughout modern history, the newspaper one read offered a shorthand expression of one's political colour, social standing and taste. Miscellaneous digests of news and opinion, newspapers have long informed (shaped) our collective and individual consciousnesses. The instant expertise, based on the tactical deployment of the telling allusion, fact or statistic, which in so many areas is a promise of the sophisticated resources of an online world, was always implied in the newspaper's model of knowledge transfer. Similarly, recent developments in e-text distribution, like Google's selling of contextual advertising space wrapped around other people's content, now extended to the marketing and distribution of e-books, are a direct development from newspaper economics. What has changed is the scale and the fine-tuning of the newspaper's functions as its economies and its implied reading culture shift from paper to screen and as its conceptual model sets a standard for the electronic delivery of other textual forms than those associated with the news.

---

10 'Times Online RSS Feeds', *Times Online*, http://www.timesonline.co.uk/tol/audio_video/rss/ [accessed 8/10/2007].

References

Aarseth, Espen J. 1997. *Cybertext: Perspectives on Ergodic Literature*. Baltimore: Johns Hopkins University Press.

Andrén, Anders. 1998. *Between Artifacts and Texts: Historical Archaeology in Global Perspective*. Contributions To Global Historical Archaeology. Trans. Alan Crozier. New York: Plenum Press.

Anon. 1911. 'The New York Public Library: How the Readers and the Books Are Distributed in the New Building'. *Scientific American* 104.21 (27 May): 527.

Anon. 1971. 'Keepers of Rules Versus Players of Roles'. Rev. of *The Impact of Computers on Organizations* by Thomas I. Whistler, and *The Computerized Society* by James Martin and Adrian R. D. Norman. *Times Literary Supplement* 21.5: 585.

Appiah, K. Anthony. 2005. 'Humane, All Too Humane'. *Profession 2005*. New York: Modern Language Association.

Baddeley, Alan. 1986. *Working Memory*. Oxford: Clarendon Press.

— 2000. 'The Episodic Buffer: A New Component of Working Memory?' *Trends in Cognitive Science* 4.11: 417-23.

— 2003. 'Working Memory and Language: An Overview'. *Journal of Communication Disorders* 36.3: 189-203.

— 2004. *Your Memory: A User's Guide*. Buffalo: Firefly Books.

Barber, Karin. 2007. *The Anthropology of Texts, Persons, and Publics: Oral and Written Culture in Africa and Beyond*. Cambridge: Cambridge University Press.

Barthes, Roland. 1986. 'The "Death" of the Author'. In *The Rustle of Language*, trans. Richard Howard. 49-55. New York: Hill and Wang.

Bateson, Gregory. 2002. *Mind and Nature: A Necessary Unity*. Cresskill NJ: Hampton Press.

Bayley, J. 1999. *Iris: A Memoir of Iris Murdoch*. London: Harper Collins.

Bellow, Saul. 2006. 'The Art of Fiction', interviewed by Gordon Lloyd Harper, *The Paris Review Interviews*, I, intro. by Philip Gourevitch. New York: Picador.

Bender, Todd. 1973. 'Computer Assisted Editorial Work on Conrad'. *Conradiana*, 5/3: 37-45.

— 1976a. 'Computational Bibliography'. In *The Computer in Literary and Linguistic Studies. Proceedings of the Third International Symposium*, ed. Alan Jones and R.F. Churchhouse. 329-37. Cardiff: The University of Wales Press.

— 1976b. 'Literary Texts in Electronic Storage: The Editorial Potential'. *Computers and the Humanities* 10.4: 193-99.

Bernard, Claude. 1865. *An Introduction to the Study of Experimental Medicine*. Trans. Henry Copley Greene. New York: Dover, 1957.

Berrie, P., G. Barwell, C. Tiffin and P. Eggert. 2003. 'Authenticated Electronic Editions Project'. In Cole and Craig 2003: 114-22.

— P. Eggert, G. Barwell and T. Tiffin. 2006. 'Authenticating Electronic Editions'. In Burnard, O'Brien O'Keeffe and Unsworth 2006: 436-38.

Bird, Helen, Matthew A. Lambon Ralph, Karalyn Patterson, John R. Hodges. 2000. 'The Rise and Fall of Frequency and Imageability: Noun and Verb Production in Semantic Dementia'. *Brain and Language* 73.1 17-49.

Bjelland, Karen. 2000. 'The Editor as Theologian, Historian, and Archaeologist: Shifting Paradigms within Editorial Theory and their Sociocultural Ramifications'. *Analytical and Enumerative Bibliography* 11.1: 1-43.

Blake, Norman and Peter Robinson. 2000. 'The General Prologue on CD-ROM (2000): General Editors' Preface'. In *The General Prologue of The Canterbury Tales on CD-ROM*, ed. Elisabeth Solopova. Cambridge: Cambridge University Press. www.canterburytalesproject.org/pubs/GPGenEdintro.html [accessed 8 February 2010].

Blayney, Peter, ed. 1996. *The Norton Facsimile: The First Folio of Shakespeare*. 2nd edn. New York: W.W. Norton.

Bliss, T.V. and T. Lomo. 2006. 'Long-lasting Potentiation of Synaptic Transmission in the Dentate Area of the Anaesthetized Rabbit Following Stimulation of the Perforant Path'. *Journal of Physiology* 232: 331-56.

Bowers, Fredson. 1969. 'Practical Texts and Definitive Editions'. In *Two Lectures in Editing: Shakespeare and Hawthorne*, ed. Charlton Hinman and Fredson Bowers. 21-70. Columbus OH: Ohio State University Press.

Bringhurst, Robert. 2006. 'The Voice in the Mirror'. In *The Tree of Meaning: Thirteen Talks* (Kentville, NS: Gaspereau Press). 107-38.

Brothman, Brien. 1999. 'Declining Derrida: Integrity, Tensegrity, and the Preservation of Archives from Deconstruction'. *Archivaria* 48: 64-88.

Brown, John. 1958. 'Some Tests of the Decay Theory of Immediate Memory'. *Quarterly Journal of Experimental Psychology* 10: 12-21.

Brown, Matthew P. 2004. 'Book History, Sexy Knowledge, and the Challenge of the New Boredom'. *American Literary History* 16.4: 688-706.

Brown, Susan et al. 2006. 'Between Markup and Delivery; or, Tomorrow's Electronic Texts Today'. In *Mind Technologies: Humanities Computing and the Canadian Academic Community*, ed. Raymond Siemens and David Moorman. 15-31. Calgary, Alberta: University of Calgary Press.

Burnard, Lou. 1992. 'Tools and Techniques for Computer-assisted Text Processing'. In *Computers and Written Texts*, ed. Christopher S. Butler. 1-28. Oxford: Blackwell.

Burnard, Lou, Katherine O'Brien O'Keeffe and John Unsworth, eds. 2006. *Electronic Textual Editing*. New York: Modern Language Association.

Burrows John. 2002. '"Delta:" A Measure of Stylistic Difference and a Guide to Likely Authorship,' *Literary and Linguistic Computing* 17: 267-86.

— 2003. 'Questions of Authorship: Attribution and Beyond.' *Computers and the Humanities* 37: 1-26.

— 2007. 'All the Way Through: Testing for Authorship in Different Frequency Strata'. *Literary and Linguistic Computing* 22: 27-47.

— and Anthony J. Hassall. 2006. 'Sarah and Henry Fielding and the Authorship of The History of Ophelia'. *Script and Print* 30: 69-102.

Burrows, Toby. 1997. 'Toward a Typology of the Electronic Text.' Paper presented at the Conference of the Bibliographical Society of Australia and New Zealand, Perth, October 1997 docker.library.uwa.edu.au/~tburrows/bibsocpaper.html [accessed 19 January 2009].

Busa, R., S. J. 1976. 'Guest Editorial: Why Can a Computer Do So Little?' *Bulletin of the Association for Literary and Linguistic Computing* 4.1: 1-3.

Buzzetti, Dino. 1996. 'Digital Editions: Variant Readings and Interpretations'. In *ALLC-ACH '96 Abstracts. University of Bergen June 25-29 1996*. 254-56. Bergen: University of Bergen.

Caldwell, T. Price. 1989. 'Molecular Sememics: A Progress Report'. *Meisei Review* 4: 65-86.

— 2000. *Meisei Review* 15: 155-62.

— 2002. 'Topic-Comment Effects in English' *Meisei Review* 17: 49-69.

— 2004. 'Whorf, Orwell, and Mentalese'. *Meisei Review* 19: 91-106.

— 2006. 'The Epistemologies of Linguistic Science: Reassessing Structuralism, Redefining the Sememe'. *Meisei Review* 21: 27-39.

Canterbury Tales Project. www.canterburytalesproject.org [accessed 8 February 2010].

Capurro, R. and B. Hjørland. 2002. 'The Concept of Information'. *Annual Review of Information Science and Technology* 37.1: 343-411.

Catach, Nina, ed. 1988. *Les éditions critiques. Problèmes techniques et éditoriaux.* Paris: Université de Besançon.

Cerquiglini, Bernard. 1999. *In Praise of the Variant: A Critical History of Philology*. Trans. Betsy Wing. Baltimore: Johns Hopkins University Press.

Chesnutt, David R. 1991. 'Historical Editions in the States'. *Computers and the Humanities* 25.6: 377-80.

Chaucer, Geoffrey. 1400-1405. *Ellesmere Chaucer*. Huntingdon Library. www.huntington.org/huntingtonlibrary.aspx?id=6074&terms=chaucer [accessed 8 February 2010].

Chklovskii, D. B., B. W. Mel and K. Svoboda. 2004. 'Cortical Rewiring and Information Storage'. *Nature* 14.431 (October): 782-88.

Cole, C. and H. Craig, eds. 2003. *Computing Arts*. Sydney: University of Sydney and the Australian Academy of the Humanities.

Corpus of Middle English Prose and Verse, quod.lib.umich.edu/c/cme/ [accessed 8 February 2010].

Cowan, Nelson. 2000. 'The Magical Number 4 in Short-term Memory: A Reconsideration of Mental Storage Capacity'. *Behavioural and Brain Sciences* 24: 87-185.

Craig, Hugh. 2004. 'Stylistic Analysis and Authorship Studies.' In Schreibman, Siemens and Unsworth 2004: 273-88. Oxford: Blackwell.

Crane, Gregory. 2006. 'What Do You Do with a Million Books?'. *D-Lib Magazine,* 12.3. www.dlib.org/dlib/march06/crane/03crane.html [accessed 9 February 2010].

—, David Bamman and Alison Jones. 2007. 'ePhilology: When the Books Talk to Their Readers'. In Siemens and Schreibman 2007: 29-64.

Croft, P. J., ed. 1973. *Autograph Poetry in the English Language: Facsimiles or Original Manuscripts from the Fourteenth to the Twentieth Centuries*. London: Cassell.

Crowder, Robert G. and Richard K. Wagner. 1992. *The Psychology of Reading: An Introduction*. 2nd edn. New York: Oxford University Press.

Cummings, James. 2006. 'REED [the Records of Early English Drama Project] and the Possibilities of Web Technologies'. In *REED in Review: Essays in Celebration of the First Twenty-Five Years*, ed. Audrey Douglas and Sally-Beth MacLean. 178-99. Toronto: University of Toronto Press.

— 2007. 'The Text Encoding Initiative and the Study of Literature'. In Siemens and Schreibman 2007: 451-76.

Curio, Gabriel, Georg Neuloh, Jussi Numminen, Veikko Jousmäki and Riitta Hari. 2000. 'Speaking Modifies Voice-Evoked Activity in the Human Auditory Cortex'. *Human Brain Mapping* 9.4 (April): 183-91.

Dahlström, Mats. 2000. 'Drowning by Versions'. *Human IT* 4: 7-38.

— 2001. 'Trycket från trycket. Fixerade, mindre editioner eller mindre fixerade arkiv?'. In *Bok og Skjerm. Forholdet mellom bokbasert og digitalt basert tekstutgivelse*, ed. Jon Gunnar Jorgensen, Tone Modalsli, Espen S. Ore and Vigdis Ystad. 61-80. Oslo: Fagbokforlaget.

— 2004. 'How Reproductive is a Scholarly Edition?' *Literary and Linguistic Computing* 19.1: 17-33.

Damasio, Antonio R. 1994. *Descartes' Error: Emotion, Reason, and the Human Brain*. New York: Avon Books.

Davis, Tom. 1998. 'The Monsters and the Textual Critics'. *Textual Formations and Reformations*, ed. Laurie E. Maguire and Thomas L. Berger. 95-111. Newark NJ: University of Delaware Press.

Day, Ronald E. 2001. *The Modern Invention of Information: Discourse, History, Power*. Carbondale IL: Southern Illinois University Press.

Deegan, Marilyn and Peter Robinson. 1994. 'The Electronic Edition'. In *The Editing of Old English. Papers from the 1990 Manchester Conference*, ed. D.G. Scragg and Paul E. Szarmach. Cambridge: D. S. Brewer.

Deegan, Marilyn. 2006. 'Collection and Preservation of an Electronic Edition'. In Burnard, O'Keeffe and Unsworth 2006: 358-70. New York: Modern Language Association of America. www.tei-c.org/About/Archive_new/ETE/Preview/mcgovern.xml [accessed 8 February 2010].

Dening, Greg. 1998. *Readings/Writings*. Melbourne: Melbourne University Press.

DeRose, Steven J., David G. Durand, Elli Mylonas and Allen H. Renear. 1990. 'What is Text, Really?' *Journal of Computing in Higher Education* 1.2: 3-26.

Derrida, J. 1973. *Speech and Phenomena and Other Essays on Husserl's Theory of Signs*. Trans. David B. Allison. Evanston: Northwestern University Press.

di Franco, Ani. 2002. 'My IQ'. In *So Much Shouting / So Much Laughter*, disc 2. Buffalo NY: Righteous Babe Records.

Dillon, Andrew. 2004. *Designing Usable Electronic Text*. 2nd edn. Boca Raton FL: CRC Press.

Donaghy, M. 2001. *Brain's Diseases of the Nervous System*. 11th edn. Oxford: Oxford University Press.

Donald, Merlin. 1991. *Origins of the Modern Mind: Three Stages in the Evolution of Culture and Cognition*. Cambridge MA: Harvard University Press.

Edwards, Paul N. 1996. *The Closed World: Computers and the Politics of Discourse in Cold War America*. Inside Technology. Cambridge MA: MIT Press.

Eggert, Paul. 1990. Introduction to *The Boy in the Bush*, by D. H. Lawrence; ed. by M. L. Skinner. Cambridge: Cambridge University Press.

— 1994. 'Document and Text: The "Life" of the Literary Work and the Capacities of Editing'. *TEXT* 7: 1-24.

— 1998. 'The Work Unravelled'. *TEXT*, 11, 41-60.

— 2004. 'The Way of All Text: The Materialist Shakespeare'. In Modiano, Searle and Shillingsburg 2004: 155-68.

— 2005. 'Text-encoding, Theories of the Text, and the "Work-site"'. *Literary and Linguistic Computing* 20: 425-35.

— 2009. *Securing the Past: Conservation in Art, Architecture and Literature*. Cambridge: Cambridge University Press.

Engelbart, Douglas. 1962. *Augmenting Human Intellect: A Conceptual Framework*. Summary Report AFOSR-3233, Office of Scientific Research, U.S. Air Force. Menlo Park CA: Stanford Research Institute. www.dougengelbart.org/pubs/augment-3906.html [accessed 17 April 2009].

Erasmus, Desiderius. 1976/1514-6. *The Correspondence of Erasmus: Letters 298 to 445, 1514 to 1516*, ed. R.A.B. Mynors and D.F.S. Thomson. Collected Works of Erasmus, vol. 3. Toronto: University of Toronto Press.

Ericsson, K. Anders and Walter Kintsch. 1995. 'Long-term Working Memory'. *Psychological Review* 102.2: 211-45.

ESE. 1994. *ESE Discussion on Critical Editing and the Nature of an Electronic Archive*.

Espinel, C. H. 1996. 'De Kooning's Late Colours and Forms: Dementia, Creativity and the Healing Power of Art'. *Lancet* 347: 1096-98.

Evans, G. Blakemore, ed. 1974. 'Sir Thomas More: The Additions Ascribed to Shakespeare'. *The Riverside Shakespeare*. 1683-1700. Boston: Houghton Mifflin.

Faulhaber, Charles B. 1991. 'Textual Criticism in the 21st Century'. *Romance Philology* 45.1 (August): 123-48.

Federmeier, Kara D. and Marta Kutas. 1999. 'A Rose by any Other Name: Long-term Memory Structure and Sentence Processing'. *Journal of Memory and Language* 41.4 (November): 469-95.

Ferrer, Daniel. 1995. 'Hypertextual Representation of Literary Working Papers'. *Literary and Linguistic Computing* 10.2: 143-45.

Finkelstein, David and Alistair McCleery. 2006. *The Book History Reader*. 2nd edn. Abigdon UK: Routledge.

Finneran, Richard, ed. 1996. *The Literary Text in the Digital Age*. Ann Arbor: University of Michigan Press.

— and George Bornstein. 1994. 'Towards a Hypermedia Edition of the Poems of W. B. Yeats'. In *Résumés/Abstracts. Colloque international / International Conference Consensus ex Machina? Association for Literary and Linguistic Computing/Association for Computers and the Humanities*. Paris, 19-23 April 1994. 73-4. Paris: INaLF, CNRS/ENS.

Fish, Stanley. 1980. *Is There a Text in This Class? The Authority of Interpretive Communities*. Cambridge, MA: Harvard University Press.

— 1980/1973. 'What is Stylistics and Why Are They Saying Such Terrible Things About It?'. In Fish 1980: 68-96.

Flanders, Julia. 1998. 'Trusting the Electronic Edition'. *Computers and the Humanities* 31: 301-10.

— 2009. 'Data and Wisdom. Electronic Editing and the Quantification of Knowledge'. *Literary and Linguistic Computing* 24.1: 53-62.

Forsyth, Richard, David Holmes and Emily Tse. 1999. 'Cicero, Sigonio, and Burrows: Investigating the Authenticity of the *Consolatio*'. *Literary and Linguistic Computing* 14: 393.

Foucault, Michel. 1989/1969. 'What is an Author'. Trans. Josué Harari. In *The Critical Tradition*, ed. David H. Richter. 978-88. New York: St. Martin's Press.

Fraistat, N. and S. E. Jones. 2003. 'Immersive Textuality: The Editing of Virtual Spaces'. *TEXT* 15: 69-82.

Freud, Sigmund. 2002. *The Psychopathology of Everyday Life*. Trans. Anthea Bell. London: Penguin.

Gabler, Hans Walter, ed. 1984. *Ulysses: A Critical and Synoptic Edition*. New York: Garland Publishing.

— 1989. 'Naissance de lédition: de l'ordinateur comme sage-femme'. In *La Naissance du Texte*, ed. Louis Hay. 53-62. Paris: José Corti.

Gadamer, Hans-Georg. 1998. *Praise of Theory: Speeches and Essays*. Trans. Chris Dawson. New Haven CT: Yale University Press.

Galison, Peter. 1994. 'The Ontology of the Enemy: Norbert Wiener and the Cybernetic Vision'. *Critical Inquiry* 21.1 (Autumn): 228-66.

Gants, David L. 1994. 'Toward a Rationale of Electronic Textual Criticism'. Paper. ALLC/ACH Conference, Paris, 19 April 1994.

Garrard, Peter. 2005. 'The Effects of Very Early Alzheimer's Disease on the Characteristics of Writing by a Renowned Author'. *Brain* 128: 250-60.

— R. J. Perry and J. R. Hodges. 1997. 'Disorders of Semantic Memory'. *Journal of Neurology, Neurosurgery and Psychiatry* 62: 431-35.

— Ralph M. A. Lambon, K. Patterson and J. R. Hodges. 2005. 'Semantic Feature Knowledge and Picture Naming in Dementia of Alzheimer's Type: a New Approach'. *Brain and Language* 93: 79-94.

— L. M. Maloney, J. R. Hodges and K. Patterson. 2005. 'The Effects of Very Early Alzheimer's Disease on the Characteristics of Writing by a Renowned Author'. *Brain* 128.2: 250-60.

Genette, Gérard. 1982. *Palimpsestes: la littérature au second degré*. Paris: Seuil.

Geschwind, Norman. 1979. 'Specializations of the Human Brain'. *The Brain*. 108-17. A Scientific American Book. San Francisco: W. H. Freeman.

Given-Wilson, Chris, ed. 2005a. *The Parliament Rolls of Medieval England 1275-1504: PROME*. 16 Vols. Woodbridge, London: Boydell Press, National Archives.

— 2005b. *The Parliament Rolls of Medieval England 1275-1504: PROME*. Published on CD-ROM and Internet. Leicester: Scholarly Digital Editions.

Gleason, Jean Burko and Nan Bernstein Ratner, eds. 1998. *Psycholinguistics*. 2nd edn. Fort Worth: Harcourt Brace.

Gobet, Fernard and Gary Clarkson. 2004. 'Chunks in Expert Memory: Evidence for the Magical Number Four ... or is it Two?' *Memory* 12.6: 732-47.

Goodglass, H. 2001. *Boston Diagnostic Aphasia Examination: Stimulus Cards-Short Form*.

Graber, Stefan. 1998. *Der Autortext in der historisch-kritischen Ausgabe. Ansätze zu einer Theorie der Textkritik*. Bern: Peter Lang.

Grafton, Anthony. 2002. 'How Revolutionary Was the Print Revolution?'. *American Historical Review* 107.1: 84-87.

Greetham, David. 1991. '[Textual] Criticism and Deconstruction'. *Studies in Bibliography* 44: 1-30.

— 1999. *Theories of the Text*. London: Oxford University Press.

— 2007. 'Electronic Textual Editing' (Review of Barnard Lou, Katherine O'Brien O'Keefe, and John Unsworth, eds., *Electronic Textual Editing*, New York: Modern Language Association of America, 2006), *Textual Cultures* 2.2: 133-36.

Greg, W. W. 1950–51. 'The Rationale of Copy-Text'. *Studies in Bibliography* 3: 19-36.

— 1998/1932. 'Bibliography — An Apologia'. In *Sir Walter Wilson Greg: A Collection of His Writings*. Ed. Joseph Rosenblum. 135-57. Lanham MD: Scarecrow Press.

Groden, Michael. 1977-79 Gen. ed., and Hans Walter Gabler, David Hayman, A. Walton Litz, and Danis Rose eds. The James Joyce Archive. [Facsimile ed. of James Joyce's manuscripts] 63 vols. New York: Garland, 1978.

— 1998. 'Perplex in the Pen—and the Pixels: Reflections on the James Joyce Archive, Hans Walter Gabler's *Ulysses*, and 'James Joyce in Hypermedia'. *Journal of Modern Literature* 22.2 (Winter): 225-31.

Hacking, Ian. 1990. *The Taming of Chance*. Ideas in Context. Cambridge: Cambridge University Press.

Haddon M. 2003. *The Curious Incident of the Dog in the Night-time*. London: Jonathan Cape.

Hamming, R. W. 1980. 'The Unreasonable Effectiveness of Mathematics'. *American Mathematical Monthly* 87.2 (February): 81-90.

Hartsuiker, Robert J., Roelien Bastiaanse, Albert Postma and Frank Wijnen, eds. 2005. *Phonological Encoding and Monitoring in Normal and Pathological Speech*. Hove and New York: Psychology Press.

Hayles, N. Katherine. 1999. *How We Became Posthuman: Virtual Bodies in Cybernetics, Literature, and Informatics*. Chicago: University of Chicago Press.

— 2001. 'What Cybertext Theory Can't Do'. *Electronic Book Review*, posted 15 February 2001, modified 8 March 2003 at www.electronicbookreview.com [accessed 21 April 2004].

— 2002. *Writing Machines*. Cambridge, MA: MIT Press.

— 2003. 'Translating Media: Why We Should Rethink Textuality'. *Yale Journal of Criticism* 16: 263-90.

— 2004. 'Print is Flat, Code is Deep: The Importance of Media-Specific Analysis'. *Poetics Today* 25.1: 67-90.

— 2005. 'Translating Media'. In *My Mother Was a Computer: Digital Subjects and Literary Texts*. 89-116. Chicago: University of Chicago Press.

Hayward, N. 2006. 'Humanities Computing'. *Ecdotica* 3: 271-73.

Hearle, Noah. 2007. 'Sentence and Word Length'. http://hearle.nahoo.net/Academic/Maths/Sentence.html [accessed 9 February 2010].

Hebb, D.O. 2002/1949. *The Organisation of Behaviour: A Neuropsychological Theory*. Philadelphia PA: Lawrence Erlbaum Associates.

Hedstrom, Margaret. 2002. 'Archives, Memory, and Interfaces with the Past'. *Archival Science* 2: 21-43.

Hockey, Susan. 1996. 'Creating and Using Electronic Editions'. In Finneran 1996: 1-22.

— 2000. *Electronic Texts in the Humanities: Principles and Practice*. London: Oxford University Press.

Holmes, David. 1994. 'Authorship Attribution'. *Computers and the Humanities* 28: 87-106.

Hoover, David. 2004. 'Testing Burrows's "Delta"'. *Literary and Linguistic Computing* 19: 453-75.

— 2005. 'Hot-Air Textuality: Literature after Jerome McGann'. *Text and Technology* 14: 71-103.

— 2007. 'The End of the Irrelevant Text: Electronic Texts, Linguistics and Literary Theory'. *Digital Humanities Quarterly* 1.2. digitalhumanities. org/dhq/ [accessed 9 February 2010].

Huidobro, Vincente. 1925. 'El Creacionismo'. www.vicentehuidobro.uchile. cl/manifiesto1.htm [accessed 9 February 2010].

— 1925. *Manifestes: manifeste, manifest, manifes, manife, mani, man, ma, m.* Paris: Editions de la revue mondiale.

Huxley, Aldous. 1928. 'Introduction'. In *Printing of To-day: An Illustrated Survey of Post-war Typography in Europe and the United States*, by Oliver Simon and Julius Rodenberg. 1-15. London: Peter Davies.

James, Henry. 1976. *The American*. The version of 1877 revised in autograph and typescript for the New York Edition of 1907. Reproduced in facsimile from the original in the Houghton Library, Harvard University, with an introduction by Rodney G. Dennis. London, Scolar Press.

Johannessen, K. and T. Nordenstam. 1995. *Culture and Value: Philosophy and the Cultural Sciences*. Kirchberg am Wechsel: The Austrian Ludwig Wittgenstein Society.

Karlsson, Lina and Lina Malm. 2004. 'Revolution or Remediation? A Study of Electronic Scholarly Editions on the Web'. *Human IT* 7.1: 1-46. www. hb.se/bhs/ith/1-7/lklm.pdf [accessed 8 February 2010].

Kay, Martin. 1967. 'Standards for Encoding Data in a Natural Language'. *Computers and the Humanities* 1.5: 170-77.

Kellogg, Ronald T. 2004. 'Working Memory Components in Written Sentence Generation'. *The American Journal of Psychology* 117.3: 341-61.

Kincaid, J. Peter, Robert P. Fishburne, Jr., Richard L. Rogers and Brad S. Chissom. 1975. *Derivation of New Readability Formulas for Navy Enlisted Personnel*. Millington, TN: Chief of Naval Training.

Kintsch, Walter. 1998. *Comprehension: A Paradigm for Cognition*. Cambridge: Cambridge University Press.

Kirschenbaum, Matthew G. 2001. 'Materiality and Matter and Stuff: What Electronic Texts Are Made Of'. *Electronic Book Review*, posted 1 October 2001, modified 30 November 2003 at www.electronicbookreview.com [accessed 21 April 2004].

— 2002. 'Editing the Interface: Textual Studies and First Generation Electronic Objects'. *TEXT: An Interdisciplinary Annual of Textual Studies* 14: 15-51.

— 2004a. '"So the Colors Cover the Wires": Interface, Aesthetics and Usability'. In Schreibmann, Siemens and Unsworth 2004: 523-42.

— 2004b. 'Extreme Inscription: Towards a Grammatology of the Hard Drive'. *TEXT Technology* 13.2: 91-125.

— 2008. *Mechanisms: New Media and the Forensic Imagination*. Boston: MIT Press.

Lancashire, Ian. 1989. 'Working with Texts'. Paper. IBM Academic Computing Conference, Anaheim, 23 June [unpublished paper].

— 1996. 'Editing English Renaissance Electronic Texts'. In Finneran 1996: 117-43.

— 1999. 'Probing Shakespeare's Idiolect in *Troilus and Cressida* I.3.1-29'. *University of Toronto Quarterly* 68.3: 728-67.

— 2004a. 'Cognitive Stylistics and the Literary Imagination'. In Schreibman, Siemens and Unsworth 2004: 397-414. Oxford: Blackwell.

— 2004b. 'Cybertextuality'. *TEXT Technology* 2: 1-18

Lance, G.N., and W. T. Williams (1967), 'A General Theory of Classificatory Sorting Strategies, I. Hierarchical Systems,' *Computer Journal*, 9: 373-80

Lashley, Karl S. 1958. 'Cerebral Organization and Behavior in the Brain and Human Behavior'. *Proceedings of the Association for Research in Nervous and Mental Diseases* 36: 1-18.

Laslett, Peter. 1971/1965. *The World We Have Lost*. 2nd edn. London: Methuen.

Laufer, Roger. 1989. 'Edition critique synoptique sur écran: l'example des Maximes de La Rochefoucauld'. In *Les éditions critiques. Problèmes techniques et éditoriaux*, ed. Nina Catach. 115-25. Paris: Université de Besançon.

Lavagnino, John. 1996. 'Reading, Scholarship and Hypertext Editions'. *Text: Transactions of the Society for Textual Scholarship* 8: 109-24. Repub. *The Journal of Electronic Publishing* 3/1 (1997) quod.lib.umich.edu/cgi/t/text/text-idx?c=jep;view=text;rgn=main;idno=3336451.0003.112 [accessed 8 February 2010].

Lebrave, Jean-Louis. 1987. 'Rough Drafts: A Challenge to Uniformity in Editing'. *Text: Transactions of the Society for Textual Scholarship*, 3: 135-42.

— 1988. 'L'écriture interrompue: quelques problèmes theoriques'. In *Les éditions critiques. Problèmes techniques et éditoriaux*, ed. Nina Catach. 126-42. Paris: Université de Besançon.

— 1991. 'L'hypertexte et l'avant-texte'. In *LINX. Texte et ordinateur: les mutations du lire-écrire*, ed. Jacques Anis and J.-L. Lebrave. 101-17. La Garenne-Colombes: Éditions de l'Espace Européen.

—1994. 'L'hypertexte et l'avant-texte'. In *Les sentiers de la création*, ed. Maria Teresa Giaveri and Almuth Grésillon. 171-89. Reggio Emilia: Edizioni Diabasis.

Lerer, Seth. 2002. 'My Casaubon: The Novel of Scholarship and Victorian Philology'. In *Error and the Academic Self: The Scholarly Imagination, Medieval to Modern*. 103-74. New York: Columbia University Press.

Levelt, Willem J. M. 1989. *Speaking: From Intention to Articulation*. Cambridge, MA: MIT Press.

— Ardi Roelofs and Antje S. Meyer. 1999. 'A Theory of Lexical Access in Speech Production'. *Behavioral and Brain Sciences* 22: 1-75.

Lieberman, Philip. 2000. *Human Language and Our Reptilian Brain: The Subcortical Bases of Speech, Syntax, and Thought*. Cambridge, MA: Harvard University Press.

Liu, Alan. 2004. 'Transcendental Data: Towards a Cultural History and Aesthetics of the New Encoded Discourse'. *Critical Inquiry* 31: 49-84.

Logan, George, David T. Barnard and Robert G. Crawford. 1986. 'Computer-Based Publication of Critical Editions Some General Considerations and a Prototype'. In *Computers and the Humanities. Today's Research Tomorrow's Teaching. Conference Pre-Prints*, ed. Ian Lancashire. 318-26. Toronto: University of Toronto.

Lord, John B. 1979. 'Some Solved and Some Unsolved Problems in Prosody'. *Style*, 13.4: 311-33.

Love, Harold. 2002. *Attributing Authorship*. Cambridge: Cambridge University Press.

Maguire, Laurie E. 1996. *Shakespearean Suspect Texts: The 'Bad' Quartos and Their Contexts*. Cambridge: Cambridge University Press.

Manicas, Peter T. 1998. 'Social Science, History of Philosophy'. In *Routledge Encyclopedia of Philosophy Online*, ed. E. Craig. London: Routledge. www.rep.routledge.com/ [accessed 8 February 2010].

Manning, Christopher D. and Hinrich Schütze. 1999. *Foundations of Statistical Natural Language Processing*. Cambridge, MA: MIT Press.

Manovich, Lev. 2001. *The Language of New Media*. Cambridge, MA: MIT Press.

Marantz, Enid J. 1988. 'Hypotextes et hypertextes. Étude génétique et genettienne des avant-textes et du texte Proustiens'. *Texte. Revue de critique et de théorie littéraire* 7: 129-51.

Marr, D. 1982. *Vision*. New York: Freeman.

Martens, Gunter. 1995a. '(De)Constructing the Text by Editing: Reflections on the Receptional Significance of Textual Apparatuses'. In *Contemporary German Editorial Theory*, ed. Hans Walter Gabler, George Bornstein and Gillian Borland Pierce. 125-52. Ann Arbor: University of Michigan Press.

— 1995b. 'What is a Text? Attempts at Defining a Central Concept in Editorial Theory'. In *Contemporary German Editorial Theory*, ed. Hans Walter Gabler, George Bornstein and Gillian Borland Pierce. 209-31. Ann Arbor: University of Michigan Press.

Masani, Pesi R. 1990. *Norbert Wiener 1894-1964*. Basel: Birkhäuser.

Masterman, Margaret. 1962. 'The Intellect's New Eye'. In *Freeing the Mind. Articles and Letters from "The Times Literary Supplement" During March-June 1962*. 38-44. London: The Times Publishing Company.

McCarty, Willard. 2002. 'A Network with a Thousand Entrances: Commentary in an Electronic Age?' In *Classical Commentary: Histories, Practices, Theory*, ed. Roy K. Gibson and Christina Shuttleworth Kraus. 359-402. Leiden: Brill.

2003. 'Data modelling for a history of the book?' Humanist Discussion Group, 16/509 (26 February 2003) www.digitalhumanities.org/humanist/Archives/Virginia/v16/0501.html [Accessed 17 May 2010].

— 2004. 'Modeling: A Study in Words and Meanings'. In Schreibman, Siemens and Unsworth 2004: 254-70.

— 2005. *Humanities Computing*. Basingstoke UK: Palgrave Macmillan.

— 2006. 'Presence and Genre in Digital Scholarship'. Paper delivered at Master Classes in Textual Studies, De Montfort University, 1 June.

McCulloch, Warren S. 1988/1960. 'What is a Number, That a Man May Know it, and a Man, That He May Know a Number?' The Alfred Korzybski Memorial Lecture 1960. In *Embodiments of Mind*. Cambridge MA: MIT Press. www.generalsemantics.org/ [accessed 17 April 2009], Programs & Publications, Programs, Korzybski Memorial Lectures.

McDayter, Mark. 2005. 'In Praise of Procedural Markup: Some Thoughts on the Encoding and Rendering of Texts'. Consortium for Computers in the Humanities / Consortium pour ordinateurs en sciences humaines (COCH-COSH) Annual Conference, CFHSS Congress, University of Western Ontario, London, Ontario.

McDermott, Anne. 1996. *Samuel Johnson: Dictionary of the English Language on CD-ROM*. Cambridge: Cambridge University Press.

McGann, Jerome J. 1983. *A Critique of Modern Textual Criticism*. Charlottesville and London: The University Press of Virginia.

— 1991. *The Textual Condition*. Princeton: Princeton University Press.

— 1994. 'The Complete Writings and Pictures of Dante Gabriel Rossetti: A Hypermedia Research Archive'. *Text: Transactions of the Society of Textual Scholarship* 7: 95-105.

— 1995. 'The Rationale of Hypertext'. www2.iath.virginia.edu/public/jjm2f/rationale.html, dated 6 May 1995 [accessed 8 February 2010]. Republished as chapter two of McGann 2001.

— 1996a. 'The Rationale of HyperText'. *TEXT: An Interdisciplinary Annual of Textual Studies* 9: 11-32.

— 1996b. 'Imagining What You Don't Know: The Theoretical Goals of the Rossetti Archive'. www.iath.virginia.edu/~jjm2f/old/chum.html; web.mit.edu/comm-forum/papers/mcgann.html [accessed 19 January 2009].

— 1997. 'The Rationale of Hypertext'. In *Electronic Text: Investigations in Method and Theory*, ed. Kathryn Sutherland. 19-46. Oxford: Clarendon Press.

— 2001. *Radiant Textuality. Literature after the World Wide Web*. New York: Palgrave Macmillan.

— 2004a. 'A Note on the Current State of Humanities Scholarship'. *Critical Inquiry* 30: 409-13.

— 2004b. 'Marking Texts of Many Dimensions'. In Schreibman, Siemens and Unsworth 2004: 198-217.

— 2005a. 'Information Technology and the Troubled Humanities'. *TEXT Technology* 14.2: 105-21.

— 2005b. *The Complete Writings and Pictures of Dante Gabriel Rossetti A Hypermedia Research Archive*. www.rossettiarchive.org/ [accessed 19 January 2009].

— 2007. 'Database, Interface, and Archival Fever'. *PMLA* 122.5: 1588-92.

McGurk, H. and J. MacDonald. 1976. 'Hearing Lips and Seeing Voices'. *Nature* 263: 746-48. See 'The McGurk Effect'. www.faculty.ucr.edu/~rosenblu/VSMcGurk.html [accessed 8 February 2010].

McKenzie, 1999/1985. *Bibliography and the Sociology of Texts*. Cambridge: Cambridge University Press.

— 2002/1992. '"What's Past is Prologue": The Bibliographical Society and the History of the Book'. In *Making Meaning: 'Printers of the Mind' and Other Essays*, ed. Peter D. McDonald and Michael F. Suarez. 259-75. Boston: University of Massachusetts Press.

McLeod, Randall [as Random Cloud]. 1982. 'The Marriage of Good and Bad Quartos'. *Shakespeare Quarterly* 33.4: 421-31.

Medawar, Peter. 1982. 'Hypothesis and Imagination'. In *Pluto's Republic*. Oxford: Oxford University Press.

Milic, Louis T. 1966. 'The Next Step'. *Computers and the Humanities* 1.1: 3-6.

Miller, B. L. and C. E. Hou. 2004. 'Portraits of Artists: Emergence of Visual Creativity in Dementia'. *Archives of Neurology* 61: 842-44.

Miller, George A. 1956. 'The Magical Number Seven, Plus or Minus Two: Some Limits on our Capacity for Processing Information'. *Psychological Review* 63: 89-97.

Modiano, R., L. F. Searle and P. Shillingsburg, eds. 2004. *Voice, Text, Hypertext: Emerging Practices in Textual Studies*. Seattle: University of Washington Press.

Montfort, Nick. 2004. 'Continuous Paper: The Early Materiality and Workings of Electronic Literature'. The Modern Language Association Annual Convention, Philadelphia, 28 December 2004, nickm.com/writing/essays/continuous_paper_mla.html [accessed 8 February 2010].

Moore, Christopher, Alan Galey, and Stan Ruecker (2008). 'Registers of Usage: Results from Usability Testing of the Electronic New Variorum Shakespeare.' Paper presented at the Society for Digital Humanities/Société pour l'étude des médias interactifs annual conference at the 2008 Congress of the Social Sciences and Humanities, University of British Columbia. June 2-3, 2008.

Moretti, Franco. 2000. 'Conjectures on World Literature'. *New Left Review* 1: 54-68.

— 2005. *Graphs, Maps, Trees: Abstract Models for a Literary History*. London: Verso.

Murdoch, Jean Iris. 1954. *Under the Net.* London: Chatto and Windus.
— 1978. *The Sea, The Sea.* London: Chatto and Windus.
— 1980. *Nuns and Soldiers.* London: Chatto and Windus.
— 1983. *The Philosopher's Pupil.* London: Chatto and Windus.
— 1988. *The Book and the Brotherhood.* London: Chatto and Windus.
— 1990. *The Message to the Planet.* London: Chatto and Windus.
— 1994. *The Green Knight.* London. Chatto and Windus.
— 1995. *Jackson's Dilemma.* London: Chatto and Windus.
Mysak, Edward D. 1966. *Speech Pathology and Feedback Theory.* Springfield IL: Charles C. Thomas.
Nagel, Alexander and Christopher S. Wood. 2005. 'Interventions: Toward a New Model of Renaissance Anachronism'. *Art Bulletin* 87.3: 403-15.
Nelson, Theodor H. 1987. *Literary Machines.* South Bend IN.
— 2003. 'A File Structure for the Complex, the Changing, and the Indeterminate'. In *The New Media Reader*, ed. Noah Wardrip-Fruin and Nick Montfort. 134-45. Cambridge MA: MIT Press. Original publication in *Association for Computing Machinery: Proceedings of the 20th National Conference*, 1965, ed. Lewis Winner, 84-100.
Nestle, Eberhard, Kurt Aland et al. 1993. *Novum Testamentum Graece.* Stuttgart: Deutsche Bibelgesellschaft.
Nunberg, Geoffrey. 1996. 'Farewell to the Information Age'. In *The Future of the Book*, ed. Geoffrey Nunberg. 103-38. Berkeley CA: University of California Press.
Ohm, T. G., H. Muller, J. Braak and J. Bohl. 1995. 'Close-meshed Prevalence Rates of Different Stages as a Tool to Uncover the Rate of Alzheimer's Disease-related Neurofibrillary Changes'. *Neuroscience* 64: 209-17.
Ore, Espen S. 1999. 'Elektronisk publisering: forskjellige utgaveformer og forholdet til grunntekst(er) of endelig(e) tekst(er)' in *Vid Texternas Vägskäl. Textkritiska uppsatser*, ed. Lars Burman and Barbro Ståhle Sjönell. 138-44. Stockholm: Svenska Vitterhetssamfundet.
— 2004. 'Monkey Business – or What is an Edition?' *Literary and Linguistic Computing* 19.1: 35-43.

Ott, Wilhelm. 1988. 'Software Requirements for Computer-Aided Critical Editing'. In *Editing, Publishing and Computer Technology: Papers given at the Twentieth Annual Conference on Editorial Problems*, ed. S. Butler and W.P. Stoneman. 81-103. New York: AMS Press.

Oxford University Press. 2007. 'Better writing'. AskOxford.com, www.askoxford.com/betterwriting/plainenglish/sentencelength/ [accessed 8 February 2010].

P[egues], F[ranklin] J. 1965. 'Editorial: Computer Research in the Humanities'. *The Journal of Higher Education* 36.2 (February): 105-08.

Peterson, L. R. and M. J. Peterson. 1959. 'Short-term Retention of Individual Verbal Items'. *Journal of Experimental Psychology* 58: 193–98.

Pichler, A. 1995. 'Transcriptions, Texts and Interpretation'. In Johannessen and Nordenstam 1995: 690-95.

— and G. Lanestedt. 2007. 'Humanistisk forskning og publisering i en digital kontekst: Europeiske filosofimiljøer trekker veksler på semantisk metadata-tagging'. *Human IT* 9.2: 29-51, etjanst.hb.se/bhs/ith//2-9/apgl.pdf (abstract in English) [accessed 8 February 2010].

Pierce, John R. 1980/1961. *An Introduction to Information Theory: Symbols, Signals & Noise*. Rev. edn. New York: Dover.

Pinker, Steven. 1994. *The Language Instinct: How the Mind Creates Language*. New York: HarperCollins.

Plachta, Bodo. 1999. 'In Between the "Royal Way" of Philology and "Occult Science": Some Remarks About German Discussion on Text Constitution in the Last Ten Years'. *TEXT* 12: 31-47.

Polanyi, Michael. 1969. *Knowing and Being*. Ed. Marjorie Grene. Chicago: University of Chicago Press.

Poore, Quintin E., Lisa J. Rapport, Darren R. Fuerst and Pamela Keenan. 2006. 'Word List Generation Performance in Alzheimer's Disease and Vascular Dementia'. *Aging, Neuropsychology and Cognition* 13.1 (March): 86-94.

Popper, R. K. and J. C. Eccles. 1977. *The Self and its Brain*. New York: Springer-Verlag.

Porlock, H. 1995. 'Why Can't Critics Reveal Whether a Book is Worth Reading?' *The Sunday Times*, 22 October.

Posner, Michael I. and Marcus E. Raichle. 1994. *Images of Mind*. New York: Scientific American.

Potter, Rosanne G. 1985. 'Reasonable Computer-assisted Research on Literary Texts: The Problem of "Messy Data Sets"'. In *La critique littéraire et l'ordinateur - Literary Criticism and the Computer,* ed. Bernard Derval and Michel Lenoble. 95-110. Montréal: Derval and Lenoble.

Rabinovitz, Lauren and Abraham Geil. 2004. 'Introduction'. In *Memory Bytes: History, Technology, and Digital Culture,* ed. Lauren Rabinovitz and Abraham Geil. 1-19. Durham NC: Duke University Press.

Reed, Charlotte M. and Nathaniel I. Durlach. 1998. 'Note on Information Transfer Rates in Human Communication'. *Presence* 7.5 (October): 509-18.

Renear, A. 1997. 'Out of Praxis: Three (Meta)Theories of Textuality'. In Sutherland 1997: 107-26.

— Jerome McGann and Susan Hockey. 1999. *What is Text?: A Debate on the Philosophical and Epistemological Nature of Text in the Light of Humanities Computing Research,* Position papers originally presented at the 1999 ACH/ALLC Conference. www.humanities.ualberta.ca/Susan_Hockey/achallc99.htm [accessed 8 February 2010].

Richards, I. A. 1924. *Principles of Literary Criticism.* International Library of Psychology, Philosophy and Scientific Method. London: K. Paul, Trench, Trubner & Company, Ltd.

Richards, Thomas. 1993. *The Imperial Archive: Knowledge and the Fantasy of Empire.* London: Verso.

Roberts, Helen I. 1959. 'St. Augustine in "St. Jerome's Study": Carpaccio's Painting and Its Legendary Source'. *Art Bulletin* 41: 283-97.

Robinson, Peter, ed.

— 1994. 'Collation, Textual Criticism, Publication, and the Computer'. *Text: Transactions of the Society for Textual Scholarship* 7: 77-94.

— 1996a. 'Is There a Text in These Variants?' In Finneran 1996: 99-115.

— 1996b. '...But What Kind of Electronic Editions Should We Be Making?' In *ALLC-ACH '96 Abstracts. University of Bergen June 25-29 1996.* 81-2. Bergen: University of Bergen.

— 1996c. *The Wife of Bath's Prologue on CD-ROM.* Cambridge: Cambridge University Press.

— 2000. 'The One Text and the Many Texts'. *Literary and Linguistic Computing* 15/1: 5-14.

— 2002. 'What is a Critical Digital Edition?' *Variants. The Journal of the European Society for Textual Scholarship* 1: 43-62.

— 2003a. 'Where We Are with Electronic Scholarly Editions, and Where We Want to Be'. In *Jahrbuch für Computerphilologie* 5: 125-46. computerphilologie.uni-muenchen.de/jg03/robinson.html [accessed 19 January 2009].

— 2003b. 'The History, Discoveries and Aims of the Canterbury Tales Project'. *The Chaucer Review* 38.2: 126-39. Preprint at www.canterburytalesproject.org/pubs/PR-ChauRev.pdf [accessed 19 January 2009].

— 2004. " Where We Are with Electronic Scholarly Editions, and Where We Want to Be". In *Jahrbuch für Computerphilologie* 5. 123-143, computerphilologie.uni-muenchen.de/ejournal.html [accessed 8 February 2010].

— 2007a. 'Electronic Editions Which We Have Made and Which We Want to Make'. In *Digital Philology and Medieval Texts*, ed. Arianna Ciula and Francesco Stella. 1-12. Pisa: Pacini Editore.

— 2007b. 'Current Directions in the Making of Digital Editions: Towards Interactive Editions'. *Ecdotica* 4: 176-91.

— 2007c. 'A Specification towards Distributed Editions 2.1'. Draft at www.itsee.bham.ac.uk/DistributedEditions/UTv21.pdf [accessed 19 January 2009].

— 2008. 'Documenting Texts and Text Sources for Exposure and Retrieval'. Working paper at vmr.bham.ac.uk/media/vmrdocuments/architectformal091008.pdf [accessed 8 February 2010].

— 2009. 'What Text Really is Not, and Why Editors Have to Learn to Swim'. *Literary and Linguistic Computing* 24.1: 41-52.

— and Marilyn Deegan. 1994. 'The Electronic Edition'. In D. G. Scragg and P. E. Szarmach (eds.) *Editing Old English Texts*. Woodbridge, Suffolk: Boydell and Brewer.

Robinson-Riegler, Gregory and Bridget. 2004. *Cognitive Psychology: Applying the Science of the Mind*. Boston: Pearson.

Rockwell, Geoffrey. 2003. 'Graduate Education in Humanities Computing'. *Computers and the Humanities* 37: 243-44.

Rose, Danis Rose, ed. 1997. *Ulysses: A Reader's Edition*. London: Picador Press.

Rosenbach Foundation, Philip H. and A. S. W. 1975. *Ulysses: A Facsimile of the Manuscript*. 3 Vols. New York: Octagon Books, 1975.

Ross, Donald Jr. 1981. 'Aids for Editing "Walden"'. *Computers and the Humanities* 15.3: 155-62.

Rudman, Joseph. 1998. 'The State of Authorship Attribution Studies: Some Problems and Solutions'. *Computers and the Humanities* 31: 351-65.

Rudman, Joseph. 2000. 'Non-Traditional Authorship Attribution Studies: Ignis Fatuus or Rosetta Stone?' *BSANZ Bulletin* [Bibliographical Society of Australia and New Zealand Bulletin] 24: 163-76.

Ryan, Marie-Laure. 1999. 'Cyberspace, Virtuality, and the Text'. In *Cyberspace Textuality: Computer Technology and Literary Theory*, ed. Marie-Laure Ryan. 78-107. Bloomington: Indiana University Press.

Sabor, Peter. 2004. Introduction to *The History of Ophelia*, by Sarah Fielding. Peterborough (Ontario): Broadview.

Santos, Paulo J. and Albert N. Badre. 1994. 'Automatic Chunk Detection in Human-Computer Interaction'. 69-77. *Proceedings of the Workshop on Advanced Visual Interfaces*, Bari, Italy, 1-4 June 1994. New York: Association for Computing Machinery. www.acm.org [accessed 7 February 2010].

Schreibman, Susan. 2002. 'Computer-Mediated Texts and Textuality: Theory and Practice'. *Computers and the Humanities* 36: 283-93.

— 2003. 'Next Generation Student Resources: A Speculative Primer'. *Electronic Book Review*, posted 8 November 2003, modified 13 November 2003. www.electronicbookreview.com [accessed 8 February 2010].

— Ray Siemens and John Unsworth, eds. 2004. *A Companion to Digital Humanities*. Oxford: Blackwell.

Searle, John. 1980. 'Minds, Brains and Programs'. *Behavioral and Brain Sciences* 3.3: 417-57.

Shakespeare, William and others. 1910. *The Book of Sir Thomas More, Harleian MSS. 7368, c. 1590-96*. Tudor Facsimile Texts, Folio series [London].

Shannon, C. E. 1948. 'A Mathematical Theory of Communication'. *The Bell System Technical Journal*, July-October, 27: 379-423, 623-56. cm.bell-labs.com/cm/ms/what/shannonday/shannon1948.pdf [accessed 8 February 2010].

Shillingsburg, Miriam J. 1983. 'Relying on the Weird: Dangers in Editing by Computer'. In *Sixth International Conference on Computers and the Humanities*, ed. Sarah K. Burton and Douglas D. Short. 654-58. Rockville, Maryland: Computer Science Press.

Shillingsburg, Peter L. 1980. 'The Computer as Research Assistant in Scholarly Editing'. *Literary Research Newsletter* 5/1: 31-45.

— 1993. 'General Principles for Electronic Scholarly Editions'. sunsite.berkeley.edu/MLA/principles.html [accessed 19 January 2009].

— 1996a. *Scholarly Editing in the Computer Age. Theory and Practice*. Third Edition. Ann Arbor: University of Michigan Press.

— 1996b. 'Principles for Electronic Archives, Scholarly Editions, and Tutorials'. In Finneran 1996: 23-35.

— 2005. 'Practical Editions of Literary Texts'. *Variants. The Journal of the European Society for Textual Scholarship* 4: 29-55.

— 2006a. 'The Dank Cellar of Electronic Texts'. In *From Gutenberg to Google: Electronic Representations of Literary Texts*. 138-50. Cambridge: Cambridge University Press.

— 2006b. *From Gutenberg to Google: Electronic Representations of Literary Texts*. Cambridge: Cambridge University Press.

— 2009. 'How Literary Works Exist: Convenient Scholarly Editions'. In Special Cluster: Digital Textual Studies: Past, Present and Future, ed. Amy Earhart and Maura Ives. *Digital Humanities Quarterly* 3.3. digitalhumanities.org/dhq/vol/3/3/000054/000054.html [accessed 7 February 2010].

Siemens, Ray G. 1996. 'The New Scholarly Edition in the Academic Marketplace'. *Text Technology* 6.1: 35-50.

— 2001. 'Unediting and Non-Editions'. *Anglia - Zeitschrift für englische Philologie* 119.3: 423-55. Reprint, with additional introduction, of 'Shakespearean Apparatus? Explicit Textual Structures and the Implicit Navigation of Accumulated Knowledge'. *TEXT: An Interdisciplinary Annual of Textual Studies*, 14 (2002): 209-40. Electronic pre-print published in *Surfaces*, 8/106: 1-34. www.pum.umontreal.ca/revues/surfaces/vol8/siemens.pdf [accessed 8 February 2010].

— 2005. 'Text Analysis and the Dynamic Edition? A Working Paper, Briefly Articulating Some Concerns with an Algorithmic Approach to the Electronic Scholarly Edition'. *Text Technology* 14.1: 91-8 texttechnology.mcmaster.ca/pdf/vol14_1_09.pdf [accessed 8 February 2010].

— and Susan Schreibman, eds. 2007. *A Companion to Digital Literary Studies*. Oxford: Blackwell.

Sigurd, Bengt, Mats Eeg-Olofsson and Joost van Weijer. 2004. 'Word Length, Sentence Length and Frequency – Zipf Revisited'. *Studia Linguistica* 58.1 (April): 37-52.

Solopova, Elizabeth, ed. 2000. *The General Prologue on CD-ROM*. Cambridge: Cambridge University Press.

Spurgeon, Caroline. 1930. 'The Imagery in the Sir Thomas More Fragment'. *Review of English Studies* 6: 257-70.

Squire, Larry R. 1987. *Memory and Brain*. Oxford: Oxford University Press.

Stubbs, Estelle, ed. 2001. *The Hengwrt Chaucer Digital Facsimile,* Leicester: Scholarly Digital Editions.

Sutherland, Kathryn, ed. 1997. *Electronic Text: Investigations in Method and Theory*. Oxford: Clarendon Press.

Sweller, John. 1988. 'Cognitive Load during Problem Solving: Effects on Learning'. *Cognitive Science* 12: 257-85.

Sweller, John. 2006. 'Commentary: The Worked Example Effect and Human Cognition'. *Learning and Instruction* 16: 165-69.

Tanselle, G. Thomas. 1989. 'Reproductions and Scholarship'. *Studies in Bibliography* 42: 25-54.

— 1989. *The Rationale of Textual Criticism*. Philadelphia: University of Pennsylvania Press.

— 1990. 'Textual Criticism and Deconstruction'. *Studies in Bibliography* 43: 1-33.

— 1991. 'Textual Criticism and Literary Sociology'. *Studies in Bibliography* 44: 84-144.

— 1995a. 'The Varieties of Scholarly Editing'. In *Scholarly Editing. A Guide to Research*, ed. D.C. Greetham. 9-32. New York: The Modern Language Association of America.

— 1995b. 'Critical Editions, Hypertexts, and Genetic Criticism'. *The Romanic Review* 86.3: 581-93.

— 2006. 'Foreword.' In Burnard, O'Keeffe and Unsworth 2006: 1-6. www.tei-c.org/About/Archive_new/ETE/Preview/tanselle.xml [accessed 8 February 2010].

Taylor, Gary. 1988. 'The Rhetoric of Textual Criticism'. *TEXT: An Interdisciplinary Annual of Textual Studies* 4: 39-57.

Thaller, Manfred. 1996. 'Text as Data Type'. In *ALLC-ACH '96 Abstracts. University of Bergen June 25-29 1996*. 252-54. Bergen: University of Bergen.

Todd, R. 2001. 'Realism Disavowed: Discourses of Memory and High Incarnations in "Jackson's Dilemma"'. *Modern Fiction Studies* 47: 674-95.

Tufte, Edward. 1997. *Visual Explanations: Images and Quantities, Evidence and Narrative*. Cheshire CT: Graphics Press.

Turing, A. M. 1950. 'Computing Machinery and Intelligence'. *Mind* 59.236: 433-60.

UNESCO (United Nations Educational, Scientific, and Cultural Organization). 2003. *Charter on the Preservation of the Digital Heritage*. portal.unesco.org/ci/en/files/13367/10700115911Charter_en.pdf/Charter_en.pdf [accessed 8 February 2010].

van der Weel, Adriaan. 2005. 'Bibliography for the New Media'. *Quærendo* 35.1-2: 96-168.

Vanhoutte, Edward. 2006. 'Prose Fiction and Modern Manuscripts. Limitations and Possibilities of Text-encoding for Electronic Editions'. In Burnard, O'Keeffe and Unsworth 2006: 161-80. www.tei-c.org/About/Archive_new/ETE/Preview/vanhoutte.xml [accessed 8 February 2010].

Vigliocco, G. 1997. 'Grammatical Gender is on the Tip of Italian Tongues'. *Psychological Science* 8:14.

Vincenti, Walter G. 1990. *What Engineers Know and How they Know It: Analytical Studies from Aeronautical History*. Baltimore: Johns Hopkins University Press.

Wentersdorf, Karl P. 2006. 'On "Momtanish Inhumanity" in "Sir Thomas More"'. *Studies in Philology* 103: 178-85.

Werstine, Paul. 2008. 'Past is Prologue: Electronic New Variorum Shakespeare'. *Shakespeare* 4.3: 224-36.

Whittlesea, B. W. 2002. 'False Memory and the Discrepancy-attribution Hypothesis: The Prototype-familiarity Illusion'. *Journal of Experimental Psychology: General* 131: 96-115.

Wiener, Norbert. 1950/1967. *The Human Use of Human Beings: Cybernetics and Society*. New York: Hearst.

— 1956. *I Am a Mathematician: The Later Life of a Prodigy*. Garden City NY: Doubleday.

— 1961/1948. *Cybernetics or Control and Communication in the Animal and the Machine*. 2nd. edn. Cambridge, MA: MIT Press.

Wigner, Eugene P. 1960. 'The Unreasonable Effectiveness of Mathematics in the Natural Sciences'. Richard Courant Lecture in Mathematical Sciences. *Communications on Pure and Applied Mathematics* 13.001-14: 1-14.

Wilson, A. N. 2003. *Iris Murdoch as I Knew Her*. London: Hutchinson.

Windelband, Wilhelm. 1998/1894. 'History and Natural Science'. Trans. James T. Lamiell. *Theory and Psychology* 8.1: 5-22.

Wood, Albert B. 1955. *A Textbook of Sound*. 3rd edn. New York Macmillan.

Wittig, Susan. 1978. 'The Computer and the Concept of Text'. *Computers and the Humanities* 11: 211-15.

Woolf, Virginia. 1976. *The Waves: The Two Holograph Drafts*. Ed. J. W. Graham. London: The Hogarth Press.

Woolf, Virginia. 2006. *The Waves*. Intr. by Ann. Molly Hite; ed. Mark Hussey. Orlando: Harvest / Harcourt.

Yates, Frances A. 1966. *The Art of Memory*. Chicago: University of Chicago Press.

Zeki, Semir. 2006. 'The Neurology of Ambiguity'. *The Artful Mind: Cognitive Science and the Riddle of Human Creativity*, ed. Mark Turner. 245-70. Oxford: Oxford University Press.

www.ingramcontent.com/pod-product-compliance
Lightning Source LLC
Chambersburg PA
CBHW050556170426
43201CB00011B/1712